La Mia

FAMIGLIA

NEVER LET THEM STEAL YOUR NAME

ANTHONY SCARPO

Testimonials For
LA MIA FAMIGLIA

A fascinating story of honor and family by a fascinating person. Having had the privilege of knowing Tony and his family for more than four decades, and now knowing details of his family life previously unknown to me, it is with admiration for his parents, his family, he and their legacy that I write this acknowledgment.

> \- **Anthony Cabrera, Senior Managing Counsel, the Coca-Cola Company**

As an Air Force F-16 pilot I love tradition, toughness, and overcoming difficult odds. I've been Tony's Pi Kappa Alpha fraternity brother and good friend for over 38 years, so I thought I knew all there was to know. To be precise, before this book I thought I knew the true Tony. Wow, was I wrong, but now the mystery is resolved. He masterfully gives us a glimpse into another side of Tampa and insight into his 'normal' which is a family's life that made me not want to put this book down.

> \- **Joe "Hooter" Feheley, Lt Col, USAF**

I am a history buff at heart and have always enjoyed Tampa's rich history, good and bad. Since meeting Tony many years ago, I've gotten a peek behind the curtain of what it was like to grow up living that history. His story is an insiders version of the true events that shaped the Tampa Bay Area and contribute to the local color. As a Spine Surgeon, I appreciate attention to detail; in this regard Tony Scarpo never fails to exceed expectation.

> \- **Dr. Geoffrey Cronen**

CONTENTS

To my loving wife Barbara for her patience, kindness and support as I spent twelve months preparing and writing this memoir. Recalling the memories and events of my past created both a challenge and a flood of emotions, but her love and dedication kept me focused and on point through the entire project. I love you. To my beautiful daughters Olivia and Sophia from whom all love radiates, I love you.

Introduction

AS A YOUNG BOY growing up in Tampa, Florida, I always thought my life was normal. It was the Sixties, a time of unrest, rebellion, hippies, drugs, free love, and the Vietnam War. I went about my daily life like most kids my age: attending school, riding bikes, going to church, roaming the wide-open spaces surrounding our farmhouse. In some ways, however, it felt different, strange, even odd at times. I often asked myself: *Is this the way it is for everyone? Are all families like ours?*

You see, we lived on the outskirts of Tampa Bay surrounded by thousands of wooded acres. Our little farmhouse (with no air-conditioning and the bare minimum of luxuries) sat in the middle of five acres my father had managed to purchase for $6,000. We lived far from any neighbors or any type of neighborhood and rarely associated with any of the kids from our elementary school. Wild pigs and deer ran freely. We explored rock quarries, and dodged alligators, snakes, and quicksand.

My normal was a mom and dad, two younger sisters, and a very large and very loud extended Italian family. My normal was a stable of horses, a yard alive with chickens and one ferocious banty rooster, and a pen filled with pigs. I owned a pony named Cindy. Cows grazed our property, and rabbits built dens in the hopes of escaping the foxes and the hawks and the blade of the plow. Our friends were the likes of Pizza Joe, Bob the Butcher, Mac the Barber, and an odd cast of characters who worked the carnival circuit during the summer and homesteaded the land next to ours during the winter. In essence, I had nothing to compare our lives to, so my version of everyday life was just that: normal.

My father came from a strong and powerful Italian heritage, the son of immigrants. He was the middle son of eleven children who grew up on a farm in Pennsylvania. Both of my grandfathers were Italian immigrants who barely spoke English, Antonio Scarpo and Luigi Ciccarelli, my namesakes.

Grandfather Scarpo worked on the railroad and met my grandmother Rosa, an Irishwoman with flaming red hair and an equally fiery disposition. They settled in Spangler, Pennsylvania. Like most uneducated, hardworking immigrants, Antonio chose a new line of work, digging for coal in mines that were as deep as they were dangerous. When a terrible accident made working in the mines impossible for him, Antonio, desperate for a new way to earn a living and clearly an entrepreneur at heart, opened Tony's Tavern at the base of the very mountain in which he had once worked.

Out of necessity, it became a family affair. All the Scarpo children had jobs in Tony's Tavern. My father's first job was to clean the spittoons, a disgusting job for a young boy, but, in an age of hard work and parental respect, no one asked questions. You did what you were told. In the end, the long hours helping in the tavern proved the catalyst for my father's own dream of one day owning his own bar.

Experience was a hard teacher. My grandparents did their best to raise their children to be strong and vibrant Americans, even as they leaned on rules and philosophies gleaned from the old country, encapsulated in statements like: *"You can be anyone and do anything you set your mind to,"* and *"Always walk with your head high."* The most powerful of them was:

"Never let them steal your name."

Packed into that sentence was generations' worth of tradition.

When all else failed, your good name was all you had! You could overcome all adversity, survive the biggest setback, and be anything as long as you kept your name and protected it from all who wished to cause you harm.

My family's journey would eventually lead my father to open his first tavern in Sulphur Springs, Florida. This area was home to the historic Sulphur Springs Pool and the Tampa dog track. Not just any dog track, but an enormous betting and gambling empire that was sanctioned by the city of Tampa and the State of Florida. My father had long inherited the entrepreneurial spirit and street smarts of his Italian father. He watched money pour in and out of that establishment, and for a young man trying to raise a family without a dime in his pocket, it presented a huge opportunity.

After some time, my father figured out how to tap into the fortunes that were generated by the Tampa dog track. The towering structure and fast lanes represented a daring opportunity that would change the course of our family's destiny forever and put us directly at odds with the largest crime family in Florida. Long known for being the head of the Tampa Mafia, Santo Trafficante Jr. made it clear that all who encroached on their turf would pay the price. As a result of this decision, we would live in fear for years to come and work painstakingly to beat the odds of a certain death. I was thrust into a world that no boy would or could ever imagine, a world steeped in crime, violence, and corruption. This became my "normal." With fear and adrenaline my only strength at times, I found myself having to grow up fast, forced into the adult role of protector of my family at the young age of 13. In the end, I was faced with two choices, to survive or suffer the consequences: Live or Die.

CHAPTER ONE

ONE CHANCE ONLY

I SAT THERE IN a rustic-style, nondescript booth. No cushions, hard surface finished in worn-out stain. Fists clenched atop the red-and-white checkered tablecloth. My heart was pounding, thundering in my ears, drowning out the sound of the restaurant's other patrons. It was one o'clock in the morning, but the place was full of students from the University of South Florida. Outside was a chilly February night in North Tampa.

My best friend Bobby sat on the other side of the booth, looking at me expectantly. We had been friends since we were 13. His parents emigrated from Hungary during the early days of the Cold War. Bobby was a first-generation American, and we were connected by our families' strong Old-World European values. He had yet to question me on why we were here. He knew this was going to be bad, and he was on board, waiting for my lead and behind me all the way.

Bobby and I, both of us 19 years old, had been sitting there for half an hour, untouched bowls of salad in front of us, glasses of Coke going warm and flat, surrounded by boisterous late-night conversation, but I couldn't hear it because sirens were going off inside my head. The waitress had mostly given up on us. My entire body felt hot and cranked up tight like a spring, muscles of my forearms straining against my skin. If that spring snapped, like the hammer of my dad's snub-nose .38, there would be no holding back.

My gaze kept going from Bobby, to the checked tablecloth, to the salad I couldn't bring myself to touch, to the kitchen window where the restaurant owner and maybe three other cooks moved in and out of view, and then to Bobby again. My vision narrowed, as if I were looking down a tunnel.

I had no idea what to do. I had no plan. I was working on pure emotion and fast adrenaline. My instincts were sharp, and my mission was clear. I kept telling myself, be patient, wait for it. As moments passed like hours, the unexpected, full rush of adrenaline pushed its way to my head one last time. I felt on fire, and my field of vision tightened almost to a pinpoint. The double salon-style doors leading to the kitchen swung open toward us, and I knew it was him. The Tall Man, the man I was looking for, came out of the kitchen, dressed like a chef, and walked right past us toward the bathroom.

Bobby and I looked at each other and then back toward the bathroom and said, "Let's go!" There was no question my friend was with me. We moved at lightning speed, sliding out of the booth, unnoticed by the other patrons, and made our way to the bathroom in a split second.

The Tall Man was enormous, over 6'4", in his mid-thirties and meaty, and here I was, all of 5'9", and Bobby, about the same height but stockier.

Inside the bathroom, Bobby hung back near the door.

The guy stood at the urinal, unzipped.

I knew his name. He didn't know mine.

I stepped up to the urinal next to him, hands trembling as I pretended to unzip, heart thundering so loud I could barely hear my own words. "How you doing?"

He nodded absently at me.

I asked his name, not sure why, maybe to confirm, even though I already knew it.

He answered.

My throat tightened like a fist as I said, "You'll never hurt another woman again!"

Then I leaped on him and started punching. He was big and tried to fight me off, but his surprise could not stand against my rage, especially with his dick still in his hand sending an errant stream of piss across the wall. Bobby fell upon him right alongside me, punching. The guy might have been making sounds, but he didn't scream. If he had, we'd have been undone. He might have tried to fight back, but only briefly, because my first blows had slammed all the strength out of him, left him reeling and dazed. But I remember the subdermal sound of his nose breaking, the wet click of it under my knuckles, the snap of his teeth smashing together. When the guy went down, we kicked him over and over.

Then I dropped upon the man's chest, straddling him, pummeling his face, slamming his head back onto the tile floor over and over. His eyelids fluttered, barely conscious. Blood spurted from his lips, from his nose.

Then my hands were around his neck, squeezing.

Blood covered my arms to the elbows. It spattered our clothes, our faces. My best friend had another man's blood all over him.

It is a memory that still haunts me to this day.

Instinctively, I let go of his throat and heaved myself upright, standing over him, repeating to Bobby, "We gotta go, we gotta get out of here." My chest hurt. My breath burned.

The guy lay moaning, gasping, spitting blood.

I stood over him and said, "I'm going to let you live, motherfucker. But I'm coming back one day to finish you off."

The look in his swelling eyes told me he had heard me, that the threat had settled into him and would take root.

We lunged for the bathroom exit door and burst out into the darkened, smoke-filled restaurant, two gore-spattered men straight out of a horror movie. Screams erupted all around, chaos building. We charged for the front door, waitresses and customers throwing themselves out of the way.

A ragged cry from behind us made me pause at the door. I looked back and saw the guy crawling on his belly out of the bathroom, his face a bloody mess, trying to scream for help. Shouts of alarm went up.

Out into the cold Tampa night we ran for our getaway car, my father's Lincoln Town Car parked about a block away. Shouts of pursuit rose behind us. A glance over my shoulder showed me two guys in chef's uniforms, one carrying a meat cleaver, one with a long kitchen knife, and maybe a third.

The night was dark, moonless, and this area of North Tampa was forested with oak trees and sawgrass palmetto, mixed with low-lying wetlands. The restaurant was situated on a two-lane, paved road, the only paved road in the area. Streetlights were few and far between. The cover of darkness was our only ally.

As we pelted toward our escape, it hit me. The moment I touched the door handle of that shiny new Lincoln, the interior lights would come on and give away our location. Someone might identify the car as we drove off. I grabbed Bobby's jacket and yanked him off the roadside into a thick grove of palmetto bushes. Behind us, an engine roared to life. Bright headlights cut a harsh glow through trees and palm fronds.

We ran hunched over to stay concealed below the tops of the low-lying palmetto, which grew to only about four feet high. I didn't know how deep we ran into that palmetto brush—the area of the grove was maybe a couple of square blocks—but eventually we stopped and threw ourselves under a thick clump of it. As I lay there on my stomach, my heart pounded so hard it felt like it was choking me. I could see my breath puffing out of me, so loud I could barely hear Bobby gasping for breath beside me.

Ten yards away, a pickup truck with blazing headlights and squealing tires roared down one of the dirt side-roads that served as tributaries to the paved highway.

"Why didn't we take the car?" Bobby whispered, still gasping.

"They would have seen the lights."

"What now?"

"We hide. Maybe they'll give up." A million scenarios cascaded through my head. They would sneak up on us and catch us and hack us to bits in this palmetto field. They would wait for us all night long and catch us going back to the car and kill us. They would call the police, and the police would catch us, and we would go to jail.

"What about the car?" Bobby asked.

To me, our voices sounded like bullhorns, but I couldn't talk any quieter. "No one knows that's our car. The car can sit there all night." My dad wouldn't get home from work until 4:00 a.m.

anyway. No one knew where we were. "If we have to stay here until the sun comes up, we stay here." If that happened, it was going to be one seriously cold night.

In the distant woods, the pickup turned a corner, circling our hiding place.

Somewhere among the squirrels in my fevered brain, a coherent thought formed, chilling me further. Rattlesnakes didn't just favor palmetto groves; they made their nests there.

A sober thought hit me. Here was Bobby, my best friend, following my lead without question, and I had put him in mortal danger. "I'm sorry!" I said, all but choking.

"It's okay."

I kept telling him, "I'm sorry!"

And he kept saying, "It's okay." Then he said, "Now shut up!"

So I shut up, and we lay there in the dark, listening to the pickup truck full of men with weapons circling our hiding place like a shark. We heard voices in the distance.

The mosquitoes must have smelled the blood on us or something, because they swarmed us. There is nothing more relentless, more unstoppable, than a swarm of Florida mosquitoes. Their high-pitched whine filled my ears, brushed my face. They crawled in my nose, my ears, all over my arms.

Hiding there on my belly in the dark and quiet, covered in another man's blood, I prayed to God that He'd let us see another dawn, asking myself over and over again, *What did I just do?*

Then we waited.

Chapter Two

A Grandfather Comes from Italy

I AM THE GRANDSON of immigrants.

My maternal grandfather Luigi Ciccarelli, an Italian immigrant from Naples and a shoemaker, barely spoke English. I have no memories of him; he died when I was a baby. In addition to the skills he employed as a shoemaker, he did odd jobs for his Catholic church in the Cleveland parish where they lived, and tried to raise my mother and her three older sisters as a widower. It was the neighbors and the local nuns who helped get them through. From stories my mother told me, Luigi was a tough but quiet man, hard-working, but he taught his girls to survive. That was my mom: a dyed-in-the-wool Catholic, a survivor.

My paternal grandfather was Antonio Scarpo Sr., an Italian immigrant from Bari, Italy, a southern port city on the Adriatic Sea. He came to America when he was in his teens to work on the railroad. He sent much of his pay back to Italy to help his family, but he never returned to his beloved country. The details of the whys and reasonings never made it down to me, only this bare scattering of facts.

When I was a boy, Grandfather Scarpo had a full head of white hair and walked with a limp, the result of a mining accident. I was named after him. In my early memories, he was gentle and kind and always played games with the grandchildren. Much like my maternal grandfather Luigi, Grandfather Scarpo was, by other accounts, also a rough-and-tumble man, and he passed these qualities down to his eight sons. It does take a certain degree of tenacity and courage to leave home, move to a different country where you don't even speak the language, and carve out a living.

As a young bachelor, Antonio worked his way through life, drifting from boarding house to boarding house, until he found himself in a particular lodge overseen by a woman named Rosa Beaver. Rosa was a Kentucky Irish fireball, standing all of five feet tall, complete with flaming red hair and the temper to match. She was married, with two children, but still young and beautiful, and I suspect my grandfather was smitten with her quickly.

Living in the close quarters of a boarding house, however, Antonio soon found that Rosa's husband was abusive.

One day, Antonio could not stand to witness this behavior anymore, and he interceded to stop the violence. I don't have details, but given how hard a man my grandfather was, and the penchant among the men of my father's generation for brawling, it's easy to imagine how the confrontation all went down.

"You're not going to beat her anymore," he may have said, either in broken English or in Italian.

And, as all abusers do, Rosa's husband told him to get lost.

Perhaps at that point, my grandfather liberally applied some well-placed knuckles and gave the man a beating he never forgot. Or maybe, as all abusers are, the man was a coward and fled at the first threat. Whatever the exact facts, suffice to say that Rosa's husband disappeared from her life following the encounter, a relationship developed between Antonio and Rosa, and they were soon married. Their relationship could be evidence that love doesn't need spoken language, because Antonio never really spoke much English, and I don't know that my grandmother spoke much Italian. In spite of all that, they would eventually have nine children together, with two from her previous marriage, for a grand total of eleven.

With a family to support now, Antonio moved them to Spangler, Pennsylvania, so he could work in the coal mines. In the coming years, he bought a small plot of land, and the family raised chickens, cows, rabbits, even kept a few horses to help work the soil.

It strikes me now how hard Antonio's family must have worked, all of them, because by the time my father, Arthur, was born in 1937, the middle of all those children, the Great Depression had fallen hard on everyone. My grandfather would work the coal mine, then come home to farm work as well. The children were all raised to work on the farm, but as they got older, they had three choices for livelihood: the farm, the coal mines, or military service.

Lots of immigrants worked the Pennsylvania coal mines. Like today, it was immigrants who did much of the hardest, most dangerous work. Immigrants and expatriates naturally form communities in new lands, and Spangler was no exception. A community of Italian immigrants coalesced, bringing with them many aspects of their cultural heritage, the good and the bad—attitudes, religion, food, and less savory things that I'll come to shortly.

My father took me to visit the old farm when I was 13 or 14. I remember the forested swells of hills and mountains. The town of Spangler itself seemed more rustic than civilized. There is a significant Italian community still there, maintaining Old World culture and dedication to the Catholic Church. When I was there in 1974 or '75, it seemed as if the town and the people were frozen in time, as if unwilling to tread too quickly through the Twentieth Century.

As with many minority immigrant communities struggling to find their place in a new country, the Italian community of Spangler, Pennsylvania, was an insular one. They had to look after one another, because no one else would. Stepping outside of expectations, though, had consequences. Antonio's non-Italian wife made him an outcast, even among his own people. He had married outside the clan.

I sometimes imagine my father growing up in this environment, the middle of eleven children, seeing the subtle or not-so-subtle social cues from fellow Italians, seeing how his father dealt with them, and learning lessons that informed his own choices later in life, lessons about forging ahead with your own dreams, come flood or damnation. No doubt, some of these lessons came down to me through the fabric of my own family, imbued in the stories we told, the food we ate, the fights we chose, and the fights we didn't.

~

Most of the Italians that settled in Spangler, Pennsylvania were immigrants from Naples, Bari and Sicily; however, they brought something else with them during the 1920s and '30s—the Mafia. But then, this was just a little backwoods town in coal mine country, right? My father always said it was too small to truly call it "the Mob," but Pete Antonucci, the leader of this gang, ran that town, possibly even that whole area of Pennsylvania. Everybody knew who Pete Antonucci was, and they gave him a wide berth.

My grandfather walked every day from the farm to the coal mine. On a particular day, as he was walking home after a full day of dangerous, back-breaking work, a car pulled up next to him, and in the car was Pete Antonucci, along with two goons. Antonio knew them, and they knew him.

"Get in," they said.

Antonio politely declined.

"Get in. Now," they said.

"Why?" Antonio said.

"We're going for a ride."

Knowing who these men were, Antonio would have been experiencing a rising wave of fear. He barely spoke English. He had a wife at home, and a passel of kids. Maybe he had eight of them by now, most of them still small. But he had no choice but to get in the car.

Pete Antonucci shoved a shotgun into his hand. "You're going to be a lookout."

"What for?" Antonio said.

"We're going to rob a pay train."

Antonio's growing fear bloomed into panic. He couldn't get involved with this. If he went with these men, there would be no going back. None. And he had no illusions that they would make him one of them. To them, he was a just a lowly farmer, somebody expendable, somebody to exploit. He handed back the shotgun. "No. I won't do it."

Why they let him out of the car is a mystery. Having revealed their plan, they could have just as easily shot him or made him disappear.

When he came home, he was terrified. My father was about 10

years old then, and he still remembers the haunted fear on his father's face. My father listened as Antonio told Rosa what had happened. Even at age 10, my father knew who Pete Antonucci was.

Now, as an adult, I know exactly what my father was feeling in that moment, because I've felt it, too.

Sometime later, the pay train was robbed. The truck, the getaway car used to rob the train, was discovered abandoned on my grandfather's farm. As an Italian immigrant, Antonio was immediately a suspect. Fortunately, his boss at the coal mine, an American, stepped up to provide an alibi. Antonio worked 13-15 hours a day in the coal mine. He couldn't be one of the culprits.

Even though the police backed off after this, the message from Pete Antonucci was clear. "You defy me, you face the consequences." Antonio knew better than to believe this would all blow over. He was petrified for the safety of his family, terrified that his wife or his children would be used to coerce him, or worse, that they would come to harm.

A week or a month later, on a day off from the coal mine, Pete Antonucci showed up at Antonio's farm. My grandfather went outside to meet him face to face, this man in a pin-striped suit and fedora, looking like a mob boss straight out of a movie, big and intimidating. My father watched them through the window and heard their conversation.

"Why did you turn me down, Tony?" Antonucci said.

Antonio could only think of one excuse at the time. "I never shot a gun before. I don't know how. You were going to give me a gun to shoot something or somebody, and I wouldn't know what to do."

Antonucci grinned. "Oh, well, if you don't know how to shoot a gun, let me show you how to shoot a gun." He pulled his .45 from his jacket and looked around. The yard was full of chickens, pecking at the dirt, wandering, scratching, clucking. Antonio and Rosa kept hundreds of chickens, perhaps making a little extra money selling eggs in Spangler. Antonucci drew a bead on one and pulled the trigger, blowing the chicken's head clean off.

Watching from the windowsill, my father jumped at the noise. His mother, watching from behind him, went still.

"That," Antonucci said, "is how you shoot a gun." He put the gun back in his jacket. "You need to learn, 'cause I'll be back to ask for your help again." Then he left, and this incident put the whole family in a panic.

As an adult, I know exactly how this feels, too.

Antonucci made one more attempt to coerce my grandfather into working for him, the nature of which I don't know, but he refused again. Several days later, Antonucci called him on the phone and said, "I want to invite you and your family to a chicken dinner."

"A what?" Antonio said.

"You know, a chicken dinner." Then Antonucci laughed and hung up.

Soon afterward, the family returned home from some excursion, possibly church, possibly some other errand, to find that every single one of their chickens, all of them, hundreds of them, were dead, slaughtered. Their bloody carcasses were scattered across the yard, in the livestock pens, in the barn.

My father remembers the terror of that moment, that realization, that sense of violation of someone coming to their home while they were away and doing such a heinous act. Those kids looked at their father, the strongest man they knew, and he only stood there, stunned, trying to keep a lid on his own panic. He tried, but little Arthur or as they sometimes called him, "Bud," 10 years old, could still see it. This kind of violence could only escalate, and it was only a matter of time before someone really got hurt, all because my grandfather said *No* to a powerful man!

It turned out, someone did get hurt.

Maybe weeks, maybe months, maybe a year later, Pete Antonucci ended up on a school playground, dead, shot between the eyes. Nobody in town knew how or why. My dad doesn't remember the time frame, only the events and the terror surrounding them, and the relief that came with news of Antonucci's death. It was like the family could breathe again.

None of Pete Antonucci's gang bothered my grandfather or his family again, but there was more tribulation to be had before the family left Pennsylvania.

CHAPTER THREE

LEAVING PENNSYLVANIA

YEARS HAD PASSED SINCE Pete Antonucci's demise. Antonio's family no longer lived in fear and everyone returned to their day-to-day routine as if nothing had ever happened. Sometimes it's best to put these things out of your mind, pretend they never happened. After all, we all find ways to cope with the fear. The family still lived with the everyday hardships of poverty, barely getting by, all while the country was recovering from World War II. Art's two oldest brothers went to work in the coal mine, before they were shipped off to war. Rationing made basic things scarce. They grew much of their own food, but Antonucci had destroyed much of the family's livelihood by killing all their chickens. Despite all the hardships, they all lived with the relief of no longer being in the crosshairs of organized crime.

Antonio used his encounter with Antonucci as a life lesson for his sons. He told them what happened. He told them what Antonucci wanted him to do.

He told them, "If you're ever approached like that, you play dumb."

"Dumb how?" my uncle Gene replied.

"I told Antonucci I don't know how to use shotgun."

"But you *do* know how, Dad."

"*Si*, Son. But *he* didn't know that. I let him think I was idiot. They say bad things about me. They mock me. They say I was not real Italian. I was giving Italians bad name."

"Somebody said that to me, I'd punch him in the face!" my dad exploded.

"That's your pride talking. It's good to be proud, Son, but bullets don't give a damn how proud you are. When Antonucci and his henchmen were following me, I just say, '*Si, signore*,' and '*No, signore*.' But I didn't agree to nothing. Because I knew that I was dirt to them. They didn't want me in their gang. They just wanted to use me, just like they use everybody. I tell you, it stuck my gut to sit there and pretend to be less than I was. But that was the only way I survive. It was the only way you still have papa. So listen to me. Are you listening!"

"We're listening, Dad."

"Somebody like Antonucci show up, you play dumb. You hear me?"

"Yes, Dad."

"Pride not worth making my kids into orphans. Right?"

"Right."

"All right then. Now get to work!"

If there is anything wired into the personality of an Italian man, it is pride. Navigating that moment, swallowing his pride and still managing to refuse was some kind of stroke of genius in that moment. But had he not done so, his kids would have grown up without a father.

This incident took root in my father so deeply it might have been carved into his soul, even if he didn't think about it until decades later. In many ways, it formed the foundation of my family's story. When a real live gangster shows up at your doorstep or stops you on the road and says, "You're working for me now," what do you do?

And why the Scarpo family? Why did Antonucci choose my grandfather? Was it accidental? These incidents are carved into my soul, too, even though I never lived in Spangler, Pennsylvania. I'll venture to say that many of my own life decisions go all the way back to Spangler as if I were somehow transported in time, hovering over all that transpired, learning and watching.

After a few years of normalcy following Antonucci's death, everything changed again for Antonio's family, on the day a runaway coal cart crushed Antonio's leg. Medical care being what it was back then and the family with little money, his leg never properly healed. The injury kept him from working in the mine ever again, but without some sort of livelihood, his family would starve.

After much thought, Antonio pulled together what little money he had and opened Tony's Tavern. It was on the road where all the miners passed going to and from work, at the bottom of the hill in the tiny little town of Spangler, not more than a few dozen square blocks. He sold pizzas, sandwiches, and beer. Everybody knew Tony the Italian, the nice guy from the coal mine.

One thing was clear to my grandfather, however: he was an outcast. To the Italian community, he was not fully Italian, as he had married an Irishwoman. To the local community, he was a foreigner who could barely speak English, a dumb dago. They did love his pizzas and sandwiches, though, and they certainly drank his beer.

As a teenager, my father cleaned spittoons and swept the floor in Tony's Tavern. He watched his father interacting with the Italian community, and with the other miners. Did that sense of being an "outsider" seep into his bones, too? He grew up watching the bar business, seeing how his father was treated, both good and bad, wondering if he was doomed.

In Spangler, young men went to work in the mines or they enlisted in the military. The family's farm could not support eleven adult children. My father Art had to make his own way. He tried the mines briefly, but he quickly understood what they had done to his father. It was dangerous, back-breaking work down there in the pitch dark. You simply worked until you couldn't anymore, and then the company discarded you, often left you to die. If a mine accident or a cave-in didn't get you, black lung would. He saw the short, broken lives of the miners all around him, exploited for someone else's profit, and thought, *I can't do this. I won't do this.*

As the middle child, Art was stuck. The oldest brothers were heroes, having joined the Army and gone off to war, and the youngest kids were babies, requiring all the attention. He was lost in the middle.

When his brother Al came back from the Army, the town threw a parade for the war hero. After his discharge, he opened a trucking business, distributing produce around the area.

As Art grew older, so did the desire to get out of Spangler. It was a town without opportunities. The fires of World War II had barely cooled when the Korean War broke out. Art didn't want to die in a mine, nor did he want to find himself in a distant land riddled with Chinese bullets.

He asked his brother Al if he needed any help unloading watermelons. By this time, Al's trucking business was busier than he could manage. So, he hired his little brother, and the two of them made a team. Al was the big-rig driver, and Art was the labor.

One of their major routes was Cleveland, and Art soon discovered Al had ulterior motives for going to Cleveland. It turned out that Al had a sweetheart named Pearl, a Polish immigrant living in the Cleveland suburbs. Unbeknown to anyone in the family, they were planning to get married. Al and Art would finish their deliveries and then go to Pearl's house for dinner. It was abundantly clear Al and Pearl were crazy about each other.

On one visit, Pearl took Art aside and said, "I'd like to introduce you to one of my neighbors. Her name is Sandella."

Art shrugged and said, "Sure."

So, Pearl took him across the street to where four sisters lived with their widowed father, the Ciccarellis. Art and Sandella hit it off instantly. Both of them had immigrant fathers from Italy. Both of them had been raised in the Catholic Church. She was all suburbia and raised by the Catholic nuns; he was an unbridled country boy. They made their way.

Al and Pearl got married first, but Art and Sandella were not far behind. That secured my father's first step out of Spangler, out of spittoon-cleaning detail, out of the coal mines.

It was an Italian wedding, a beautiful thing. Lively music, classic folk songs, plenty of wine and wonderful food. But it was a wedding on a budget. Times were still tough for Art's parents in Pennsylvania. Sandella's father Luigi was a shoemaker and a church handyman, suffering from declining health. Sandella's sisters voted and offered the newlyweds a deal. They could live there with her father and take care of him, take care of the house.

For Art, this was a natural arrangement. His own father had come from the same region of Italy, and Luigi, as hard as he was, was still softer and gentler than Art's own father.

Antonio was a firm believer in discipline and corporal punishment. His eleven children included seven scrappy boys. Keeping them in line required a hard, callused hand. For Art, Luigi must have been a breath of fresh air.

In the meantime, Art now had a family to support. His work experience was farm work and coal mining, neither of which were to be found in Cleveland. But he also had experience in Tony's Tavern, so he found work as a bouncer, before bouncers were even a thing. They probably called him a doorman. He had been watching his father handle drunks for years, so he knew how to apply force when someone got out of line. But this was a meager income. Needing something steadier and more lucrative, he learned the electrician trade and found work. Electrician by day, doorman by night. My mom worked in a local five-and-dime. That was their life.

Until they had a son, Anthony Louis Scarpo, yours truly. The namesake of both Italian grandfathers.

When I was still just a baby, my grandfather Luigi suffered a stroke and died. Unfortunately, I can't remember him, but the stories my mother told painted a picture of an amazing grandfather and loving man. Art and Sandella were now faced with a decision. The Ciccarelli house was old, and while Art worked hard to keep it up, he lacked the money for repairs. To make matters worse, back in Pennsylvania, Antonio's health was also declining. His injured leg, which had never properly healed, was deteriorating and dragging down his health with it. The doctor told Antonio that he had to get out of the Pennsylvania climate and go south. He couldn't handle the cold anymore.

~

At some point near the end of his life, Antonio sat Art down for one of those conversations that leave indelible imprints, marks so deep they get passed on to grandchildren. It's probable this conversation took place in Italian or broken English.

"Never let anyone steal your name," Art's father told him. "People can steal your fortune. They can steal your house. They can steal your wife. They can steal your car. They can do all these things, but no one can steal your name. It's yours. It's the only thing you have in this world that can't be taken from you. But *you* have to take it, and you've got to build it. You've got to do the best you can with it, because that's all you have in life." Antonio sat quietly for a while, gathering his thoughts. "Also, you have to be careful, son, because in one way or another, everyone steals from you."

"Dad, what the heck do you mean by that?" Art said. "Why does everyone steal from me?"

"They knew I couldn't speak English. They knew that. In the coal mines, the only way you got paid is when you sent your coal bucket up."

Deep down in the earth, the miners worked to fill their coal buckets, and they would send them to the surface in a train. A miner marked his personal carload with a medallion stamped with his number and sent the load up on the train.

"You never knew," Antonio continued, "when that train came all the way up, did the boss man swap your coin with his son's, or his uncle's, or somebody else's. It happened all the time. I worked like a slave, breaking my back every day in those mines. I knew I had sent ten loads up, and at the end of the day, I got paid for six."

The resentment still simmered.

"You're trying to do the best you can, work hard, provide for your family, and everywhere around you, everywhere you looked, always, somebody was on the take. There was always corruption."

When I asked my father why my grandfather told him this, my father said, "He always wanted me to be aware of the fact that when you think everyone's playing by the rules, they're not. Many times, they're looking out for themselves."

The "rules" don't benefit immigrants. They never have. The people who break the rules don't care that the immigrant is fighting, struggling for his or her family. An Italian immigrant who doesn't speak English must be stupid. He's just a dago, a wop, an easy mark. At various points in American history, Italians and Irish people weren't even considered "white." Prejudice and racism were prevalent in those days but rarely publicized like today. The stigma was real, and it was just as painful.

Art never forgot that the deck was always going to be stacked for somebody else. Always.

This was the litany that my father drilled into me for as long as I can remember:

Family.

Reputation.

Name.

In the face of a world set against you, these things were to be protected at all costs.

~

So, Antonio, Rosa, and their eleven children cooked up a plan to move the whole family south. But where? Miami, Florida, jumped to the top of their list.

Several of the siblings banded together and hit the road for a reconnaissance mission to Miami. They arrived in the great southern city, but for whatever reason, perhaps crowding and traffic, they decided against it and headed back north on Interstate 95.

They stopped in a little town called DeLand, just a bit north of Orlando, to visit a friend, and it turned out they liked DeLand quite a bit. They reported back to Antonio by telephone, and it was decided that that was where the family was heading, a new migration.

Meanwhile, for reasons unknown, the reconnaissance party in DeLand decided to cross the Florida peninsula to check out Tampa.

One look at all that warm sun, the ocean, the palm trees, the beaches, the beauty of Tampa Bay, and they vetoed DeLand.

Tampa had a bustling Italian population, plus many Spanish and Cubans. Cubans fleeing Castro's revolution flooded into Florida, and many of them settled in Tampa. The Latin connections were strong, especially in Ybor City. In the early 1960s, Ybor City was home to vibrant, thriving Italian and Spanish communities. Cigar factories ran night and day, employing mostly women and older men to roll cigars. The air smelled of tobacco and fresh-baked Cuban bread, a true delicacy only known to Florida and Cuba at the time.

To the reconnaissance party, Tampa felt *right*. And so, the Great Scarpo Migration began. The eldest children and their spouses went first, found jobs, and established themselves, which laid the foundation for the next stage. My grandparents and their youngest children migrated in 1959 or 1960.

Art and Sandella had roots in Cleveland now, plus a baby. It wasn't until late 1961, shortly after I was born, that they sold their house in Cleveland, packed me up in the station wagon, and headed for Florida.

The Scarpo family migration went as well as could be expected. They were a hardworking, resourceful bunch, and they had each other for support. The men got jobs. The women got involved with church and community. One of the things that never happened was integration with the established Italian community. The Italians in Tampa had decades to get settled and build ties. In spite of the cultural connections, we were still outsiders. There were enough Scarpos, though, with my grandfather as the patriarch that we formed our own Italian clan, occasionally inviting others to join in. Those we invited in became family, as I'll discuss later. The move to Tampa was considered a great success. Escaping the cold was reason enough to celebrate.

The city of Tampa is divided into South Tampa, North Tampa, Ybor City, and the affluent part of town. North Tampa was where the city met the country. Outside the northern city limits lay forest and swamp, the realm of the rednecks, the country folk, the "crackers." Where that term came from is uncertain, but it's used to refer to Florida's early white settlers. It may have come from the cracked corn used to make moonshine, or it might come from the sound of the bullwhips used by the small farmers and cattle ranchers who made up the bulk of those early settlers.

South Tampa and Ybor City were home to the Italian, Cuban, and Spanish communities. The Latin roots of these groups crossed ethnic boundaries and created a sense of Latin pride that helped bind the communities together.

But where the north and south parts of Tampa met, the edges

grated. Distrust, racism, and fear made a thick stew, and the best that could be achieved most of the time was an uneasy coexistence.

I don't know when I was old enough to understand the significance of it—all I knew was that people were kind and the streets were bustling—but gambling was everywhere. Back-room poker games and gambling dens thrived. Bolita was just something everyone played. But anywhere there's organized gambling, like Las Vegas, there's organized crime, and just like in Pennsylvania, a large Italian immigrant community had brought the Mafia with it. Most people associate the Mafia in America with Chicago and New York, but unbeknown to many, Tampa boasted the southernmost headquarters for the American Mafia and was just as powerful as the other two big cities.

The bolita rackets formed the backbone and battleground of organized crime in Tampa. *Bolita* is Spanish for *Little Ball*. It can be described as a combination of lottery and bingo, where players place bets well in advance on which of the one hundred numbered balls will be drawn from the bin, not unlike today's Powerball. Bolita started in Florida during the nineteenth century among Florida's Latin and black communities. By the mid-twentieth century, it was a huge industry. It was perfect for organized crime because it is easily rigged, and profits were easy to skim.

My family gambled, but they didn't play bolita. There were plenty of other means available: dog and horse racing, dice, poker, bookmaking, pool. The men of the family picked this up early, but it was not something the women engaged in.

In late 1961, my father bought a duplex in South Tampa, and we settled in. He worked as an electrician to support his family, and he had dreams of opening his own tavern like his father.

Some of my earliest memories are of family gatherings. Sunday spaghetti dinners, Christmas, Easter, birthdays. I remember noise. I remember a profusion of Italian language flying back and forth. I remember the men playing a game called *Morra*. It could best be described as the Italian version of Rock Paper Scissors, but it took quick wit and sharp skills to play. Such a thing might sound trivial to some, but this was serious business. It was intense, it was loud, it was competitive, and it was all in Italian. I remember all the children sitting and watching this, fascinated. It was more than a way to pass the time, however. For them, it was a way to hold on to Italian customs and culture, and to maintain family bonds. Even the inevitable arguments were part of that bond.

The Scarpo clan settled into Tampa and thrived.

Before long, my sister Diane was born.

None of us understood the significance of this for many years, but Sandella, my mother, was already showing little signs—moments of clumsiness, dizziness, and disorientation—of the insidious ailment that would ultimately change her life. All of this could be easily ignored, for now, troubling as it might have been in the moment for my mother.

What my parents were focused on instead was the opportunity for my father to fulfill his dream. What they didn't expect was the terror, anguish, and heartaches that would come with it, for all of us, his family...

CHAPTER FOUR

AN "INVITATION" FROM THE MOB

SOMETIMES IN LIFE, you get a break. Just like that, your life can change in an instant. And so it was in 1962, when my father began building his dream of owning his own tavern, like his father had before him.

He had been working in Tampa as an electrician for a couple of years when the opportunity came along to purchase a small, home-town tavern called The Springs Tap, an unassuming beer and wine bar in Sulphur Springs, a rural community just north of Tampa. He scraped together what money he had, along with a small loan from his father, Antonio, and just like that, he was running his very own bar.

The Springs Tap was a modest establishment, tiny by modern standards. Like Tony's Tavern, my dad sold pizzas and beer but added a hometown favorite known to all the locals and Latins in the area, the Cuban Sandwich, that perfect combination of fresh-baked Cuban bread from Ybor City, thinly sliced sweet ham, shaved pork, swiss cheese, lite mayo, mustard, and a pickle all pressed firmly on a hot grill. The young man from Pennsylvania learned quickly how to make the best Cuban sandwich in town. Within a short time, my father was doing very well with his menu, but he did not have a liquor license. Beer and wine only. In those days, the coveted liquor license cost a great deal of money and was handed down from the higher-ups in the beverage department as if it were an edict from the Almighty. That was the grand prize of the bar business. Get your hands on one of those and you were set for life. However, at the time, that was a difficult and distant thought for my dad.

The old Springs Tap building is still there, but nowadays it has been absorbed into a much larger one, a sprawling carpet store. Since the days of the dog track and the Springs Tap, the town of Sulphur Springs has lost its luster. People no longer walk the neighborhood sidewalks, and crime has taken over. The towering edifice that was once the dog track sits frozen in time, rusting, a relic of a bygone era.

Sulphur Springs was far outside of the Latin communities of Ybor City and South Tampa. This was across the border in cracker country, and the relations between the immigrant communities of South Tampa and the old-time white settlers were far from cordial. Sulphur Springs is more or less a suburb of Tampa now, but in those days, it was much more rural. No one spoke Italian, no one spoke Spanish. Here my father found himself in a situation much like Tony's Tavern in Spangler, looked down upon by the deeply entrenched, rural locals who patronized his place. A pool table and a shuffleboard table were not enough for them to embrace him as one of their own.

They said things like, "It was really stupid for an Italian to cross the line and come up here." Anyone going north of Kennedy Boulevard knew this. Being new to Tampa, he had no idea such a line existed.

They told him, "You're a dumbass wop, but your pizza is good, and your Cuban sandwiches are even better."

In the 1960s, Tampa had no major sports teams; no football, no baseball, no soccer. But there was horse racing, dog racing, jai alai, and all kinds of illegal gambling. One major advantage of the Springs Tap, however, was its location, across the street from the biggest dog-racing track in the area.

It must have been an exhausting time for my father, because he worked as an electrician and a lineman during the day and ran the Springs Tap at night. He would come home at 2:00 or 3:00 a.m., sleep for a few hours, get up, and do it again. To him, it was all worth the sacrifice, raised on the farm with a full understanding of hard work and a determined work ethic. For the first time in his life, there was a steady income flowing in to the family. All the hours of hard work seemed to be paying off.

In the midst of this success and sacrifice, an unforeseeable tragedy struck our family.

My younger sister Diana Rose died of crib death in March 1963. I was too young to remember this, but I do remember the sorrow, the pervasive grief the whole Scarpo family experienced.

I also remember my mom disappearing shortly after Diana Rose's death. I did not learn this until years later, but the death of her daughter sent her spiraling into depression and finally a mental breakdown. She had to be institutionalized for a while. To treat her depression, she was subjected to electroshock therapy, which resulted in brain lesions that may have contributed to her later illness.

But during this time, all I remember is that my mom was gone, and my dad was drowning in grief. Family members must have been taking care of me while my dad continued to work. With no real savings to speak of and the unexpected cost of funeral expenses, he could not even afford to bury his daughter. So, the patrons of the Springs Tap passed a plate and collected enough money to help out. I have a memory of him going to the funeral home, begging them to let him make payments on his daughter's funeral, promising to pay them on time.

Dealing with this kind of grief was foreign to him. A young father with a dead daughter. I cannot imagine how he got through it, working two jobs, without sleep, and having to support his wife with her breakdown as well.

Selling pizzas, Cuban sandwiches, and 25¢ beers was not going to be enough. The desperation must have grown, and the sense of despair must have taken over with every bill he couldn't pay, every time he had to rely on the support of his family. Pride grates at accepting help. At some point, panic must have set in as well as the overwhelming fear that he was not going to make it.

~

Art and his brothers had a code, inculcated by their father. It wasn't the Mafia's code. It wasn't a neighborhood code. It was unique to the Scarpo family. The pillars of that code are pride, respect, and family.

As a young man, he was built like a boxer. Medium height, enormous hands, and broad, thick shoulders, a brick callused by years of hard work.

My father never went looking for a fight. He wasn't a bully. But if a fight came to him, he would not shy away. Years in the bar business taught him how to manage drunks and belligerence. He developed a keen eye for body language—eyes, posture, demeanor. If something bad was going to happen, he recognized it immediately and could explode into action like no one else I've ever seen. The best way I can describe it is that he was closely attuned to his instincts and intuition.

My uncle Tony lived in a nice, double-wide trailer in Tampa. My father and I were visiting him one evening when I was maybe 7 years old. The owner of the trailer park was a decent enough guy when he was sober, but, like a lot of people, booze turned him into a raging asshole. Everybody knew him. Even my dad knew him from coming into the bar. That evening, my dad and I were in the car leaving Uncle Tony's house and were trying to pull onto Nebraska Avenue. Our car and the trailer park owner's got in each other's way, both of us trying to turn in opposite directions. With the windows down, I could hear him swearing, slurring, "Goddammit, I can't see!" Unaware that we were people he knew, he yelled at us in a drunken slur, "Get the fuck out of the way! What the fuck is your problem?" Then again, maybe he did know who we were.

That was the first time I had ever heard the word *fuck.*

Quicker than the man could say another word, my dad slammed our car into Park, lunged out, ran around the car, reached through the driver's window, seized the man by the throat, yanked him half out of the car, and punched him once in the face—hard. "You just said *fuck* in front of my son. Now say you're sorry."

Half-dazed, dangling out of the window, my dad's hand around his throat, the man gurgled, "I'm s-s-sorry! I'm sorry!"

My dad shoved him back into the car. "Now get the hell out of here."

The man drove away.

That's how brutally and fast my dad could act when his code was triggered. He never called the police to manage a fight or an altercation. He handled everything himself. Always. And this little story was just one example. Over decades of his working the bar business, scenarios just like this occurred literally more than a hundred times. He protected his family. He protected his patrons, and he especially protected my mother when she was working at the Springs Tap.

I often wondered where his explosive volatility came from, this sudden, almost animalistic, launch into action. It went all the way back to my grandfather, Antonio. Antonio raised eight handsome, physically fit hellions. They were a scrappy bunch, and Antonio was not shy about applying his fists when his sons got out of line. This set the stage for the brothers to fight like hell with one another—and with anyone who crossed them. Back in Spangler, among the locals, the Polish, the Irish, and the Italians, they were treated as outsiders. Their pride would not let them allow a slight to go unanswered. Such fights often ended with one man left standing.

Always he tried to keep us all insulated from the seedier side of his business—cussing, fights, bad behavior—especially my sisters. When I was a teenager, my sister Debbie, maybe 13 years old at the time, went with him to the bar. This was an unusual occurrence, but it was in the middle of the day, a time that's usually calm.

When he and Debbie walked in the door, a group of men jumped him. He threw a signal to Madelyn, his manager, to run Debbie to safety in the back office, then he launched himself into two of his attackers, fists flying. It turned into a huge brawl, complete with crashing tables and chairs. Madelyn waded into the fray with a baseball bat, slamming it hard into one man's back.

In a crying panic, Debbie ran back out of the office to watch her father taking a bloody beating.

Between my father's ferocity and the manager's baseball bat, however, they turned the tables on the attackers, beating them to a bloody pulp in front of a girl who'd never seen that kind of violence before. They dragged the attackers outside and threw them into a pile on the sidewalk.

My dad remembers this event with terrible guilt that his daughter had to see this kind of violence at such a young age.

My sisters and I were often startled by what he could do in the name of protection and defense, but this brutality he so often displayed with drunks and surly customers was dedicated to the bar side of his life. At home, he was a gentle giant.

That being said, as a teenager I was no angel, and on occasion, I did cross the line. I usually realized this half a moment too late as the tone of his voice changed and his eyes squinted. When that line was crossed, he did spank me a few times, usually with a belt, but I deserved it every time. I look back now at those times as a boy when I terribly disrespected my mother or my sisters, or when I stole an eight-track tape from a department store, and how he came after me with the combination of anger and disappointment in his eyes. His hand was iron, but I always knew that when he came after me, it was because I had violated his code, the same code that he was trying to instill in me.

~

The history of the Mafia in the United States has more twists and turns than the most ambitious crime novel. Volumes have been written about it, but most of those books focus on the mob in Chicago and New York. Al Capone and the Five Families of New York spring easily to mind, but most of the American general public are unaware of the Trafficante crime family.

In the early twentieth century, Tampa, Florida became the southernmost headquarters of the American Mafia. Tampa was a major port, perfect for running bootleg liquor and narcotics. It had a large community of Italians from which to recruit its soldiers.

In the days of Prohibition, the heart of organized crime in Tampa was Ybor City, a thriving community of hardworking immigrants, the cigar factories that exploited them, and the speakeasies and gambling halls that entertained them.

Organized crime's influence infiltrated every level of Tampa's government. Strategically chosen police officers were on the take, as were their superiors, prosecutors, judges, and politicians. Not all of them were corrupt, to be sure, but enough that the wheels of the Mafia's illicit dealings were well greased. Cops who turned a blind eye, prosecutors who soft-balled charges, judges who offered laughably lenient sentencing, politicians who cozied up to known criminal bosses, these allowed criminal operations to proceed with minimal bumps in the road. When the murders became too brazen, the public too frightened, law enforcement would make some very public arrests, rounding up "the usual suspects." But the rap sheets of many of these characters often included dozens of arrests, often with charges of petty crime and questionably short sentences.

For decades, the Tampa underworld was a tangled web of murders, vendettas, shifting alliances, and factions vying for power. The ripple effects reached across the country as younger gangsters murdered old-time Mafia bosses and seized their territories.

The first gangster to consolidate power in Tampa was Charlie Wall, an Anglo, who ran bolita, prostitution, and bootleg liquor operations. Beginning in the late 1920s, he oversaw the largest organization in Tampa's underworld, a reign that lasted almost thirty years. His only real competition was Sicilian gangster Ignacio Antinori. The two mob bosses fought a brutal, ruthless turf war for a decade, scattering the streets and back alleys of Tampa with dead mafiosi, leading the 1930s to be called the Era of Blood.

Charlie Wall won this feud, at least temporarily, in 1940. Antinori was entertaining a young female companion at Tampa's Palm Garden Inn when a gunman blew his head off with a sawed-off shotgun. The assassin was sent by the Chicago Syndicate in retribution for a shipment of poor-quality narcotics. Antinori's death might have been a great triumph for Wall, but by this time, their two organizations had largely spent themselves in the war against each other.

This opened the door for Santo Trafficante Sr. to step in, another Sicilian mobster, with ties to Charles "Lucky" Luciano and Thomas Lucchese of the New York Mafia families. Trafficante was another thorn in Wall's side from the 1930s until both of their deaths in the mid-1950s. Charlie Wall's biggest loss of influence was surrendering the bolita rackets to Santo Trafficante Sr., in 1945. When he was semi-retired, Wall testified before Congress about organized crime activities in Tampa. By 1955, his power in the underworld was all but gone, largely usurped by Santo Trafficante Sr. and his son, Santo Jr. In April 1955, he was murdered in his own home, probably by the Trafficante crime family, an event that marked the beginning of Italian Mafia dominance of Tampa's underworld.

Before the elder Santo's death of stomach cancer in 1954, he had been grooming his son, Santo Jr., as his successor. In the 1930s and '40s, he sent the younger Santo to New York to work with the Lucchese and Profacio mob families to learn the rackets, to learn how the game was played. The younger Santo became a well-liked and respected figure in Mafia circles, so when the elder Santo designated him as his heir, the transition was smooth and expected.

It should be noted that the Trafficante crime family was not strictly a Tampa-based organization. Their reach extended to New York, Europe, Mexico, and Cuba.

In the 1940s and '50s, Cuba became the Mafia's playground. With the cooperation of a succession of corrupt Cuban regimes, the Mafia owned and operated five-star resorts and casinos all over Havana. The Trafficantes were at the forefront of the Italian mob's operations in Cuba. Santo Trafficante Jr. owned interests in several Havana resorts, with heavy involvement in gambling and prostitution as well.

The mob's grip on Cuba ended with Castro's revolution in 1959. Their widespread influence, cultivated by the corruption of the Fulgencio Batista regime, perhaps in part spurred the revolution. On the eve of Castro's forces rolling into Havana, Santo Jr. delayed his departure from Cuba to scrape together as much money as possible from the family's crumbling operations, but he was arrested and jailed before he could get out of the country. While in Cuban prison, he was scheduled for execution. He was ultimately released, but the circumstances of that release are unclear. One strange and interesting turn is that Jack Ruby, the man who killed Lee Harvey Oswald, was known to have visited Trafficante in Cuban prison. Whether Ruby helped secure Trafficante's release, or whether it was the efforts of Santo's lawyers, or a personal deal that he made with Castro, Santo was released and returned to Florida.

Santo Trafficante Jr. was for a long time on the FBI's list of biggest hoodlums in America. Despite that, his extensive Cuban connections led him to be recruited by the CIA in their efforts to assassinate Fidel Castro. It is not known whether he ever went through with the attempt to kill Castro, but he was nevertheless a central figure in the complex web of CIA, Mafia, and Cuban collusion.

And all that brings us into the 1960s. By that time, various organized crime factions owned most of the bars and lounges in Tampa. These places were mob hangouts, centers of communication, narcotics trafficking, and prostitution. They could also be battlegrounds. Successful independent club owners were often annexed into Mafia operations, or at the very least became victims of protection rackets.

Why do I tell you all this? Because the young man from Pennsylvania could have never known at the time that he would soon be targeted by the biggest, most notorious crime family in the South.

~

With the bills racking up from my mother's hospitalization and the debt of my sister's funeral, my father was working himself to death, applying more and more of his time to the Springs Tap. It wasn't making ends meet, however. My mother could not work for him during this period, so he had to hire waitstaff, further cutting into a narrow profit margin. Things were growing desperate. Sandwiches, pizza, and beer were not enough to keep his family afloat.

But the culture of Tampa was steeped in gambling. Across the street was the biggest dog-racing track in the region. The Tampa dog track was such an economic powerhouse and entertainment draw that an interstate exit was built specifically for it. Thousands of people came weekly, even daily, to gamble on the dogs.

My father saw the fortunes being made across the street every night, and he wanted a piece of this action. The bright lights of the track flashed like a beacon for an opportunist like my dad, so he dipped his toe in the well and started out with low-level book-making. He would take bets in the Springs Tap and send a runner across the street to make the bets. Whatever the result of the bets, he would keep a small percentage. Once word got out, this side enterprise grew quickly. He did not get into other areas of book-making, like sports; he put his efforts strictly in the dogs. Racing was the answer.

He handled the bookmaking in various ways, such as writing orders in code on restaurant tickets. Customers would order "a pizza," or a "Cuban sandwich," or a "Schlitz beer," and those notes would be code for particular dogs and races. Those tickets, great piles of them, would go into a cigar box.

This operation worked so well in part because his patrons wanted to bet on the dogs, but exhaustion or laziness would keep them on their stools, sitting at the bar sipping a beer. They worked hard all day, and once they plopped themselves onto a barstool, they didn't want to move again. The bookmaking allowed them to make bets without having to venture across the street.

With this proximity to the track, he got to know many of the dog owners as they patronized his bar. He would listen closely as they got drunk and talked about their dogs. He listened to which dogs were lightning fast, which were on steroids, which were sick, which were soon to be put down. A common practice among dog owners was to take a dog that was nearing the end of its useful career, but still running, and inject that dog with a huge, potentially lethal dose of steroids, then race it immediately. Most often it would win that race. One last hurrah for that dog. If it survived, it would be retired or killed.

With this kind of information, he knew exactly how to make his own bets.

These two extra sources of income were soon enough to keep his family afloat, along with some gravy for his trouble.

In many ways, the dog-racing became his connection to the local clientele. Because the Scarpos came from Pennsylvania, they never connected with the local Italian community. For one reason or another, my father found himself on the outside, just like his father in Spangler. Whether by choice or circumstance, this was the hand he was dealt. And he learned how to play it well.

So, he had to make his own way, and he did it with his cracker country patrons. They worked hard. Then they drank beer. Plenty of it. They played the horses. They played the dogs. Instead of continuing to treat him as the "dumb dago," their attitudes slowly changed. "Art's Italian, but he's all right." He still looked Italian, clean-shaven with a full head of jet-black hair, but over the years, his accent shifted to a Southern drawl.

I have vivid memories of the Springs Tap from when I was about 6 or 7 years old. He would take me to the bar during the day, before he opened, to help him clean up, to sweep the floors, to dust the shuffleboard table. I loved that table, the smell of its fine sifting of shuffleboard sand, fascinated by the way the pucks moved. The smell of cigar and cigarette smoke must have been embedded in the old wood paneling. I still remember red-vinyl and chrome bar-stools, the counter bright with a stainless-steel rail large enough to handle many pitchers of beer. And there was a large pizza oven, and there were few things I loved more than the smell of fresh-baked pizza. Back then, I thought the place was enormous. I still remember many of the patrons—the plumber, the mailman, the store clerk, the mechanic. He always made sure I was out of there before anyone really started drinking. In some ways, these loyal customers became our extended family, the beginning of some-thing bigger.

It's probably because his bookmaking operation was so low-lev-el, focusing only on dog-racing, that he was able to operate under the radar for so long. But all this changed when, on a particular day in 1966, two men of Italian descent summoned my father for a meeting.

~

I don't know the circumstances of how this meeting came about. He may have been invited, he may have been forced, or he may have been thinking he was going out to dinner with friends, but he found himself in a scene straight out of *The Godfather.*

Two men he had never seen before asked him to join them for a cup of coffee. The meeting was to take place at Ayers Diner on Hillsborough Avenue. When my dad entered the well-known restaurant, he was escorted back to a dimly lit banquet room. Wondering why the main diner tables weren't sufficient, he heard the door slam behind him. There, sitting at a four-top, were two men waiting to meet him. He noticed several other men scattered throughout the room, all standing with their eyes focused intently on him, each man standing at attention as if waiting for some sort of signal.

One of the seated men wore wire-rimmed glasses, reminding my dad of a character called Mr. Peepers from a 1950s sitcom. His hair was perfectly slicked, his suit perfectly creased. He took off his glasses to clean them, and every movement was meticulous, methodical. He gestured for my father to sit down, which he did.

"Do you know who I am?" the man said.

"No, I don't," Art said, thinking this might be the most uptight man he had ever met. The way he held his coffee cup, the way he straightened the dinnerware. Everything was in its place and meticulously adjusted.

"My name is Henry. This is my brother Fano." The man gestured to the other, a blunt-faced ape of a man. Fano just grunted.

These two were a study in contrasts. Fano looked as dim-witted and thuggish as Henry looked sharp and utterly in control. Henry, the brains; Fano, the knuckle-dragger. In these first moments, Art's instincts kicked in, and he recognized them both as pure killers.

Henry took off his glasses and leaned forward. "We know what you're doing."

"Uh, what is it you think I'm doing?" Art said.

"We know about your bookmaking and the dog track," Henry said.

Fano leaned back and cracked his thick knuckles.

Art wanted to jump out of that seat and run, but he did not dare. His mind was already making connections. Just like what happened to his father, here were two real live mobsters, and they wanted something from him. "I don't know what you're talking about."

Henry sighed. "Look, *paisan*. We run this town, not you. We know what you're doing, and we don't like independent operators. We're here to make you a one-time offer. *Capisci*? Everyone needs protection and we want to give it to you."

Protection? Art knew exactly what they were talking about. These were the words of gangsters. Those were the same words used in movies. This was an invitation that once accepted could never be undone.

Art had been in Tampa long enough to know the names of its mobsters, and that the Trafficante family were the lords of the underworld. But the Springs Tap was seven miles north of central Tampa. What were these guys doing out here in redneck country?

Whether he did this consciously, I can't say, but he turned on a switch deep inside him and responded in a thick Southern drawl. "Naw, fellas," he said, "I just run numbers for a few of my family members and a few customers. Especially that old guy in the wheelchair who can't get out, and that guy who has the crutches, and then my brothers."

Henry looked at him with his piercing eyes staring right into his soul. "We've already checked into your numbers. We know the truth. We already see the volume you do. Don't try to bullshit us. We know everything. That's my job, Art. Don't insult me. Do you understand?"

My grandfather's words came back to him. *I was nothing to them. Expendable. You don't agree to nothing.* "Naw, boys, I dunno where you're getting yer information from, but you got it all wrong. Just a few numbers for buddies and brothers. What do you want a piece of that for? It's just chump change."

Henry's face reddened, his jaw tightening. Like a gorilla, Fano picked up a fork and squeezed it, like he was going to use it to jab out Art's eyes.

Henry fixed Art with a long, ice-cold gaze. "Then why don't you let us help you take a step into the big time?" His tone was affable, but the threat already hung between them.

"Well, ya know, I'm doing all right," Art said. "Don't think I'm much interested in the big time."

"You don't want to make more money?"

"'Course I do. Don't ever'body? Look, I really wish I could help you guys, but I don't think we got much to talk about." He started to get up to leave, but Fano stabbed the fork into the tabletop. Art sat back down. "Look. Gentlemen. It'll cost you more in gas to come up here to collect than I'm taking home running numbers for a dozen people. You got me? It's just a hobby. I swear to God."

Henry shrugged. "All right then. So, you're running a few numbers for family and friends. I can respect that." Then he leaned forward again. "So here's the deal. Knock it off. Right now. Don't *ever* do it again. And by the way, you're an embarrassment to all Italians, talking and acting like some redneck hick. Where's your pride? Where's your respect? You must be an embarrassment to your father."

A chill went through Art like he'd been doused with ice water. Those piercing eyes gazed right through him. Unable to speak, knowing it would mean certain death, he remembered his father. *Hold your pride. Don't speak. There will come another time. I do not want my son to grow up without his father. Be still.* All these memories from Antonucci came rushing back to him as if this moment in time was destined to happen. He was a mouse, and this man was a python that would devour him without a second thought.

That was the moment it came home to him just who these men were.

Henry and Epifano "Fano" Trafficante were the younger brothers of Santo Trafficante Jr. Henry oversaw the family's gambling rackets. For many years he was considered the family's Number Two man. Fano was Henry's dim-witted muscle. Fano was never formally inducted into the family's organization but remained a thug, a mere "associate." Santo Trafficante himself would never come out of the shadows to threaten a small-time bookie like my dad, but he *would* send his top lieutenants, his brothers.

Henry leaned back again. "Do we understand each other, Mr. Scarpo?"

Art nodded.

"How's your wife these days? Heard she was in the hospital for a while."

Art's guts turned to lead. "Doing well."

"And that boy of yours. A chip off the old block, I'll bet."

"A chip off the old block," Art said, his mouth dry as beach sand, wishing more than anything in the world to get the hell out of there.

Henry glanced at Fano, and the two of them stood. "Well, you take care of that family now."

Then they put on their hats, straightened their suits, and walked toward the front door. My dad sat there, unable to move, unable to think. The blood all drained from his face.

He asked himself, *What the hell just happened? What have I done?*

CHAPTER FIVE

THE HOUSE ON SKIPPER ROAD

THE ENCOUNTER WITH THE Trafficantes must have shaken my father to the core. The stories his father had told him of Pete Antonucci must have been forefront in his mind. He now had a son who was almost the same age he himself had been when his father encountered Antonucci.

What do you do when the brother of Santo Trafficante Jr., a lieutenant who was a "made man," demands that you attend a private meeting and gives you a direct order? What goes through your mind when you realize that you are now on the radar of the largest reputed crime family in the South? New York had the Five Families. Chicago had its Syndicate. Tampa had the Trafficantes.

By this time, my father was the only person left sitting in the banquet room. Happy to be alive and counting his blessings, he slowly rose from his chair, not knowing if the steps he took to exit the restaurant would be his last. He made his way to the car and told himself over and over again, it was time to stop. *I can't mess with these people. They mean business.*

My father ceased his lucrative bookmaking enterprise, but soon found himself back in the same boat that spurred him to launch it in the first place. The Springs Tap was not big enough. He knew

49

this. Somehow, he needed to expand. His customer base was expanding, but without the additional income from bookmaking, he knew it would be a tough road ahead.

So, he sold the Springs Tap and bought a different establishment, naming it Art's Bar and Grill. In those days, the seller of a bar or a lounge would always carry the mortgage note. This made it relatively easy to buy a business. My dad just needed to make enough money to pay his business mortgage payment and he would be set. Unlike the Springs Tap, Art's Bar and Grill was much bigger, with a stage for live music and entertainment and back rooms that he later employed for various other activities, which I'll come to shortly. He was able to sell beer, wine, and food just like before. By this time, my mom's health had returned, and the doctor encouraged her to go back to work, knowing that a busy mind would lessen the pain of losing her daughter.

Cracks about crackers notwithstanding, the people north of the line became my father's people, these rednecks and country folk. His clientele from the Springs Tap mostly followed him over to Art's Bar and Grill. By this time, many of them had become his friends, his clan, his posse. As I grew up, I came to know many of them by name. Bill Silvers, "Pizza Joe," Buddy Blanks, Carl the Bug Man. They were working men who stayed in our lives until they died.

Around the same time, he sold the duplex in South Tampa and bought some land in what was then the country. I find it interesting that he sold the Springs Tap and the South Tampa duplex shortly after his meeting with the Trafficante brothers. There must have been a long-term strategy that set in, maybe trying to drop off the Trafficantes' radar. There had to be a master plan in place, but maybe more importantly, he just wanted to move to the country, deep into an area of Tampa where no one lived or even traveled. Here he could carve out his own kingdom, make his own rules.

Nowadays, Skipper Road is thoroughly urbanized, absorbed along with what used to be separate towns north of Tampa like Sulphur Springs. Practically within spitting distance is the University of South Florida, which now hosts one of the premier medical schools in the United States. Back then, it was only a few years old, founded in the late fifties and opened for classes in 1960.

But in those days, Skipper Road was a dead-end dirt track into the forest. Enormous oak trees dripping with Spanish moss, palm groves, bottlebrush trees, crepe myrtle, Carolina laurel cherry, large pine trees, swamp, underbrush so thick you had to crawl through it like a raccoon.

The property my father bought consisted of five acres with a farmhouse that lacked both air-conditioning and heat, so he installed a kerosene floor furnace to keep us comfortable in the winter. I remember the only relief from sweltering Florida summers was to open all the windows and let the cross-breeze flow through the house. It was like trying to cool a sauna with a fan.

The house on Skipper Road soon became home. My parents enrolled me in Mort Elementary School. My sister Antoinette was born.

The endless forest was paradise for an adventurous boy. My playground stretched forever. That it also was home to alligators and water moccasins makes me wonder nowadays how I survived. But out there on Skipper Road, there were no Trafficantes. No mob. No gangsters.

~

I was outside, 8 or 9 years old, in the carport when Uncle Tony—my favorite uncle, and I was his favorite nephew—showed up pulling a horse trailer behind his pickup truck. A big brown eye looked at me from inside the horse trailer.

As Uncle Tony got out of the truck, I said, "What the heck is this?"

He circled around to the rear of the trailer and unlatched the gate. "Well, I won this in a card game, and I don't know what to do with it." He winked at me, then went into the trailer. Moments later he emerged leading a Shetland pony. My jaw dropped.

"Wow!" I said.

"I named it Cindy after your mom."

That's when my mom came out of the house, all of 5'3", with a fiery temper usually aimed at my uncle Tony. "Tony, what in the *hell* do you think you're doing?"

Stunts like this were not out of character for my favorite uncle. My mom would get so mad at him, only to break down in laughter as the craziness would continue.

"Isn't she beautiful?" Uncle Tony said. Light tan color with a hint of white, just big enough for me to ride.

"She's beautiful!" I said.

My mom crossed her arms. "Tony. Get this damn animal out of here."

"Sorry, the pound doesn't take them this big," he said apologetically.

I was jumping up and down. "Mom! It's a pony!"

She sighed. "I know it's a pony."

Cindy became the first horse that found its way onto our place on Skipper Road. We kept it tied up near the house while my father fenced in the entirety of the two or three acres in back.

So that's how I became a horse rancher at 9 years old. My father taught me how to run the operation. Several more horses came along, eight in all. I fed them, cleaned them, brushed them, trimmed their hair. I was too small to take care of their hooves, but everything else was mine to do. I cleaned and oiled the saddles and blankets.

After Cindy's arrival, an entire farm blossomed. Along came a baby cow named Charlie Brown. Then came a handful of pigs named Arnold and Arnold's Family.

Six months later, Uncle Tony showed up again, this time with a hundred chickens. And then rabbits. Here I am, 9 years old, and surrounded by all these amazing animals. As the oldest child, I was the one who tended them. My sisters Debbie and Antoinette were too young. Antoinette was still an infant.

Over time, with me "helping," my father built more fences and pens, a chicken coop, then rabbit runs.

I loved all that, but tending all those critters was hard work for a boy that size. Carrying water and feed for them was heavy lifting. Taking care of the chickens was my least favorite activity. A hundred chickens raised a terrible stink, and the banty rooster was my nemesis. He was a tiny little thing, but he had the heart of a gladiator. Every time I entered that pen with him became a showdown. He would come after me with his spurs and beak, and I would swing my arms or a bucket to try to drive him away. I secretly hoped that a snake would get him.

On one such day, I entered the pen to gather the eggs and

spotted what looked like a firehose hanging from the ceiling near the egg nests. At first, I didn't care much but then realized it was moving, very slowly. Jumping back, I noticed the bulges along its length. This six- or seven-foot rat snake had eaten all of the eggs. I ran back to the house, grabbed my .410 shotgun, returned, and *BAM!* It gave a whole new meaning to the term scrambled eggs. I'm guessing that snake ate four dozen eggs or more. It was disgusting but it had to be done. Every time I returned to gather the eggs, I never knew if I'd find another rat snake in the chicken coop.

Antoinette was too young to remember, but my sister Debbie and I discovered the hard way what all these farm animals were for. When my dad shot and butchered Arnold and Arnold's Family, Debbie cried and I stood there in shock. Charlie Brown, our beloved cow, also went the way of the deep freezer, *and* the chickens sometimes, *and* the rabbits. We did all that work ourselves. My father did the killing, and I was dragged into helping with the butchering, along with various other Scarpo family members.

Learning where our meat came from was one of many ways I lost my innocence. Butchering livestock is not a pretty picture, especially for a kid. It is knives and blood, skin and meat and stinking viscera. The copious volume of blood contained within a steer shocked me. Watching a formerly living creature, one you've become attached to, be killed and hacked into smaller and smaller parts is not an experience easily forgotten.

But the farm on Skipper Road was also about life. On two occasions, I got to watch my pony Cindy give birth. I still remember watching those colts emerge, seem to come awake and aware, pawing their way free of membranes and slime, wobbling to their feet, and taking those first unsteady steps on gangly legs. Dad made me hand out cigars to all the friends and family members, following the old Italian custom for when one's wife has a baby.

Those horses were an unending source of enjoyment and bonding for me and my whole family. Scarpo relatives or my dad's friends would come over to visit, and we would all go riding. I felt like I was in a John Wayne movie, forging a path into the wilderness. I sat tall in the saddle, full of pride that these horses were my responsibility. And we did live on the edge of what felt like wilderness. We would go riding for hours, night and day, deep into the woods, through the swamp, venturing occasionally onto the newly built campus of the University of South Florida. I remember getting stares from students and faculty, our group of eight to ten riders.

When I think about it now, it strikes me that my father was recreating his own childhood, the farm in Spangler, Pennsylvania. Perhaps he wanted that for his children, or maybe there was something deeper he wanted to reclaim for himself on our little farm carved out of the forest. Maybe he felt farm work was a great way to mold me into a man. I would be inclined to agree with him, because there's no question it instills a sense of responsibility for one's animals and for oneself.

~

By the time Art's Bar and Grill really got rolling, my mother was healthy enough to work, so she joined my dad working at the bar. They both worked long hours and would come home at 2:00 or 3:00 a.m. after the bar closed.

The care of my sisters and me during those hours fell to our nanny, Miss Kagan. She took me to school, fed us, read stories to us at bedtime and made sure that we sat down with her every night to watch the *Lawrence Welk Show*. She was a wonderful lady, very sweet and kind.

While Miss Kagan was taking care of the kids, another thing was happening at Art's Bar and Grill: success. My father was becoming well known in the community, very popular. Also, by this time, the entire Scarpo family, all my dad's brothers and sisters, had migrated to Florida, so family get-togethers were huge, and my parents hosted them all out there on Skipper Road. Birthday parties, Christmas parties, New Year's Eve, any excuse would do. My dad built a smokehouse, so no doubt some of Arnold's successors found their way in there. At many of these parties we must have fed fifty or sixty people, mostly family but also many of Dad's posse from the bar.

Regarding his "posse," these men were loyal to my dad, these country folks from north of Tampa. They were more like followers than friends. Maybe for them, he was a little larger than life, especially if they had seen him handle a belligerent drunk. They looked at him with a little bit of awe. This nicely fed his ego, because I think he never really felt like one of them. Maybe it went back to all those ethnic slurs that had showered him and his father during the early days, but he always felt like he was just a shade better than them. He had built this business *in spite of* them, and only then had they come over to his side. That did not make them any less loyal to him, however. They stayed with him until they died. His posse would do anything for him, as I'll discuss later.

These parties were a way of building bonds—bonds of family, bonds of loyalty.

For all the kids, maybe twenty of us at any given time, these parties were a ball. We played with the rabbits. We rode horses. We swung on the tire swing. Sometimes, we would even jump in the mud with the younger hogs. This was not a popular activity with the grown-ups.

But that's not to say the parties were all fun and games.

This mix of Italians and country folk was usually cordial, but not so much between the hard-knuckled Italians themselves. All of them were heavy-drinking people, and we're not talking about martinis. Straight whiskey, sometimes without a chaser.

All the kids and I would be running rampant around the property, through the forest, having a ball, then I would notice the noise from the adults' area growing. The laughter got louder, the conversation got louder. The air filled with tobacco smoke, mixed with that of the smokehouse. Then suddenly the laughter would turn to yelling, and then there would be a crash or an uproar, beer spraying, paper plates flying, then there would be two men in a writhing knot with fists flying, usually two of the Scarpo brothers. But then, others would jump in, whether to break it up or to help, and before you knew it, there was an all-out brawl in the grass.

As the brawl raged, my dad would calmly retrieve the garden hose with the spray nozzle. Then he raised the spray nozzle and hosed them down. "Break it up!"

If they didn't, he hosed them down until they did.

"This is my family's house! I'll beat all your asses if you do this again! So straighten up or get the hell out!"

The brawlers, sputtering and dripping, separated, laughed it off, and went to get another beer. Before long, the shouts had turned to laughter again.

Even at 8 or 9 years old, I could see what alcohol did to people. This bizarre level of aggression was just commonplace. All of us kids knew that we had crazy parents, crazy aunts and uncles. We also knew that most other families did not behave this way. Alcohol sometimes peeled back the civilized veneer and let the animal out, even in the meekest of people.

In this realm, my father was at home.

~

Our house was full of weapons.

I don't know when it started, but I remember from an early age that my dad carried a snub-nose .38 revolver in his pocket everywhere he went. When he was home, it rested on the counter. We were not to touch it.

There must have been a dozen other guns around the house, mostly shotguns. I remember a double-barrel and a Browning pump-action. I also remember Smith & Wesson pistols, and several guns that my uncles brought back from World War II and the Korean War. There were also hunting rifles and guns he told me were just my size, like the .410 shotgun with which he taught me to hunt alligators, the same one I'd used to make scrambled snake and eggs. There was also an assortment of huge knives, swords, brass knuckles, and a recurved bow and arrows.

From the age of 7, my father taught me how to use them for hunting and protection. He drilled it into me that if anyone tried to hurt us or tried to break into the house, I had to be ready to use those guns. My age didn't matter. When my dad was gone, I was the man of the house. It was a responsibility that I understood at a young age. I would play out the scenario in my mind. What would happen if a Bad Guy came to the door? What if someone wanted to cause my family harm? What would I do? How quickly could I get my gun and at what point would I shoot? To hurt? To kill? So many questions.

The woods were so deep and dangerous I was never allowed to go hunting on my own. There were always at least two of us, and even then, I had to be sharp. There were prey animals like deer, but there was plenty out there that could kill a careless child—alligators, water moccasins, and wild boars in particular.

I was so young then, some of this is hazy now, but water moccasins the length of a truck and as thick as a man's forearm lived under the bridge near one of the creeks that crossed our property.

One day while hunting, I stumbled across a huge sow tending to her piglets. The cold hand of fear struck me like a slap. I had to get out of there. As I turned to run, another wild pig, one I hadn't seen, charged me. I scurried up a tree like a squirrel, yelling for my dad. My father arrived on the scene just in time to raise his Browning semi-automatic shotgun and blast away.

Once the smoke cleared, two pigs were down, and the rest scattered into the brush.

He helped me out of the tree. "You okay?"

Shaken and frightened, I said, "Yes."

"I think we're going to have wild boar for dinner tonight."

We approached the two hogs, and I knew full well what would happen next.

He pulled out his buck knife, and within seconds he slit their throats to bleed to them out. I just stared, queasiness making me unsteady on my feet at the grisly sight. My biggest question was how the hell were we going to haul two dead, bleeding hogs out of those woods?

So life on Skipper Road was, by turns, paradise and peril. That dichotomy encapsulated much of my early life, especially in light of the unforeseen circumstances and new relationships that would soon form. My family was about to be drawn into a whole new world. One of oddities and curiosity.

CHAPTER SIX

GUESS WHO'S COMING TO DINNER

I WAS 8 YEARS old when the house next door caught fire. On Skipper Road we had a small handful of neighbors, but our houses were not shoulder to shoulder.

The commotion brought my mother and me out to look long before the fire trucks arrived. Out there in the country, we were a long way from emergency services, and 911 did not yet exist. It was strange to see a house I had passed so many times going up like a torch. We joined a number of concerned people who converged on the place. The farmhouse was rustic and fairly large, but by the time we got there, it was already engulfed in flames.

Then, an odd person in a thin scarf, like a veil, walked up to my mom and said, "Do you know if anyone is inside?"

Something was strange behind that veil. To my 8-year-old brain, she looked almost like a gorilla, but her voice was very soft and concerned, a woman's voice. She slowly pulled back her scarf and my mom's eyes opened wide.

I stared and grabbed my mom's hand.

My mom stared, too, for a long moment, speechless, before she managed to respond. "Uh, no, no one lives there anymore."

Not far away were a man and a boy, standing together. My mom saw them, too. The man's face was shiny, scaly, almost like a mask, except that it was clearly his face. He might have been a handsome guy except for that. The normal-looking boy standing beside him was about my age. We stared intently at one another.

I edged closer to my mom.

"I'm Priscilla," said the human gorilla, extending a hand covered in black hair, knuckles and all. She was shorter than my mom, with a full head of glossy, black hair that also covered her forehead and cheeks. Her mouth was strangely protuberant, like a monkey's.

My mom looked at the dark-furred hand for a long moment, then tentatively shook it, pulling away quickly.

Priscilla pointed toward the man and the boy. "That's my husband Emmitt, and my son, Tony."

The boy had the same name as me. I scrutinized him.

Priscilla gestured for them to come over, so Emmitt and Tony joined us. Emmitt smiled broadly, his scaly face crinkling in a way that looked unnatural. He wore thick, coke-bottle eyeglasses and shook my mom's hand, but she still looked terrified. I'd just stepped into *The Twilight Zone*.

"You live around here?" Emmitt said.

My mom swallowed hard and nodded.

Tony and I sized each other up.

Mom pointed to where our house lay, just a few steps away.

Emmitt said, "We live across the main road, just over there."

Mom gained more control of her voice even though the fire raged on. "Did you just move in?"

"No, we been here a few months," Emmitt said. "But we're gone on the road a lot."

"On the road?" Mom said.

"We're carnival people," Priscilla said. "We go on the road traveling with the sideshow during the summer months. In the off-season, we live here." She smiled broadly. Her teeth were also strangely arranged, like a monkey's. "They call me the Monkey Girl or the Bearded Lady, and Emmitt is the Alligator Man." The wrinkles around her eyes made her look much older than a girl.

The well of weirdness just kept getting deeper underneath me. I was trying to process this information and contain my fear at the same time. *Are you telling me our new neighbors are the Bearded Lady and the Alligator Man, standing right there and shaking my mom's hand?*

"What are *you*?" I said to Tony.

Tony shrugged. "I'm just like you, but I can do some stuff."

Priscilla grinned proudly and hugged him closer to her.

Something inside the burning house burst with a small explosion. In the distance, a siren was approaching.

"Where do you go to school?" I asked him.

"Mort Elementary," he said.

"That's *my* school."

He smiled at me. Then I recognized him. He was a grade ahead of me.

Something about Priscilla's kind manner helped put me at ease. I asked her, "Do you have hair all over?"

"Tony!" Mom said.

"I sure do," she said, ignoring my mother's admonishment, lifting her pants leg a few inches to reveal a hairy shin. Then to my mother, she said, "Don't worry, hon. I get it all the time."

Emmitt said, "It's pretty much the job."

"Why is your skin like that?" I said to him.

63

"I was born this way," he said. "It's a condition called ichthyosis."

"Ick-thee-oh-sis..." I said.

He rolled up his sleeve and showed me his arm. It really did have a texture like alligator skin.

"Cool!" I said. "Can I touch it?"

"Tony!" Mom said, growing more exasperated with my brazen curiosity.

Emmitt laughed and offered his arm for me to touch it. It was scaly and hard, but not cold like an alligator.

The fire truck rolled up. Firemen bustled around with hoses. Water sprayed, sending billows of steam and smoke into the air. We all watched the spectacle.

~

That was how we met the Bejano family.

As the fire burned down, the onlookers went their separate ways. All of the other rubberneckers gave the Bejanos a wide berth.

Back at home, my dad was surprised to learn that we had met real live carnival people, what most folks still called circus freaks. He had a wary look in his eye and responded to my enthusiastic storytelling with grunts of acknowledgment. I probably couldn't stop talking about it. I went to bed thinking about what it must be like to have hair all over one's body, or scales like Godzilla.

Priscilla had the kindest eyes I'd ever seen, and a very soft-spoken manner. Emmitt was also one of the friendliest men I've ever met. I suppose they had to be, given how society at large treated them. At first glance, they made the strangest couple.

Because of the way the Bejanos looked, my parents were

stand-offish at first. When my sisters, much younger than I was, first saw Priscilla and Emmitt, they cried and hid.

I don't remember who came over to whose house first, me or Tony, but before long we were riding our bicycles together everywhere. We both went to Mort Elementary, so we often rode to school together. It didn't matter that he was a year older than me. We were the only two young boys around Skipper Road. Up until this point, my only socialization was with relatives, when all the Scarpos would come over for the big parties. That was great, but the various families were scattered all over the Tampa area. I didn't have any local friends outside the family. Finally, I had someone to play with! This was a Big Deal.

Emmitt and Priscilla had adopted Tony, who was biologically normal. He'd learned some amazing tricks, though, during his time on the road traveling with the sideshow. Remembering his comment about knowing how to do "some stuff," I asked him one day to show me something.

He told me and my sisters, "Watch!"

And then he stretched his neck back as far as could, staring up at the sky, and we gasped as he raised a thin metal sword and slowly thrust it down his throat. Apparently, that was one of his acts: Tony the Sword Swallower in Training.

My sisters and I made horrified noises. Antoinette ran away.

This both horrified and fascinated me, as one might imagine. I kept thinking there was some sort of trick to it, that the sword wasn't really going all the way in, or something like that, but no, it was real. The sword really did go all the way down his throat into his stomach.

Tony enjoyed messing with people. One day, he came over, and my mom greeted him. My dad was there, too.

Tony said, "Hey, Cindy, want to see something?"

She knew enough to be skeptical at this point. "What is it?"

He pulled out an ice pick and held it up. "I can stick an ice pick all the way into my brain." He grinned at her.

My parents both screamed at the same time, "*NO!*"

My mom lunged to stop him, but before she could reach him he had inserted the ice pick up his nose all the way into his sinus cavity. "Ta daah!"

Everybody got a little queasy at the sight of an ice pick handle hanging from one nostril. After he slowly drew it out, I distinctly remember watching his eyes water up. I asked him about it, and he told me the pick barely missed his sinuses but irritated them to a point of tears flowing. It was all rather odd for my family to comprehend.

After that, the chance that my mom would let me try Tony's carnie tricks dropped to zero. Anything that involved sharp objects or puncturing were strictly off limits. Fortunately, Tony had a whole array of other midway gimmicks and tricks to show me, all of them designed to skim money from the passersby who visited the carnival midway. Some of them were fun to try. Almost everyone who has been to a fair knows what I'm talking about, the vast array of games or sporting booths that give you the chance to win a stuffed frog or a big teddy bear, all rigged. From the ring toss to the BB-rifle, all of them were tilted to benefit the carnival and never the gamer. Some of his tricks were pure genius at conning people out of their money. I remember his stories of how gullible people were, almost as if they were happy to give their money away. Tony and his carnie friends were happy to take that money. After all, it was all legal and in good fun.

In various ways, each and every carnie I met was a masterful con artist. The average carnival or state fair lasted a week or less, so they had to maximize their profits while the getting was good. I listened to how they talked and how they used the word "mark." Anyone who visited the midway was a "mark." I never forgot that. And as I grew older, there were times in business I was certain that I was being played or conned, and I reflected back to those days when I saw firsthand how a con artist would operate. I always made sure to stay three steps ahead of the con. Knowing the end game, I could turn the trick on them.

Tony's stories of being on the road both shocked and enthralled me. Our lives were so incredibly different. I would enthuse about go-kart racing, and he would talk about sticking a sword down his throat. He told me what it was like, even at 10 or 11 years old, to have sexual encounters with girls who were much older than him, stories that made my head spin. As I look back, it seems unreal and maybe even abusive, but to hear him tell the stories it sounded like a boy coming of age like Hermie in the classic movie *The Summer of '42*.

Before long, the Bejanos had me over for dinner, and then my family had them over to share our traditional Italian spaghetti dinner on Sunday. They were thrilled to be accepted by a normal, traditional American family, and we were happy to call them friends. As time went on, Tony and I had sleepovers. I would stay at Tony's house. He would stay at our house.

As this friendship developed, my parents kept it quiet and low-key from the wider Scarpo family and other friends, fearing the social awkwardness that would inevitably arise. But I enjoyed the weirdness of it, plus the novelty of having a friend of my own.

I have to admit, I was a terrible big brother at times. I told my sisters ghost stories featuring Emmitt and Priscilla, which gave the girls nightmares. In 1969, *Dark Shadows* was one of the highest-rated horror shows on TV. It featured a main character named Barnabas Collins, a vampire. I made sure to let my sisters know that Emmett and Priscilla were his best friends and often visited the castle. I was a troublemaker and a great storyteller even if it meant being mean to my sisters. My sisters cried and hid and told me to shut up. After all, I was the older brother. It was my job to torment them, although I'm happy to say I grew out of that.

It turned out that Priscilla and Emmitt were famous. She was born with a condition called hypertrichosis, which led to the thick black hair all over her body. She also had two rows of teeth, which contributed to the way her face was shaped. Her father placed her in the sideshow circuit at a young age. She spent her younger years performing alongside a chimpanzee.

She met Emmitt Bejano, the Alligator Man, while performing with the Tommy J. Jones Exposition in 1938. Their romance was the stuff of legend in the carnival community. In 1980, they appeared in a movie called *Carnie*, which starred Gary Busey and Jodie Foster. In their later years, they appeared on several day-time talk shows with Phil Donahue and Maury Povich. Priscilla would sometimes shave the hair on her face for this.

Whenever I visited Tony's house, I would often see Emmitt go outside and stand under a garden hose he had arranged in a tree. He would douse himself several times a day. This mystified me, like many aspects of their lives, until I worked up the nerve to ask about it. Because of Emmitt's condition, ichthyosis, he could not perspire, and in the Florida heat, sweating is a way of life.

My dad was the slowest to warm up to the Bejanos, after my sisters. Kids are quicker to accept weirdness as normal, because they don't have the wider experience to know when something is truly out of the ordinary. For little kids, everything is out of the ordinary. For them, Priscilla became simply the nice neighbor lady, Mom's friend. My dad eventually came around as well. He never mistreated the Bejanos, but his wariness took a while to subside.

～

Priscilla never let her appearance dictate how she lived her life, but she was *always* conscious of how it might affect her son's.

She came to our house one night and sat down to have a cup of tea with my mom. It was one of the rare times I ever saw Priscilla look uncertain. Mom chatted with her until she was ready to broach the subject of her visit.

By this time, Priscilla and my mom had become close friends. We were teaching the Bejanos about Italians, about Pennsylvania, about the bar business. Tony and I traded notes on the best fishing spots, the most exciting areas to explore the surrounding forest and swamp. They taught us about carnivals, circuses, and fairs, life on the road for five months a year, hitting every state with multiple shows. Among their stories were instances of vicious, bigoted aggression toward them simply because they were different. I should have been more shocked than I was, perhaps, but I was already acquainted with how badly people could behave, especially when they were drinking.

By this time, Mom had started to develop a limp, noticeably dragging one of her feet wherever she walked. For us kids, it was just the way Mom walked, but for her, it marked the acceleration of a long, painful, downward spiral.

Priscilla sighed. She wouldn't meet my mom's gaze. "There's a parent-teacher meeting for Tony at school this week..."

Mom nodded. "I have one for my Tony, too."

Priscilla nodded and sighed again. "Cindy, you're such a wonderful person. I have a favor to ask of you. Would you... Could you...go with my Tony?"

Mom looked taken aback.

Priscilla continued, "I can't go to school myself. I can't go to the PTA. I can't go see the school play. It would start a panic, even with my babushka." Whenever she went out in public, she wore a babushka over her face. "And then Tony..."

To me and my sisters, by this time, Priscilla was normal. Her body looked like a woman's, except for all that hair. She talked like a normal person. She cooked like a normal person. She was a sweet, incredible soul in an incredibly harsh world. And she was our friend. America had been at war in a distant land for almost as long as I had been alive. The Civil Rights Movement was raging. Blacks and whites were at each other's throats, especially in the South. Tampa was a steadfastly segregated city. Blacks kept to themselves. Whites kept to themselves. The Latins kept to themselves. Words like "nigger" and "wop" were commonplace. And here my family had formed a friendship with the strangest people anyone had ever seen or heard of.

Priscilla looked ready to cry, asking my mom to go to school in her stead, for her, for Tony. My mom, kind and loving soul that she was, said, "Of course I will."

So from then on, Tony came to school functions with my

family. My mom took him to parent-teacher meetings. She became his surrogate mother for all public functions outside of our little Skipper Road enclave.

~

Florida was the chosen retirement spot for carnies and sideshow folks from all over the country. They settled *en masse* in a town called Gibsonton, which lay just to the south of Tampa, for community and self-protection.

Emmitt and Priscilla chose not to live there because they wanted to have their own little patch of land, just like my dad had. They wanted to be away from everyone, where they could live on their terms. They wanted "normal."

But Gibsonton was where all their carnie friends lived. It was also home to the Showmen's Club, a private organization for all the country's carnies, circus performers, sideshow people, etc.

The Bejanos took me with them once to Gibsonton, to one of the monthly parties at the Showmen's Club, also known as Gibtown. The Showmen's Club is a building painted like a living carnival, a kaleidoscope of bright colors. Nowadays there's a carnival museum inside, with exhibits going back to the early days of Ferris wheels.

I had known the Bejano family long enough they were practically family. Tony and I were best buddies. Our parents hung out together often. The Bejanos were normal to me now. When I walked into the Showmen's Club, however, the sights knocked my little life askew. The walls were covered with photographs of famous performers and sideshow people. This place was a shrine to their history, their accomplishments, their uniqueness.

The party was in full swing when we walked in, boisterous and loud, full of tobacco smoke and the smell of beer and liquor, just like the backyard parties at my house. But my backyard parties did not have a man who stood eight feet tall, or a woman who weighed seven hundred pounds. Or a wolf-boy. It was the off-season and they had all gathered at the Showmen's Club to celebrate. Who knows, maybe it was a good year, or they just wanted to spend time together.

One man had a face that was normal on one side, but on the other it sagged grotesquely, like a melted lump of flesh with no muscle tone. He put a cigarette in the droopy side, and it seemed to reach almost to his collarbone.

"That's the Two-Faced Man," Tony said.

He remains perhaps the most hideous person I ever saw. I have since tried to Google him, but I've never found any photographs or learned his name.

My heart pounded like a frightened little boy's in a haunted house. My mouth dried up. My limbs trembled, clenched fists shaking. My chest tightened like it was cinched up with ropes, making it hard to breathe.

For a long time, I must have stared. When I finally found my inner voice again, I said to myself, *I think I need to go home.* I couldn't go into this world. I didn't know how to communicate with these people. I thought it would be okay, normal, commonplace, but it was too much for my 9-year-old self.

Nevertheless, I kept my discomfiture to myself. I stayed there with them for the duration.

Among these people, Priscilla and Emmitt were celebrities, nobility. If there was a King and Queen of the Carnies, it was them.

Because I was their guest, the other carnies treated me kindly, for the most part.

At one point, however, I went to the bathroom, and found myself alone with several drunken carnies. Whether they knew I was with the Bejanos, I cannot say. They gave me long, narrow-eyed, drunken stares that made me feel very alone, exposed, outside the protective umbrella of the Bejanos' presence.

That first jolt of terror came surging back, and I had to go outside to get some air. Tony may have realized that something was wrong at that point.

I don't recall the circumstances of our leaving the party. What I do recall is the nightmares featuring the Two-Faced Man and many of the others.

I never went with them to the Showmen's Club again.

~

The Bejanos loved their little piece of land on Skipper Road, just like we did. Their visits that happened to coincide with other visitors formed a host of stories in and of themselves. Watching the reactions of our other guests was sometimes hilarious. The reactions, the expressions, the statements, the raw cascades of emotion crossing their faces, the cussing, the running and hiding. At times, we were embarrassed, but usually we all laughed about it together.

The wildest reactions came from Dad's friends from the bar. Literally anything could come out of their mouths, especially if they had been drinking.

On one particular day, my dad enlisted two of his buddies from the bar to come over and help him move a new washer and dryer. One of them was Forrest Cooper, a jolly character with a full, bushy beard and a beer belly to match. Forrest had a boisterous, colorful personality. Like all such ventures as this, there was alcohol involved, probably a lot of it.

Due to his physical condition, Forrest ran out of gas quickly and often, at which point he would pause to whine and complain.

Priscilla came over for something, entering through the front door, and then came through the house toward the back door, where the washer-dryer debacle was underway. She and Forrest came face to face.

He jumped back and yelped, "What the hell is this?"

Priscilla smiled at him.

Forrest edged back. "Art, what the hell kind of stunt are you pulling? Is this Halloween or something?"

My dad said, "Hey, Priscilla."

"Hello, Art," she said.

Forrest said, "Hah hah, that's very funny. Now when are you going to take your mask off?"

My father was stunned, embarrassed, speechless. So was my mother.

Priscilla said, "This isn't a mask. When are you going to take yours off?"

Forrest stumbled backward and this grown man pelted full speed out the back door.

My dad apologized to her, then followed Forrest outside to catch him before he reached the Georgia state line.

Everyone inside burst out laughing.

When Dad ushered Forrest back inside to introduce him to

Priscilla properly, Forrest apologized sheepishly. Everything was fine after that.

Priscilla and Emmitt took it all in stride. After so many years in circus sideshows, they had seen everything. Even when people said terrible, thoughtless, hurtful things to them, they could put on a friendly face and go about their lives. In fact, Priscilla made it a point of personal philosophy to enjoy life to the fullest at all times, no matter her appearance.

Another time, one of my dad's friends from the bar, Pizza Joe, I believe, was at one of these parties when Priscilla came over, and he said something ungodly awful to her, but she just laughed, took down her babushka and tried to give him a kiss, to the uproarious laughter of everyone else.

Sadly, sideshow folks like Priscilla and Emmitt were well acquainted with the worst of human behavior. It sometimes happened, as carnivals and circuses toured the entire country, encountering small-town people, some with the smallest of minds, they evoked such a powerful negative reaction that the carnival people had to protect themselves. Threats, fights, sabotage, even riots were not unheard of if one of the freaks was too scary or behaved in a way perceived as "threatening" or "disturbing."

Many of them had been mocked, ridiculed, or bullied their entire lives for being different. They couldn't count on the police, because the police too often reacted or behaved just as badly. They needed to protect each other, so they found strength in numbers. They developed a universal cry for help. If any of them were ever threatened with violence, they would let loose a cry of "Hey, Rube!" As if an echo in the Grand Canyon, every carnie within earshot would immediately drop what they were doing, grab the nearest improvised weapon, like a rake or a hammer or a baseball bat, and converge on the sound of the cry, and woe unto whoever attacked them. It was truly a gang-type mentality, but it was how they protected themselves while on the road.

The longer I knew the Bejanos, the more I became acquainted with other carnival and circus people. The bonds between them were tight. They were a close-knit family, with undying loyalty to one another.

Over the years, the Bejanos started coming to our backyard parties. We went over to theirs, which consisted entirely of other carnies. It was at one of those backyard parties that I got to know the Two-Faced Man. Once I was able to get past my fear, I soon realized he was as kind as the Bejanos. I felt most sorry for him, though, because he was terrifying, truly hideous, but I sensed that he knew this and needed a friend. I learned early on that once you get past these obstacles and begin to understand human nature, we are all the same, equal under the eyes of God. I found him to be intriguing and well balanced, but I always had a hard time watching him smoke his cigarettes. For some reason, he would always insert the lit Marlboro in the sagging part of his mouth.

All of our lives became more and more intertwined. The Bejanos and other friends of theirs, other "freaks" with whom we'd gotten acquainted, might come over for a visit. We had our own little House of Oddities at times.

This was a real challenge for my mom and my sisters. They kept their cool because Priscilla was there, but even I could see it was a struggle at times. Some of the carnies' appearance was truly unsettling, their behavior too far out of the norm.

Other carnies were different from Emmitt and Priscilla. Many of them were kind people, but others lacked Priscilla's gentle soul and Emmitt's gregarious amiability. There were so many, I wish I could remember their names and stage names. Like the time I went to Gibtown, the weirdness of them, the grotesqueness, got to me as a little boy. I had nightmares sometimes of deformities and fat ladies, the tricks the circus geeks could do.

When my sisters were old enough to have sleepovers, several little girls were shocked to see Priscilla or Emmitt and in a panic, ran home screaming. They literally ran out of the house and wouldn't come back. My mom had to explain to the other parents about the Scarpo house of horrors, and it did not go over well. No matter how hard we tried to tell others about the kindness of our unusual friends, many outside families wanted nothing to do with it. In some ways, I understood, but found it sad.

That was when I heard Dad say to Mom, "This is getting to be a little too much for our children. We need to be conscious of this situation."

The carnie world had come to overlap the Scarpo world just a little too much. My mom and dad came to an understanding: the carnie relationship needed boundaries and we all needed to be more aware of other children's fears.

Nevertheless, my mom and Priscilla remained best friends until my mom died in 1997. Ours was a friendship that started with a house ablaze and lasted for years. They taught us much in life, more than the average person could learn in a lifetime.

As I look back and reflect on these experiences, I remember the prejudice and racism of the time. The world was full of it. My father and his brothers were deeply prejudiced, even as they were discriminated against themselves. There were no black people in

Spangler. The Scarpo brothers never had the opportunity, or the interest, frankly, in meeting any, until coming to Tampa. I remember being aware of that prejudice, and of the irony, even as they were trying to instill it in me.

And amid all that, this incredibly kind and sweet family entered our lives. Priscilla was a true freak. She made a living being just that. But her heart was made of the purest gold. From Priscilla especially, I learned young that I could never judge people by their appearance.

I like to think that, as my dad and his brothers got to know these "freaks of nature," they came to reconsider their own prejudices.

As I remember, I think I must have smacked head-first into the limits of my tolerance for weirdness a few times. Memories of that time still carry a strange, surreal quality in my life today. I had been in the presence of "carnival monsters," even though far worse monsters, ones that wore normal clothes and walked among us, were skirting the fringes of my little world.

CHAPTER SEVEN

THE PIT OF PARADISE

THREE O'CLOCK IN THE morning.

The sound of a huge explosion yanked me upright in the bed. The detonation shook the house, rattling windows and furniture.

Moments later, our whole family was awake, coming out of our bedrooms.

"Is everybody okay?" Mom called.

We were, but Antoinette was crying.

"What was that?" I said.

"Something blew up," Dad said.

Outside, even the frogs and crickets had gone silent.

Dad went out into the night, and I followed him to the edge of the gravel road and looked up and down. Just north of our house lay the main road, which was still paved with dirt and shells at that time. Across that and a hundred yards farther north lay the Bejanos' house. It was a straight shot across the road to the Bejanos' gate.

"Looks okay over there," Dad said.

Then I noticed the cloud of smoke rising against the starry sky, tinged by orange at the bottom. It rose from a nearby area we knew little about.

The area lay catty-corner northwest from us, across the main road, across Skipper Road from the Bejanos. From our vantage point, it looked like forest, except that an endless convoy of dump trucks, loaders, and earth movers came and went from there at all hours of the day. The rumble of the engines and the diesel smoke were endless. We had lived on Skipper Road for a short time, so we were still exploring our surroundings. But this area had a tall fence around it, with a chain-link gate about seventy-five yards from our house. It seemed off-limits to most people.

A few minutes later, the wail of sirens approached. By this time, an orange glow was spreading in the forest across the road.

Dad was getting tense. "Are those woods on fire?" The thought must have crossed his mind that a fire would jeopardize our house.

Several fire trucks barreled around the corner toward that chain-link gate.

"You stay here," Dad said to me. Then he ran across Skipper Road following the fire trucks, making his way through the first responders like he was one of them.

I stood there for a long time, even after I couldn't see him anymore.

When he came back, finally, after what seemed like hours, he said, "Everything is okay. The fire is under control."

"What happened?"

"A plane crash."

My eyes must have bugged out. "Plane crash!"

"Just a small plane. Maybe a four-seater."

"Did they die?"

He nodded. "Let's go back inside and get back to bed. There's nothing for you to see. The police are taking care of everything and the fire is under control. School tomorrow."

~

What he discovered while he was over there, though, changed everything. It was like opening the gates to our own private lost world. Very few people lived that far out on Skipper Road.

The land was owned by a company called Cone Brothers Construction. They built many of the highways and roads around the Tampa area for decades, including the interstate system of I-75, and they were mining this area near Skipper Road for fill dirt. In the process, they had dug down to limestone bedrock, and because Tampa's water table is about three feet below the surface, these large pits filled with water to become three man-made, beautiful, crystal-clear lakes, surrounded by dense forest.

This discovery excited my dad, because he loved fishing and hunting. Over time, someone had stocked the lakes with fish. There were all kinds: bass, brim, catfish, you name it. My dad's excitement over the discovery of three perfect fishing lakes led him to work a little magic.

One of his regular customers at Art's Bar and Grill was a truck driver who routinely hauled loads out of there. He gave Dad a key to the front gate.

One evening before dark, he loaded all of us into the station wagon, along with our fishing poles and tackle box, and drove us through the entrance, where he unlocked the gate and slipped inside. Down a winding dirt track, maybe a hundred yards into the property, we came to the edge of one of the lakes. I marveled at seeing it there for the first time, so bright and blue and pristine. Surrounded by trees dripping with Spanish moss, it looked absolutely primeval. It was the first time my sisters held a fishing pole.

We found a great spot on the embankment and dropped our lines in. We set out trotlines and looked for turtles. It was one of those perfect childhood nights of cool air and resplendent sunsets over the primeval forest. My sisters groaned in horror and held their noses at the worms and catfish bait—I was a man, worms and bait didn't bother me—and they squealed in delight when we hauled a flopping bass up onto the bank or spotted a turtle watching us from a few feet into the water.

When we went home that night, I remember thinking we had just found paradise. This new adventure became routine for my family. We would fish, hike, camp, ride horses, and build the most spectacular campfires. Hard to believe it was only a few hundred yards from my house and we never knew it existed until now.

The pits were supposed to be inaccessible behind the chain-link fence, but Tony Bejano lived right across the road. He already knew several ways in. Before long, we were exploring together like it was the jungles of deepest Africa. It became a paradise of adventure for two young, curious boys, a land of pirates, of Indians, of lions and gorillas, of dinosaurs.

Especially dinosaurs.

~

My dad wasted no time telling my uncles about our incredible discovery. It was a huge hit for the whole Scarpo family.

One night, my dad took me and a couple of my uncles, my favorite, Uncle Tony and Uncle Roy out to do some night fishing. I felt special because it was "no girls allowed."

The four of us loaded up in our little rowboat and ventured out onto one of the lakes. It was a gorgeous night, warm and peaceful, moon glimmering on the water. The woods shrouded the banks with blackness filled with tree frogs and crickets. The echoing sounds of nature were mesmerizing.

We set some trotlines and put our fishing poles in the water. Each of us, except for me, put on a headlamp to hold back the pitch darkness. My head was too small for the headlamp. Their beams danced and jumped around the boat, around the lake, casting off into the darkness and reflecting from the lake's tiny ripples.

But then I spotted these fireballs out there on the water, little reddish-orange orbs at the water level. The headlamp beams shifted around so quickly, I kept losing sight of the fireballs.

I poked my dad and pointed. "Hey, Dad, what are those lights out on the water?"

Dad's headlamp beam played across the surface toward where I was pointing, and a pair of fireballs appeared again. Nonchalantly, he said, "Oh, that's just an alligator."

"An alligator!" I yelled.

The men all shushed me.

"An alligator!" I whispered. "They're all over out there."

My dad looked around with his headlamp. Fireballs bloomed all around us, some of them approaching our trotlines. I suddenly found myself in a horror movie. They were swarming us! Not really, but that's what my fevered 9-year-old's mind shouted at me. Our rowboat suddenly shrank to the size of a plank. Our legs might as well have been dangling in the water for the level of panic that surged through me.

"Looks like that one's after some of our catch," Uncle Roy said casually.

"There are dozens of them!" I whispered. "What are we doing out here?"

"Fishing," Dad said. "Now just relax. We got this under control. Just relax." He pulled in one of the trotlines. The pair of fireballs followed it toward our boat.

"You know," I said, with all the mature reasonableness I could muster, "I don't think we should do this again."

Dad's voice turned hard. "You're not a sissy, are you?"

"No!"

"Then keep quiet. You're absolutely doing this again." As he reeled in the trotline, a nice catfish came up on the hook. "Now take that fish off the hook."

My hands were shaking as they reached over the side for the fish. My eyes must have been the size of hubcaps as they scanned the water for any hint of prehistoric, reptilian menace.

The alligators kept their distance, thanks to my uncle Roy smacking the water with his paddle, and we all went home with our fingers and toes intact.

That night as I lay in bed, though, I went to sleep dreaming of hungry fireballs on the water.

~

As frightened as I was that night, the memory of those alligators did not stop me from exploring. There was too much fun to be had.

Sometimes the adventures Tony and I experienced were not just in our imaginations. For weeks we had enjoyed the run of the place, imagining we were alone out there, riding our bikes through the trails and stopping on occasion to watch a deer drink at the lake's edge.

But then, one day, the sounds of voices and splashing caught our attention. We crept through the forest, stealthy as Seminole trackers, or so we imagined, toward the noise. Peering through the bushes, we saw a group of young people, probably in their twenties, maybe a dozen or so, sitting on the edge of the water, talking, sunning, and swimming.

And they were all naked.

Men and women. Women. Tony and I stared at each other, then looked back at the spectacle. I had never seen a naked woman before. None of them were having sex or acting in a perverted way, but they were out there like it was the most natural thing in the world to be naked.

My little brain went to strange places, watching them. The Manson Family murders had been all over the news for weeks, and I hadn't grasped what a cult was, but I knew it was bad. I knew cults did "bad things," so was this some sort of weird, nudist cult we were watching? What was going on here?

The sight of all those naked bodies just confused and fascinated me, especially the women.

Tony and I watched them for a long time, never letting them know we were there. Eventually we sneaked away.

Maybe those people were just communing with nature in their own way, because nature was *alive* in the Cone Brothers pits. Every wild animal you could imagine called this place home; however, we could never ignore the presence of the alligators. A few too many encounters sparked nightmares crawling with reptilian fury.

My dad and I rode our horses around that area. It seems strange now to remember, because it was so long ago. We knew to watch for alligators, though. We didn't want our horses to get hurt.

I was riding my horse Cindy through the woods around the lakes one day, alone. We came through some bushes and suddenly something lurched and jerked at Cindy's feet. Cindy let out a snort and reared, hooves thrashing, again and again. A massive alligator, at least six feet, hissed and bared its teeth at Cindy's feet. I held on with everything I had. Cindy got herself turned around and fled the alligator, and eventually I got control of her again. If I had fallen off, that would have been certain death, because that gator could have eaten me in seconds.

We saw them when we were swimming, sculling toward us, which spurred us to get our butts onto dry land. We sometimes saw them when we were riding our horses through deep water. Gators can move with shocking speed, both on land and in the water. As I reflect on those times, I pause, knowing that any day exploring the Cone Brothers pits could have been my last. The dangers were everywhere, but we took it in stride and went on with everyday life. It became normal.

Maybe we all take this for granted, but the earth under our feet is usually hard, firm, and easy to walk on. No one ever seems to question that. However, on one such day, I learned that wasn't always the case, and I became aware of it in the worst possible manner.

If you know anything about Florida and Florida sand, the water table is so high that all land saturates quickly. The Cone Brothers excavations had worked up a tremendous amount of sand that never had time to settle. Millions of years of packed soil and limestone were unearthed, leaving the area an enticing, slushy danger. The end result was numerous patches of quicksand.

Tony and I were riding a cow pony named Moonie through some knee-deep water when suddenly Moonie's step faltered and he stumbled, as if his feet were getting stuck. The ground sank under our weight.

I told Tony, "Something is wrong."

Moonie bucked and struggled but couldn't make any progress. Worse, she kept sinking.

My heart flew into my throat, because I could not easily tell where the quicksand began and ended. But there was no bottom under Moonie. She had already sunk to her belly. Tony and I bailed off—and immediately sank to our knees. The quicksand sucked at my feet as I scrambled to take hold of a tree branch and then Moonie's reins, trying to pull her toward the nearest solid-looking ground. We were pulling as hard as we could, and the horse let out a long neigh and snorted uncontrollably.

I had horrific visions of having to tell my dad one of his horses was gone, lost in the quicksand.

Soaked and exhausted, with fine sand lodged in every orifice, we managed to drag Moonie back to solid ground. Everything was okay again, until the next incident.

What strikes me now is that utter absence of caution in the face of all these dangers. My sister Debbie vividly remembers us riding our bikes or walking the two miles to Mort Elementary School through this desolate area. We had no idea what danger looked like.

On one such occasion, we were met by a man who pulled his white hippie van over to the side of the road in front of us, cutting us off. He jumped out and approached us. Was he lost? Asking for directions? No. He shouted obscenities at us, pulled his pants down, and began to masturbate. For a moment we just stared, agape, in shock. Then, realizing we were only about seventy-five yards from our house, we made a dash for it. The pervert just stood there laughing. Within moments we arrived at our driveway and screamed for our dad.

We were able to babble enough words to make him understand, and without thinking he ran into the house, grabbed his shotgun, and said, "Tony, get in the car."

We raced up and down every road in the vicinity, looking for the man. "If you see that van, you holler," he growled. There was no question that had we found that van, I would have witnessed my first murder. We never found him.

How in the hell we survived as kids remains a mystery to me.

Over time, all these misadventures added up to something for me—a sense of pervasive, underlying unease, as if I sensed evil around the Cone Brothers Pits.

We had lived on Skipper Road for a year or two when one day all hell broke loose in the pits.

Tony and I came home from school on our bikes to discover a police helicopter circling the lakes. There was bright yellow crime-scene tape everywhere. A couple of police cars lingered on the scene. Tony and I rode to his house.

Inside, he asked Priscilla, "What's going on, Ma?"

Priscilla's voice quavered. "They found a body out there in the pits."

"You mean like a *dead* body?" I said.

She nodded sadly. This had really shaken her up.

"Who was it?"

"A young woman," she said. "They haven't yet identified her."

Tony and I just stared at each other. We were still too young to understand the fullness of what that meant, but we did understand that some poor girl had been murdered and dumped.

Back in Tony's bedroom, we discussed this.

"It doesn't surprise me," Tony said.

"A murder doesn't surprise you?" I said.

"You haven't seen how bad some people act."

I frowned. "I have so!" After all the times I had been to the bar with my dad, all the brawls that erupted at our backyard parties, I had seen how badly people could behave, people I thought I knew. Oh, childlike naiveté.

Tony continued, "We're so far outside the city limits, this is a perfect dumping ground. Deep lakes, all them gators, all them thick woods."

I went home and told my parents about this, troubled in ways I didn't understand. Surrounded by all this incredible beauty of nature, something dark and sinister had just happened. Was this what evil looked like? Was it hiding just under the surface of everything?

It would have been easier to put aside had there not been another body discovered a year or so later. This second one was a man.

I heard my dad speculating, "This one was probably a mob hit." He carried on with the same line of reasoning Tony had given me. A remote location, thick woods, deep water. The gators could literally make a body disappear. "God knows how many more bodies are out there."

I may have sworn off the Cone Brothers Pits for a while; I

can't say for certain, perhaps plagued by too many imaginations of stumbling upon a corpse. On the other hand, the place held a fascination I couldn't release. What would it be like to find a dead body?

Tony and I came pretty close.

~

It was April 29, 1971, when 23-year-old Diana De La Paz disappeared. School was winding down. I was almost finished with fourth grade. She was abducted in her own car from a shopping center parking lot. Her abandoned car was found the following day, but she was not.

The story was all over the news. She came from a prominent family. Her father was well placed among Tampa's elite. Diana De La Paz's disappearance seized media attention and dominated news coverage statewide for weeks. The all-out search went on for days. The family appeared on television pleading with Diana's abductor to bring her back to her family.

A Tampa man named Carroll Paulk was arrested in Shreveport, Louisiana, on May 17, for the murder of a Shreveport woman. He had been under suspicion by Tampa police, because her car was spotted at his house, but he had disappeared, too, until he was collared in Louisiana. While in police custody, he confessed to the murder of Diana De La Paz, and told police where to find her body.

Watching the news coverage after school, transfixed on the sad events and the notion that a young girl could be abducted like that, I felt so much pain and sorrow for the grieving parents that it was hard to control my emotions. My parents were already at the bar, working. Ms. Kagan, our nanny, was making dinner. My sisters were playing.

A reporter was on the scene, reporting that the police were in the process of exhuming a body they believed to be that of Diana De La Paz. The reporter's location was immediately familiar. I recognized the shores of the lakes immediately—and froze.

"Oh, my God! *Another* one?" I said. "She's *there?*"

When I saw the location the police were digging, an embankment near the water's edge, the strength left my legs and I sat on the floor.

That was the very bank from which Tony and I had fished dozens of times.

We had been there at least twice since she had disappeared. It was one of our favorite spots. All the earth there was loose, which was how we had not noticed the freshly disturbed soil. I looked out my window and saw the same familiar sights. Police, yellow crime-scene tape, voices on walkie-talkies and helicopters overhead.

I called Tony and asked him, "Are you watching the news?"

He turned it on.

"We might have been walking back and forth over her, sitting on her," I said, sick to my stomach.

All of a sudden, it hit me. I wanted to be there. I can't say why, but I was determined to make my way onto the crime scene. Nobody knew those woods better than me and Tony.

I told him, "Meet me at the back hidden path."

Within minutes, I was at the path entrance, Tony walking up a few seconds after me.

We both looked at one another and said at the same time, "Are you sure you want to do this?"

Without further hesitation, we made our way through the brush and sawgrass, making sure to stay out of sight of the police. Ten yards from the gravesite, I froze in my tracks. There were dozens of people walking around and each one seemed to have a specific job. My job was to keep quiet and not be spotted. As they slowly unearthed the woman's body, digging and brushing the soil away by hand, gently, my eyes welled up, and I could feel the pain of all those surrounding her. What would my parents do if that were me? What if that was one of my sisters. The questions raced through my head over and over.

I just sat there, stunned, for a long time. It was like I could feel my innocence draining out of me, my eyes glued to the mound of dirt. How could this happen? What kind of evil would do this to a young woman? My parents were gone a lot. When Dad was at the bar, I was man of the house. Our house was full of weapons. Was I strong enough to use them to protect my sisters? Could I pull the trigger?

Would I find a body myself someday? What would it be like to find some person's cold, dead hand sticking out of the sandy dirt? The emotions ran high and my heart was heavy for her family.

My dad came home from the bar very late, usually 2:00 or 3:00 in the morning. That night, I waited up for him, and told him about what I had seen on the news. Then I said, "We need to move, Dad."

He just gave me that amused look that adults give to over-wrought kids.

"No, really, Dad. This is the *third one!* This place, there's something wrong. I can feel it. You need to move us."

"Just relax, son."

"No, Dad! Listen! Three murderers have come *this close* to our house! You and Mom are at the bar all the time. It's just me and my sisters here. How can I protect them?"

This last one had a barb on it. He didn't say anything, but I could see it stuck.

He told me not to worry—hollow words in light of what had just happened—and sent me to bed.

In one day, the world had become a much darker place for me, and I didn't know how to escape that.

Over the last twenty years, Cone Brothers Construction has been found guilty of fraud, bribery, money laundering, and corruption. Some of the company's principals did time in prison. One of the Cone brothers, Michael, said to be as tough as any mobster, nicknamed "Diesel" for chain-smoking unfiltered cigarettes, was exposed as a bigamist who led two separate lives with separate marriages and separate sets of children with different last names, all of whom went to the same exclusive private school and had no idea they shared the same father. Cone Brothers Construction defrauded their employees, as well as the City of Tampa and the State of Florida to the tune of millions of dollars. The Cones were rich before anyone knew what rich was.

With this level of wealth and corruption, coupled with Tampa's pervasive Mafia history, it's entirely plausible that the Cones had dealings with the Trafficantes or other mob organizations. Was the mob using the Cone Brothers pits as a dumping ground for bodies? Is there anyone still at the bottom of those lakes wearing "cement shoes" or buried out there in the forest? In the years since I lived on Skipper Road, much of the forest surrounding the lakes has been replaced by housing developments and playground.

We moved away from Skipper Road in 1973. Art's Bar and Grill was going gangbusters, and I think my dad had developed the same sense of the hidden sinister that I felt about the Cone Brothers pits.

Keen intuition runs high in our family, and the terrible events that occurred on Skipper Road and around the Cone Brothers pits made us all aware that evil found its way into our little paradise. How could we spot The Hidden Sinister, and was it going to follow us to our next home?

CHAPTER EIGHT

THE ENTREPRENEUR

WHILE I WAS BUSY being a young boy living on Skipper Road, my father was busy building his empire. And I say "empire" specifically. My mom worked there with him, which left me and my sisters to be cared for by Ms. Kagan, our wonderful nanny. My parents would come home at 2:00 or 3:00 a.m., and the nanny would leave about 5:00 a.m. I would get up and get myself ready for school. Mom would often see us off, and then my parents would sleep during the day while we were at school.

The earlier encounter with Henry and Fano Trafficante had terrified my father into dropping his lucrative bookmaking operation, which had put the business on hard times. The Springs Tap was just not big enough to provide a decent living, so he was forced to sell it. His purchase of Art's Bar and Grill, however, allowed him to expand his business substantially. Art's Bar and Grill was on Hillsborough Avenue, one of Tampa's major thoroughfares, so traffic was much higher than the Springs Tap, but even farther away from Trafficante turf. It was a larger establishment, with room for live music. He could sell beer and wine, but was repeatedly refused a liquor license, likely because of Mafia influence with the State of Florida's licensing department.

Sicilians make it a point to play grudges by the long game. My father had the audacity to tell the Trafficante crime family "no" during that fateful meeting. At the time, he couldn't have predicted the consequences of his boldness; he just did what seemed right, trying to protect his turf. He could not have known that the eyes of the mob, and specifically Henry Trafficante's, were permanently fixed on him and his business ventures.

My dad's bar attracted all kinds of clientele, most of them from the country cracker variety, as I've mentioned. Many of his patrons followed him from the Springs Tap to Art's Bar and Grill. They became his friends, dozens upon dozens of them, and he became the ringleader of his own little posse, a posse that would serve him well over the years at some critical moments.

The 1960s and '70s were the heyday of mob involvement in the bars and lounges of the Tampa area. Many of the city's most prominent lounges, such as La Tropicana and the Deep South, were owned by Mafia figures. These clubs served as meeting places and hangouts for mob soldiers and leaders, and hubs from which to administer illicit gambling, prostitution, and narcotics operations. These establishments also became battlegrounds as various criminal organizations vied for bigger pieces of the pie. The Trafficantes had scared my father, but his pride would not let him knuckle under for long. There was simply too much money to be made in side ventures related to the bar and lounge business. No one was going to tell him what he could and could not do. It must have ripped his guts out to think that the Trafficantes had made him feel less than powerful, made him feel weak. After all, he had a family to support. Who the hell were they to tell Art Scarpo what to do?

No doubt many of his friends and customers missed the

bookmaking services he used to provide and probably encouraged him. "Hey, Art! When you gonna let us bet the dogs again?" The dog track was farther away now. Having a runner going back and forth to make bets for customers was easy money, money he was leaving on the table unless he took advantage of it. No doubt, his old runners also enjoyed making a little money on the side.

So, maybe a year or so after opening Art's Bar and Grill, he ventured back into bookmaking. I can imagine he must have been incredibly secretive about this at first, waiting to see if the mob might get wind of it. When Trafficante's henchmen did not come knocking immediately, this gave him the courage to expand the bookmaking business beyond the dog track, which led into betting on boxing, baseball, and other sports. From there, he ventured into other activities.

He had become a master pool player, and playing for money became a substantial source of income, supplemented by allowing other players to run money tournaments and games, from which the house received a nice cut. These games happened every week. Male and female players traveled the bar circuit looking for games. Stacks of money changed hands, sometimes thousands of dollars, huge money for the early 1970s. Cash was always laid on the edge of the table and remained there until the game was over. The shots they pulled off, seemingly as a matter of routine, often left me speechless. The games would go on for hours, as intense and testosterone-fueled as anything I've ever seen. The shit-talking was extraordinary, like NFL players getting in each other's faces. And yes, sometimes fights would break out—these games were almost like duels of honor—but my father quashed the fights with fierce, brutal authority, just like he always did.

Occasionally, pool sharks would show up with stunningly beautiful women. When one of these pairs showed up, the woman would spend hours distracting other players in the middle of their games with peeks of cleavage and curves, suggestive poses, come-hither smiles, often coming across as nothing more than empty-headed eye candy. Hours later, the girlfriend would ask to play a round with the other player, and the other player would always jump at the chance. There was nothing like watching a woman like this bend over a pool table. Only too late, after hours of marinating in lustful fantasies, the other player would discover she was a pool shark herself. Top in her class. These women were masterful, every bit as skilled as their male counterparts, and sharp as knives.

Sometimes my dad just facilitated; sometimes he played. He was good enough to go toe to toe with these pool sharks. He knew when and who to play. He knew when to talk shit and when to keep his mouth shut. He knew who had money and who was broke. He knew who loved Jack Daniels and how many drinks it took for them to lose their edge. He would never play anyone who had less than two hundred dollars in his pocket. He wanted it all, and when he ultimately won it all, he would buy them a drink and say, "Good game. We'll play again tomorrow."

I would watch some of these guys blow their last dime on a pool game, their entire paycheck. Then my dad would loan them two hundred dollars for the week's groceries for their families at 10 percent interest.

I used to practice for hours and hours, trying to get that good. It was an art form and a skill set that I tried hard to develop. The skill, the precision, the money. All that fascinated me as a boy, along with admiration for my dad's skills. I loved watching him play. I loved it when he taught me about bank shots and English. I wanted to be like him.

Art's Bar and Grill also had two back rooms that my dad put to other purposes.

Poker and dice games in the back room were a common thing, and no doubt the house took a cut there as well. He always had a doorman and a guard. High-profile personalities from the Tampa area came looking for a good, clean game—lawyers, executives, judges, priests. Like pool, sometimes my dad played in those games, sometimes he just facilitated.

My dad had a knack for finding ways to make money with everything he touched. He had an instinctual awareness of niches that he could fill, needs that he could exploit.

There were always women around, pretty women, young women, lovely older women, well-preserved older women. Many of them smelled of booze and cigarettes, wrapped in clothes a little too tight, wearing lipstick a little too red. They were all super-friendly to cute little Tony, and as I got into my teenage years, they became even friendlier. As I grew older, I came to understand why many of those women frequented the bar.

My father was well aware of the ladies of the night and always kept an open mind about their sexual advances and business practices. He believed in letting hookers ply their trade, and if he could make a few bucks facilitating liaisons, so much the better. He was never a pimp nor would he stoop so low as to be labeled in such a way. Some of those women were hardcore hookers, others part-time prostitutes, a few just desperately lonely. He knew them all. He knew which women needed extra money, which women wanted to cheat on their husbands, and he knew the men who wanted to cheat on their wives. So, he facilitated. He looked at it as helping people. Everybody got something they wanted. Men wanted to get laid; women wanted or needed the money; and he put them together and got to make a little money for himself.

As a young boy, I didn't really become aware of any of this until I reached my teenage years and began to understand sexuality and to think more grown-up thoughts. But when I was 8 or 9 years old, my dad took me to the bar one day and showed me these back rooms. One had a poker table, the other one a bed.

"What are these rooms for? Why does this one have a bed? Do you sleep here sometimes?" I asked him.

"I rent it out sometimes," he said.

"To customers?"

"Yeah, to customers."

"Like if they get really tired or something."

"Something like that.

"There are lots of ways to make money in this business," he said. "I haven't been able to get a liquor license. That would be a big way to make money, but I can't sell liquor without a license. That's really put a dent in our income."

"Income?"

"The money we make. So, because I can't get a liquor license, I have to do lots of different things."

I often heard him talk about this, his voice full of frustration and bewilderment that someone or something, some corrupt bureaucrat, was stopping him from succeeding in the liquor business. My father eventually realized that the Trafficante mob had blackballed him from ever having a liquor license. A parting shot from "the meeting" and a bold statement that rang loud and clear.

Legally, he could only sell beer, wine, and food. The city council was corrupt to the core, beholden to the Tampa mob, and he did not know how to beat that system. I remember how hard he tried to get the coveted license, but to no avail. As a last-ditch effort, he appeared in front of the city council to state his case and it became clear that nothing he said would matter. It was then, with absolute frustration and anger, he realized the word had been put out. No liquor license for Art Scarpo. Never.

~

Accompanying him to the bank to deposit the receipts was always one of the highlights of my day. The Pan American Bank was a seven-story, blockish building right across the street from the Sulphur Springs dog-racing track. All the bank tellers knew me by name, and they always gave me a lollipop. My dad flirted with the tellers, and they flirted back. He was always given the royal treatment.

One day, these visits deviated from the routine and plunged straight down a rabbit hole that changed everything.

We went inside as usual, him carrying a bag full of money, which he deposited with the teller. He then motioned to an official-looking bank employee who met us at the entrance of an enormous vault, the kind that you see in old movies. My father flashed a stainless-steel key and we proceeded inside. Being inside the bank vault was almost like being inside a cave. I could feel the thickness of the walls around me, the silence. My dad gave the special key to the manager and he unlocked a safe deposit box, pulling it from its slot. He then turned to my father and in a ceremonious way, gently placed it in my father's hands. The man then departed.

"What are we doing?" I said.

"I want to show you something," he said.

He led me into a private room adjoining the vault and locked the door. We both took a seat in the tiny room and my dad flipped up the lid of the safe deposit box.

My eyes must have bugged out of my head.

Inside were stacks and stacks of hundred-dollar bills. I had never seen so much money in my life.

My mouth dropped open. "What is this?"

"Insurance."

"Why are you showing me this?"

"You need to know that you're protected. You and your sisters are protected if something happens."

"Protected from what?"

"In case you ever get kidnapped. Do you know what kidnapping is?"

It sounded like children taking naps to me, but the look on his face told me I was wrong.

He continued, "It's when bad guys steal a person, they take them and hide them away, and they don't let them go until their family pays a ransom."

My face must have turned pale. "Money to let them go. I saw that on *Dragnet*," I said.

"Right."

I wanted him to get to whatever point he was trying to make. I could tell he was thinking about difficult things, but he could turn his facial expression into an unreadable wall.

"If you or your sisters ever get kidnapped," he said, "I want you to know this money will protect you."

"But who would want to kidnap us, Dad?"

"Do you know what the Mafia is, son?"

"You mean like gangsters? Like on *The Untouchables*?"

He nodded. "Yeah, like that. Do you understand what they do?"

"Sure I do," I said, but I didn't really. How could I?

He said, "Gangsters work for the Mafia. They do lots of illegal stuff to make money, and if you get in their way or become a distraction to them, they don't like it. A lot of those bad men don't like me and I'm not sure they will leave us alone."

"What kinds of illegal stuff?"

"Gambling, dope, kidnapping."

"Gambling is illegal? Why don't they like you?"

So many questions racing through my head all at once. By this time, I was feeling a little dizzy.

I could see his exasperation with me building. This conversation had left the rails of what he intended. "Doesn't matter. So the mob doesn't like other people horning in on their business. Or what they think is their business, anyway. They can get pretty mean about it."

"Like on TV," I said. "With guns and stuff." In that moment, I realized why we had so many guns in the house.

"Exactly. Sometimes they just want to beat you up. But if you don't listen, they might come with guns next time. Or they might kidnap your family."

A fog moved in around my mind, a dark, clinging fog. The darkness seeped into me and soaked into my bones. My sisters and I were in danger. At this time, he had not yet told me about his encounter with Henry and Fano Trafficante. I was only beginning to understand that he was up to things that were incredibly lucrative, but also incredibly dangerous. Some of the arguments I had heard between him and my mother now made sense. She didn't like that he was into things not exactly above board, but no one was going to tell him his business, not even my mother.

"Here's the thing, Tony," he said. "You have to be a man now. You can *never, ever* tell anyone about this. Not your mother. Not your sisters. Nobody! You understand me?" His gaze drilled me to the floor.

A rapid-fire succession of possibilities shot through me. Gangsters coming to grab me on my way home from school, or my sisters. Bad guys breaking into our house. Tommy guns in violin cases. I imagined getting thrown into the trunk of a car.

"Swear to me you'll never tell a soul," he said.

"I swear," I said, my mouth dry.

I walked out of that bank in a daze, feeling like the world was full of monsters walking around like normal people.

For the next few weeks, I couldn't stop thinking about it. Were there people who wanted to do things like this to him? To *us?* Where on earth had he gotten *all that money?* I can't even speculate on how much was there. Tens of thousands of dollars, certainly, and this would have been 1969 or 1970.

This knowledge ate at me, and knowing I couldn't tell anyone made it worse. I tried to stay calm and keep my thoughts to myself, but one day the stress got to me.

Finally, my mom saw that something was chewing on me, and I just blurted it out to her. "Dad showed me a huge pile of cash in a safe deposit box." In that moment, it seemed important that she knew.

She looked as surprised as I had been. "You're sure, Tony? You're not making this up?"

I shook my head vigorously. "Ask him about it!"

When she did, a little chunk of hell broke loose. The argument was loud and long. She was furious, yelling at him.

"What the hell are you doing with all that money in a safe deposit box!"

"Relax," he said, "don't worry about it. Tony doesn't know what he's talking about."

"What the hell are you into, Art! Where did you get all that cash?"

"Don't you worry about it."

When the argument was finally over, I must have breathed a sigh of relief, but this began some of the earliest friction I can remember between my dad and me. It was my job to protect my sisters—the fact that I tormented them mercilessly notwithstanding. My dad was doing things that put us all in danger. To him, I had broken my word by telling Mom, and a man's word is *everything*. A man whose word is worth nothing is worth less than nothing. The disappointment and the frustration he directed at me made me feel guilty and resentful that I had been put in that kind of position, that I was expected to lie to my mom and provide a cover for something I didn't understand.

A slow realization came to me after the initial shock. My dad was making a *lot* of money. He was populating our little farm on Skipper Road with horses and other animals, which I knew were not cheap. He bought a nice car, a big, shiny Lincoln. I hadn't thought much about those things, except to enjoy them with my family as they came along, but at some point, it hit me: Dad must be doing a lot more than selling beer and sandwiches.

With this realization, that dark fog crept back in. Along with the darkness of happenings at the Cone Brothers pits, I couldn't help but see the evil all around us now and that it might follow my dad home like a stray dog. The world became a rougher and more sinister place, more evil. I inherited his powerful protective streak, and the irony is that as I got into my teenage years, the older I got, the more often I felt like I had to protect my family from the things his activities were bringing down on us.

This was a slow evolution, however, this fracturing, like the crack in a windshield that begins as a tiny gravel chip. This incident was the chip in the windshield. As I got older, the chip became a crack, but at this age, he was still a god to me. His word was gospel.

Chapter Nine

Broken Bones and Salvation

LIVING FAR OUT IN the country on Skipper Road had its advantages, but the one drawback was the lack of stores near our home. It was a major inconvenience to go shopping, sometimes an all-day event. So you can imagine how great it was when the first convenience store was built about a mile and a half away. It was 1971 and I was 10 years old. They called it Shop N' Go, the home of the famous Icee, my favorite treat.

Tony Bejano and I made numerous trips to the store. It became part of our new adventure. My mom loved a candy bar now and then and would ask me to buy her favorite soda, Purple Passion. Priscilla would often send Tony over there to bring back the ingredients for her favorite sandwich: baloney, cheese, and bread. Riding our bikes that distance on the main road made us feel free, grown-up, needed.

Our parents put few restrictions on Tony and me. We had our run of the Cone Brothers pits and the surrounding forests and swamps, as far as our spirit of adventure dared us to go. We rode our bikes and horses everywhere, dodging snakes and alligators. We felt like we owned our whole world.

One evening, my mom and sisters asked me if I planned to ride to the store. Always looking for an excuse to get on my bike, I said, "Sure."

I called Tony and he jumped at the idea. Armed with a list for treats, sweets, soda and ice cream, away we went. We made our way to the Shop N' Go and loaded up. It was nearing sunset, and Tony and I were about halfway home when we approached a hairpin curve, riding on the left side of the road.

A car was coming at me.

As it rounded the curve, the sun shone from directly behind me, into the eyes of the woman driving the car.

Everything turned to slow motion. The driver shielded her eyes, blinded, headed straight in my direction.

Tony swerved hard right to get out of the way. I swerved to the left.

The driver never even saw me.

The car T-boned me on my right side, flipping me high into the air.

Spinning, soaring, feeling as if I was going higher and higher, the sun in my eyes. Was I going to Heaven? Was I just going to keep spinning up and up and up and...

No, it wasn't my time.

Within an instant, the ground rushed up at me; I slammed into it, flat on my back, pain exploding everywhere. I looked down, and my legs were gone. I couldn't breathe.

Tony came flying back, his face full of panic. I remember screaming uncontrollably, "I'm dead! I'm dead!" A wave of shock overtook my body. The act of screaming helped me breathe again.

Tony took off for home at lightning speed.

The driver got out of her car, both hands clutching her mouth.

I couldn't see my legs. Where were they?

She reached under me and stretched my legs back out. I heard and felt crunching, grinding sensations inside. My legs had been bent backwards under me. A huge wave of relief went through me knowing they were still attached to my body.

She was crying and trying to talk at the same time, but I don't remember what she said, only the blood on her hands.

It seemed like hours before I saw my mom pedaling toward me on Tony's bicycle, ignoring the wobbliness from the growing symptoms of her illness. Tony was running on foot, right on her tail.

My mom was frantic, yelling at the driver. Priscilla stayed behind to watch both of my sisters. There was crying and wailing. The way they were carrying on terrified me. Was I going to die? I didn't want to try moving, afraid I might make things worse if I did, so I just lay there looking up at the sunset sky, a bizarre sense of peace and panic all at the same time, all while trying to talk to my mom as best I could.

I don't know how long I lay there before an ambulance showed up, but it was about the same time as my dad had made it from the bar. He must have been traveling a hundred miles an hour to make it there that fast. His face was white, tense, holding my mom, propping her up, as they loaded me onto a gurney.

One bit of good fortune was that University Community Hospital had just been built on the University of South Florida campus, about half a mile from where I lay. Otherwise, it would have been fifteen miles to the nearest hospital.

As the doors shut on the ambulance, I didn't yet know if I was going to live, walk again, or die.

～

Amid X-rays and examinations, a vigil coalesced around me in the hospital. Aunts, uncles, and cousins showed up. The worry in the air was palpable.

My hard, macho father looked one breath away from tears. There was something in his eyes that I didn't understand then. As an adult, knowing what I know now about the things happening in his life outside of my view, I wonder if he must have been questioning himself. His only son might be dying. He had already lost one child. Was God unhappy with the choices he was making? Was he living his life right? Maybe he was questioning his immortal soul, his salvation, his place in the world.

The doctor at University Community Hospital, Dr. Tedone, told me and my parents, "He has a concussion, and his right femur has been shattered." When he showed us the X-ray, my thigh bone looked like a shattered glass. He didn't say this to me, but I later learned that my survival was not yet a given. The concussion was severe, and there was the possibility of dangerous, undetected internal injuries or infection. I had several serious cuts on my body and my face.

"Normally, when we fix a break like this," Dr. Tedone said, "we go in and put in a bunch of steel pins. But in this case, I think that's a bad idea. The pins never really do what they're supposed to do. They're incredibly painful. Plus, that bone is still growing. Putting in pins will stunt its development and leave him with a lifelong limp."

"So, what then?" Dad said.

"I want to put him in traction. Constant tension on the leg

should help the broken pieces align themselves and knit properly. It's experimental, but I think it's his best chance to walk normally again."

"How long will he be in traction?" Dad said.

"Maybe two months, give or take. It depends on how the bone heals."

So they decided to go ahead with experimental traction, which meant that I would be flat on my back for two months, with my right leg elevated. They flooded me with painkillers and glued pads to my leg, using weights to keep it under constant tension.

If all went well with the traction, I would be in a full body cast for ninety days afterward.

I passed much of the next few days asleep, my brain fogged by the concussion and the drugs that were supposed to keep me comfortable. I remember lots of pain medication and lots of Hawaiian Punch, the only drink that I liked while in the hospital. Morning, noon, and night, Hawaiian Punch. When it became clear that my life was no longer in immediate danger, my family relaxed a bit. Classmates and teachers came to see me. All the attention made me feel almost famous. I became the kid everybody rallied around. Because of what happened to me, connections between my family, community, school, and church strengthened. But even that didn't lessen the nightmares of arcing high through the air, into the sky, seeing the ground rushing at me, and then jolting awake, feeling as if my legs were gone, which sent shock waves of pain through my legs.

My mom was there with me constantly, often holding her rosary, praying when she thought I was asleep. If not for her choice to marry, she might have become a nun herself, such was the strength of her faith.

All the women in my family were strong women, and they were all devout Catholics. They went to Mass and Bible study regularly, and they made sure all the children did, too. They made sure we received our sacraments, from baptism to reconciliation, communion, and confirmation. They made sure we went to catechism. The Scarpo men sanctioned all of this, but even at this age I couldn't escape noticing their hypocrisy, because for them, religious practice was at best a pretense, a cultural tradition rather than any belief system. Of course, they went to weddings, funerals, and major holiday services, but they were happy to relegate religion to the realm of women. Kids who complained about having to go to church were quickly set straight by the men, even though the men never went themselves.

Toward this end, I was soon visited by nuns from Most Holy Redeemer, led by Sister Dorothy Barbara. At the time of the accident, I was in the midst of preparing for my First Holy Communion, and my father declared that this preparation was to continue, so the nuns came to me weekly to continue my catechism instruction.

Sister Dorothy Barbara was an angelic vision of the divine. About 30 years old, with long dark hair, she was stunningly beautiful. I already knew her from my catechism studies, and was already taken with her, but having her visit me in the hospital filled me with a warmth I cannot describe. She was stern, like all nuns I've ever met, but there was a warmth and kindness inside that made me feel a special love for her. Because of her tremendous beauty, I couldn't help but have a boyhood crush on her and found myself falling into fantasies of adoration. She could have been with any man she wanted, but she had chosen to marry God. I never understood why she would do that, but I was always thankful she was there. When I was discharged from the hospital, she continued my lessons at home. Occasionally other nuns would accompany her to our house to help my mom with household chores, to pray for us or read to my sisters. Through them, I saw what true kindness and compassion really meant. This was what goodness was supposed to look like. I had already seen so much of the opposite—the Cone Brothers pits, a dead body, terrible behavior at the bar, the safe deposit box—she was like a breath of fresh air.

During their visits, my dad would occasionally hover, maybe to make sure I was doing my studies properly, or maybe because he was drawn to that goodness. His empire, now firmly established, was built upon human vices, but these nuns had brought divine light into our lives, and I think he could not help but measure himself against it. Maybe he thought it was too late for him, but he could make sure his son's salvation was ensured.

~

Two months in traction was not something I would wish for anybody. It was incredibly painful at times, as I was unable to move, unable even to lie on my side, the weights constantly pulling on my injured leg, creating an ache that pain medication could only dull, never wipe away.

When the doctor gave the go-ahead for my parents to take me home, I was first encased in a full body cast that started at my sternum and reached all the way down to the foot of my injured right leg and halfway down the left. The legs of the cast were connected by a brace that kept my knees locked in place. I had to wear this body cast for the next three months. It was terrible, but at least I had more freedom.

My dad built a ramp for me in the back seat of the station wagon so I could prop myself up in an approximation of normal. I could go places with them.

He was also serious about me not getting behind in school. He hired my fourth-grade teacher to come to the house and tutor me personally.

The itching under the cast was torture, so I fashioned myself a coat hanger to reach down inside and scratch. I still have scars from the times I got overzealous.

The awful thing about the body cast was that all bodily functions went through a single opening. I was stuck with bottles and bedpans for the next ninety days, which is its own special kind of gross. I could fit a T-shirt over the upper part of my body, but the legs were a special kind of problem if I wanted to have any modesty at all. So, my parents fashioned a wrap for my waist that covered my cast hole. The wrap had snaps to hold it closed on the top and the bottom, but on one occasion, they failed when Sister Dorothy Barbara was teaching me. When I discovered this, I was mortified. If she noticed, she gave no indication.

Her kindness and compassion always managed to soothe the chafing of my confinement. To her, I must have looked like a mangled mess. She believed in the inherent goodness of everyone, and her innate holiness was like a warm glow whenever I was in her presence. She brought me pictures of the Pope and one of the saints to keep beside my bed.

My lack of freedom ate at me, though. After two months of being on my back, unable to go bike riding or on deep woods adventures with Tony, I got pretty cranky. In my body cast, I was neither sitting nor lying down, but stuck in a half-reclined position. The cast was so heavy I had to be carried everywhere, and I couldn't bend at the waist or the knees. By the end of it, I did manage to learn how to lever myself into a semi-standing position and shamble like Frankenstein's monster, swinging each leg forward. Dr. Tedone hated that.

~

During my recovery, the entire family attended a family baptism for one of my cousins. We were all there in church, the entire Scarpo family, aunts, uncles, and cousins. Thirty-five or so in all. I was there in the pew with my parents and sisters, propped up like a crooked statue in my body cast.

The church was not full that day, a private event, so we all sat near the front, dressed in our finest, all these Italian men with slicked hair and fine suits, women in their beautiful dresses. It was a windy day, whistling over the church.

The priest was in the middle of the service when an explosion boomed in the back of the church, and the sound reverberated through the cavernous space of the sanctuary, echoing like thunder.

My dad and all his brothers ducked behind the pews. Right next to me, he knelt there with his snub-nose .38 in his hand, and I just stared. My uncles hunkered down, guns drawn like they were ready for war. Here I was, sitting upright like a statue, unable to bend over.

Nobody said a word.

As the silence hung, it occurred to me that the noise sounded just like a huge door slamming shut, caught by the wind. The same realization must have slowly taken hold of everyone around me. Eventually, the guns all disappeared, the men got back in their seats, facing forward as if nothing had happened. The Scarpo women seemed to take this all in stride.

The priest stood there with his mouth open, but then recomposed himself and went on with the baptism.

It wasn't until after the service when my cousin Linda reenacted that incident with exaggerated gravitas for everybody, holding her finger pistol like cops on TV, that everyone exploded with laughter. She must have been 11 or 12 at the time.

"Hey, Uncle Bud!" she called with a mischievous grin. My dad was known as "Uncle Bud." "Show us all that move you did again."

At all sorts of family gatherings, Linda would reenact the Great Shootout That Never Was, and the incident became Scarpo family legend.

∿

Ask yourself this: how many kids do you know whose family members pulled their guns out during a church service? It was as bewildering as it was absurd, so absurd that it never occurred to me that I would have been a sitting duck in a real shootout. Mafia assassinations had been commonplace in Tampa for decades, but it's only in retrospect that I can recognize how much tension my father must have been under to be that jumpy.

For the most part, though, the incident fell second in magnitude to the awfulness of my time in the body cast.

One day, I was in a lot of pain, lamenting my sorry state, stuck in my body cast. I asked Sister Dorothy, "If God is so good and kind, how could He let this happen to me?"

She just gave me that beatific smile. "It's all part of a plan, a plan for your salvation, to make you a better person, and quite possibly to bring people together."

This did not help me in the moment. It didn't make the pain go away. It didn't get the stupid body cast off me. My life had been brought to a screeching halt. These thoughts must have shown on my face, because then she said, "You will get better. You'll be back on your feet. But here's the most important thing: you're going to make a difference now for everyone who comes into your life."

In the time between her visits, though, I chewed on what she had said, and her words settled into me. My life has always been a struggle between good and bad, with both rooted deep in my soul. The lights in my life were my mom, the Church, and the nuns who cared for me. But I had already seen some of the worst of human behavior, with much worse in the years to come. I couldn't help but think that I had almost died when that car hit, that I was halfway to Heaven, but then came crashing back to earth. I came to see this incident as a second chance at life.

I have always felt the presence of God in my life, that He's been with me all along through this journey, perhaps strongest during all those moments when I inexplicably escaped death. At 10 years old, I did not understand this fully. As I grew up, I danced with the Devil many times, but I could not stand the heat or the fire. My conscience always won in the end, steering me from the wild side back onto a more positive path. At times, as I grew older, I could be very bad and very good at the same time. I was the first male

Scarpo to embrace Catholicism, rather than fall into it by default. All the other men did the lip service but relegated it to the realm of the women in the family. For me, it became a real thing, something I chose.

To this day, when I'm in the presence of or nearing something that's not right, something on the dark side, I get a sick feeling in the pit of my stomach, and I steer away from it. I often ignored this feeling while growing up and pushing limits. However, I credit Sister Dorothy Barbara's teaching for developing the goodness in me. Without it, I may have gone too far down some very dark paths.

CHAPTER TEN

LUCKY'S

MY DAD MET Bert Wallace on the pool circuit. Bert was a true pool shark, incredibly skilled—and a wheelchair-bound paraplegic.

As a young boy in Wisconsin, Bert accidentally shot himself in the back with a shotgun while climbing over a fence, paralyzing him for life.

As an older man, he was a larger-than-life study in contradictions, with a personality that could be as expansive and generous as it was hostile and excessive. In appearance, he resembled a craggy, jowled, Larry Flynt kind of character, but confined to a wheelchair. Like Larry Flynt, publisher of *Hustler* magazine, Bert was always surrounded by beautiful women. Women were his weakness, that much was clear, even to a kid like me. What surprised me was how well he managed his disability. He drove himself around in a shiny new Cadillac, specially modified for him. He cooked and cleaned and drove his own boat. There wasn't much he couldn't do. Bert did, however, have a significant vice. He practically created the stereotype of a hard-drinking, belligerent drunk. I doubt I ever saw anything but hard liquor pass his lips. When he was sober, he was kind and generous, boisterous and charismatic. When he was drunk, however, he'd routinely try to pick a fight with the biggest guy he could find.

Bert owned a lounge called Lucky's on Nebraska Avenue, about a mile and a half from the dog track. The distinction between a lounge and a bar and grill was huge. A lounge was a true nightclub, where liquor but no food was served. The profit margin for liquor was astronomical compared to food.

Bert was a shrewd salesman hampered by his weakness for hard booze. What he needed was a manager to oversee daily operations at Lucky's, someone who might mitigate the worst of his drunken impulses.

~

Around the time of my accident, my dad got an offer from someone who wanted to buy Art's Bar and Grill. Even though business was good, he was still feeling stymied by his lack of a liquor license and the prestige that went with it. All his entrepreneurial side-ventures were still not enough for him. There was more money to be made, if only he could reach it. Plus, he wanted to extend a not-so-cordial middle finger to the Trafficante mob.

On the pool circuit, Bert had taken particular notice of my dad and how he ran Art's Bar and Grill, how he could hustle the crowd. The key word here is "hustle." Bert was self-aware enough to know he needed a real manager, a good one. Every manager he had hired up to this point had been awful. They stole from him or brought with them a host of personal deficiencies that tore holes in Bert's business.

As fate would have it, the timing was great for both Bert and my dad. My dad had recently signed the sales contract on Art's Bar and Grill, and Bert needed someone to help him run his business.

Somewhere deep in their negotiations, they both left the meeting with a smile on their face. What started as an offer to run and manage Lucky's as an employee ended up being a fifty-fifty partnership for my father. He had finally hit the jackpot: ownership of a liquor lounge, albeit partial ownership. A backdoor past the Trafficantes.

My dad's job was to manage all the operations, and he brought with him all the skills and contacts he had garnered from his side-ventures at Art's Bar and Grill—the bookmaking, the backroom gambling, the pool games, the "facilitating"—and Bert got to play pool, drink his liquor at wholesale, and womanize. Bert was already running poker games and hookers and my dad was ecstatic to finally have this opportunity. He was determined to make it a huge success. The profit margin for the liquor business was enormous. Just imagine a $19.00 fifth of Jack Daniels. A fifth of liquor contains about seventeen standard shots, at $3.50 a shot. The math is clear, and serving food is a low-margin proposition. My dad's first order of business was to build a new package store addition to the front of the building. That way he could expand the liquor operations with the sit-down customer, who spent a small fortune, or the customer on the run. My dad invented the first drive-thru liquor store. Hard to believe in this day and age but at the time, it was revolutionary. Profits exploded overnight, and Bert was thrilled.

What's more, serving liquor brought a different kind of clientele than beer and wine drinkers. Up until this point, most of my dad's patrons had been local crackers and rednecks. In effect, they had become his people. Whether consciously or unconsciously, he had made himself into one of them, speaking with a Southern drawl and taking on some of their mannerisms. His posse followed him to Lucky's, but liquor sales also attracted people willing to pay more for fancy cocktails and high-shelf booze, people willing to gamble for higher stakes.

He was also delighted to be back within spitting distance of the dog track, one of his most profitable ventures. His runners were still with him, still eager to cash in on bookmaking. He took charge of all the gambling operations at Lucky's, putting him deeper than ever in the illicit activities that had grabbed the attention of Henry Trafficante. The road had been paved for massive expansion of the gambling operations. Pool games, poker, dice, bookmaking, and more. Why he did this, after the threats to him and his family, I have often tried to figure out. Was it pride? Was it greed? Both? Was he caught up in watching it all build and snowball? Was it the fact that he had managed to create his own mini-empire, complete with soldiers willing to do anything for him? These were the questions that swirled in my mind for years.

Maybe in the beginning, some of that was true, but life threw my family a major curveball around this time.

It had been clear for a few years that my mom was having increasing problems with her balance, dexterity, and cognition. When I was about 12 years old, she was diagnosed with multiple sclerosis, a debilitating disease that slowly, inexorably strips away one's physical and mental abilities, and eventually one's dignity, and at the late stages, the ability to breathe. I can only imagine the blow this must have been to my parents. One child had died, I almost died in a car accident, and now my mom had an incurable, long-term, degenerative disease. My sisters and I went through a phase of having to accept our mother's debilitating illness, and all the while I was questioning my teaching from Sister Dorothy Barbara. How could God do this to such a good person?

My mom herself went through a terrible period of denial, falling deep into depression, interspersed with periods of anger at the injustice of it all. Hadn't she been faithful enough? She soon stopped working at the bar with Dad, partly because my father did not want her around the liquor business and partly because she was losing the ability to stay on her feet for long. She tired quickly and tended to spill things.

The doctor told my dad, "You need to be in this for the long haul and you better have a fat wallet." She could go into a slow, inevitable, downward spiral that could last many years. There might come a day when she could no longer live at home. What was worse, we had no health insurance, and because of her condition, no chance of getting any. He was personally responsible for every medical bill. That fact alone made him calculate the possible costs for long-term health care, and the number was staggering—hundreds of thousands of dollars, possibly millions. So, he threw himself into every moneymaking proposition he could find, despite the danger that he was stepping on some dangerous toes in the Tampa-area Mafia.

Regardless of the danger, the synergy between Bert and my dad turned Lucky's into a goldmine. Even at a fifty-percent share, my dad began to make more money than he ever had before.

～

All the members of my dad's posse had nicknames: Pizza Joe; Ralph the Meat Man; Carl the Bug Man; Ed the Mailman; Freddy and Verlon. These men were like my uncles, these Deep South country people. They were always around, drinking, fishing and joining us for barbeques. At any time, he could have called up ten of them, and they would have done anything he asked. Their loyalty was hard-won, but it went deep.

They spent their money at his place, and he helped them in many ways. He facilitated some of their business deals, helped their families, and loaned them money.

Tampa is unique because of its conglomeration of local cultures and ethnicities. The Spanish, the Cubans, the Italians, the African-Americans, and the crackers. All these groups were more or less segregated, with uneasy overlap at the edges, yet they all found a way to coexist. Ironically, it was among the crackers that my dad found true acceptance. They became his people more so than the Italian community ever did.

Something he carefully maintained, however, was hierarchy. Through brains, determination, and audacity, he had become the emperor of his own mini-empire, which put him just a shade above them, but he would never insult them or look down on them. It was their money and loyalty that made him. Loyalty is a two-way street, and he worked hard to be worthy of it.

Lucky's was his territory, his sphere of influence, and he now had a significant group of men willing to help him defend it. All these men were aware of the Mafia influence in Tampa, the battle-grounds. The 1970s was the height of territorial wars between the various factions, and lounges like Lucky's were both strongholds and battlegrounds.

Dad's people read the newspapers, where stories of mob-related killings and trials had been part and parcel of Tampa life for decades. These men were not only his defenders, but his informants. They were all over town. They heard things. And they would be invaluable when the Trafficantes realized my dad was back in the saddle.

∼

A couple of years after beginning the Lucky's partnership, my family opened a new chapter.

The University of South Florida had become a successful institution, growing tremendously, so it began to buy as much of the surrounding land as it could. This created a demand for nearby housing, so real estate developers jumped into the market as well. Because of Skipper Road's proximity to the university, my dad was able to sell our farmhouse and property on Skipper Road for a tremendous profit. He sold everything, all the horses and other farm animals. He was done with farming. He had his eye on a higher kind of living.

Coupled with the ongoing success of Lucky's, my dad bought several acres and a house in Lutz, a community north of Tampa peppered with beautiful lakes. Because of all the lakefront property, Lutz was an affluent area, a land of watercraft and Cadillacs.

Our new house was even more secluded than Skipper Road, in an orange grove on a beautiful lake.

I was still very much a kid, at 13 years old. One of the unfortunate side effects of opening a new chapter is closing the previous one. I inevitably lost touch with Tony Bejano. We couldn't ride our bikes to school together anymore or explore the Cone Brothers pits. My mom and Priscilla remained close friends, but we didn't see the Bejanos as much after that, although we occasionally came to visit each other. As Tony grew older, he gravitated more and more toward the carnie world, and after my experiences at Gibsonton, I had had enough of that world.

Even though Dad had shown me all that money in the safe deposit box and explained its purpose, I still had little concept of the magnitude of what he was doing. He must have thought it was time for me to learn more because he would often take me to Lucky's to help out during the day and, more importantly, get to know the customers. All in all, I was just happy to have a nicer house—with air conditioning!—and a beautiful lake on which to fish, boat, and water-ski right outside my back door, plus a whole new secluded area to explore. We had hit the big time. Instead of swampy forest infested by alligators and venomous snakes, we had orange groves and beautiful lakes.

Well, we still had alligators.

We had few neighbors, so it wasn't long before we got to know them. There was maybe a total of ten kids who lived in our sprawling neighborhood. The properties all consisted of several acres, so we all lived some distance apart.

Tommy Dolan lived with his family on a nearby lake. He was a couple of years older than me and soon introduced me to the world of motorcycles. He drove a Kawasaki 200, and before long I had a Honda CB-100 of my own. Small motorcycles were all the rage then, and we rode all over that area, making little paths around the lakes and orange groves.

My dad and Bert had struck up such a friendship, and thanks to my dad's management Lucky's had become so successful, that Bert bought a property across the main road from ours, on Deer Lake. No doubt, the power of Bert's liquor license encouraged my dad to put up with the extremes of Bert's behavior, but I think mutual understanding was the basis of their friendship. Our house was situated on Lake Kell, a beautiful lake just under two hundred yards across and maybe a quarter-mile long north to south.

At the school bus stop, I met another boy named Bobby who was my age, and soon discovered he lived next door to Bert. We lived the farthest away from school, so we spent many hours on the bus together, the last to get off. All of us who lived so far out became good friends. Bobby's family was Hungarian, and as mine was Italian, we found we shared a kind of Old World set of values.

Before long we were inseparable. He had a motorcycle, too—all the rage, as I said—and we spent hours tooling around the acres and acres of orange trees.

Bert never paid much attention to me or my sisters. By this time, Dad would take me with him to the bar during the day to help with cleaning up, and Bert was often there, just as often surly and hungover as he was friendly and kind. As far as I knew, his attention was firmly rooted in booze and women, reveling in the money Lucky's was making.

But then something happened I did not expect—Bert got engaged.

His fiancée could have been actress Loni Anderson's twin sister, a buxom, blonde bombshell named Dory. She and Bert adored each other, and like my dad, she knew how to handle him when he was drunk. What a woman like that could see in him mystified me. For a 13-year-old boy, she was pure, curvaceous eye candy.

They threw a massive engagement party one weekend at Bert's house on the lake.

All the crew from the bar were there, the who's who of their clan, many dignitaries that were on the payroll, plus people from around the neighborhood. My dad's parties on Skipper Road were legendary, but this one fell into a whole new realm. I had never seen such quantities of food, beer, and liquor, along with a mountain of engagement gifts for Bert and Dory. Like all the houses on these lakes, Bert's house had its own dock, and boats were coming and going, water-skiers coming and going. My cohorts and I were riding motorcycles everywhere. Bert's magnanimity that day stretched to the kids as well. He let us play with his high-end Pioneer hi-fi stereo. I still remember the huge Cerwin Vega speakers that could rattle windows and make it sound like a live concert was happening right in front of us. He let us drive his racing boat, a sleek little craft that felt like it was powered by a rocket. It could make a circuit of Deer Lake in no time at all.

It was on that day I saw why so many people loved Bert. He could be amazingly kind and generous, like he was with us kids, with a personality too large for his skin.

Life was good in our new world. I was making friends, enjoying the perks that my dad brought home, and growing up. Finally, a real normal.

Soon, I would start the new school year and enter seventh grade. Without our knowing, a social revolution was unfolding all around us. The dark places of existence lurked very close—as well as others soon to be discovered.

CHAPTER ELEVEN

THE SCHOOL GAUNTLET: A WAR ZONE

MY FAMILY AND I moved to Lutz in the summer after sixth grade. This move happened to coincide with Hillsborough County's new, federally mandated school busing program, an effort to end racial segregation in the South. Tensions were high as neither side embraced the idea of their children being bused miles across town. Protests and anger erupted throughout the state, but the government had their final say in this debate. As the brain-trusts mapped out our future in an effort to ease race relations, they had in fact set the wheels in motion to create greater tension and increased violence throughout the school system. We had become their lab rats in a social experiment gone wrong. No one, not even our parents knew what was in store for us and sadly, very few even asked questions.

I was raised in a household full of prejudice, surrounded by it at family gatherings and backyard parties, and especially at the bar. My dad, my uncles, and all the men from the bar used the word "nigger" and other racial slurs routinely. I often overheard them saying disparaging things about them. I have no knowledge of their prior conflicts or how they were raised but I felt a distrust early on that seemed confusing. But that never felt right to me. I was the kid who thought blacks and whites should get along. I was a child of the Sixties. I looked up to Martin Luther King Jr. and John F. Kennedy. If I had learned anything from the Bejano family, it was not to judge people by the way they looked, by the color of their skin. Tampa was very much a segregated city—and largely remains so to this day. The whites, the Latins, the Italians, the blacks, each had their own part of town, and there was distinct friction at the borderlines.

The assassination of Dr. Martin Luther King Jr. was only five years in the past. The civil rights movement was still front and center in the public consciousness, a contentious issue in Florida on the best of days. But it wasn't something I thought about much at 12 or 13 years old. Kids were just kids. That being said, I hadn't grown up around any black kids. I didn't know any. I was curious, but at the same time, how much of what I'd heard shaped my mind. There weren't any black people out on Skipper Road or in my elementary school; that was cracker country.

Black people frequented Lucky's package store because my father cashed their payroll checks and sold them liquor and beer. There was always a mutual respect between the black community and my dad, but segregation was still a real thing. They were only allowed in the package store side; the lounge side, sitting down with white customers—most of whom were unabashedly racist and very country—those things were off-limits. It was still true, even in the seventies, that black people who "went where they shouldn't go" were putting themselves in physical danger. In the package store, my father would tell them, "I can only protect you on this side of the wall but I can't protect you on the other side." He was referring to his hard-nosed, redneck customers who loved to fight.

The irony was that *I* was about to go to the "other side" myself.

The new federally mandated school busing program was going to take us kids from Lutz and haul us seventeen miles—about 45-60 minutes each way—to one of the schools in the black part of town, Nathan B. Young Junior High in East Tampa. My stomach must have been a basket full of butterflies on that first day. I was going to *junior high*. I wasn't in elementary school anymore. Nathan B. Young was a new school where I knew nobody, and riding with a bus full of strangers to boot. At first, it did seem odd to be traveling so far from home to attend school but like all kids, I just went with the flow.

I was still the new kid in the Lutz neighborhood, and I still knew practically no one. It was at the bus stop across the main road that I met Bobby, who would soon become my best friend. Among others, there was also Tommy Dolan, whom I'd already met, and his two sisters, Rebecca, who was a little older than me, and Kathy, who was my age. Few kids lived in the area, so they were all curious about me. All that attention was like pressure on my skin. Before long, though, the extended bus rides gave us the opportunity to get to know each other. The Lutz kids all lived at the "end of the line." The last bus stop.

That first bus ride, alone with my thoughts and trepidations, was an eternity. It took us down unfamiliar streets into a part of Tampa I'd never seen before. Skipper Road was hardly the "nice" part of town, but the kind of poverty I saw rolling past the grimy bus window shocked me. The houses were run-down shotgun shacks desperately in need of paint, roofs and porches sagging, hunched in the sun on patches of bare earth, not a blade of grass to be seen. Everywhere I looked were black faces and looks of surprise at the bus full of white children. Were their eyes as big as mine?

I was on an alien planet.

When I got to school, however, my nervousness went away. The school building felt bright and safe, and the teachers were kind and friendly, like teachers should be. When I was inside the school building, I could begin to imagine that it felt normal. My classes were interesting, and I have always loved learning. I jumped right into that aspect of my school life and I excelled.

The mix of students was about 50 percent white, 50 percent black. We shared the same building but nothing else. Each group kept uneasily to itself. To the black students, we must have been invaders, horning into their turf. From the first day, I was not alone in getting the distinct impression the white students were not welcome.

The school day could almost feel normal amid classes and other activities, but underneath it all, tension was building. The black students spoke differently, acted differently. The underlying resentment of our intrusion was palpable every day, and it grew. The Darwinian, survival-of-the-fittest mentality was most prevalent among the boys. Middle school is probably the most difficult time of transition for any kid, but adding the racial friction made it into its unique kind of hell.

Physical education class was the worst. Because of my small size, I always felt like a tiny worm on a great big hook surrounded by sharks. The black kids tried to push me around; I tried to stand my ground. If there was anything I had learned from my dad, it was to never back down. Our P.E. fields were broad and open with no fences or borders in sight.

The perimeter of the school property was lined with houses and apartments full of poverty-stricken families, with nothing separating us from them. Among these tenements was a population of teenagers who did not go to school, a rough conglomeration of dropouts and gang members. They hovered around the outskirts of the P.E. ground, heckling and taunting us. We were prey animals surrounded by hyenas. As the school year progressed, they grew bolder, venturing onto the school grounds to provoke or frighten us even more. I used to think, *Oh my God, I don't dare get too close to the boundary.* Whenever I was on the P.E. field, I made sure I was never a straggler. God forbid you were that lone puppy out there surrounded by coyotes. The coaches and teachers seemed to ignore them or at least tolerate them, but these hoodlums always knew when no adults were around.

The tension among the students grew as the school year went on. The intimidation by the black kids was an endless barrage of smack talk that left me constantly uneasy, walking on tiptoes and looking over my shoulder. On one hand, I started to get used to it, but then fights began to erupt between black and white students, small at first but escalating, a constant process of establishing hierarchy and social boundaries. The resonance with stories like *Lord of the Flies* still haunts me.

Greg Perez was a boy who stood out. At 13, he stood taller than all the rest of us and was into bodybuilding. He looked older, more muscular. He was a pleasant, soft-spoken kid of Puerto Rican ancestry, born and raised in Tampa. He was always shy, but happy to talk if someone else talked first. Because he stood out in a physical way, he became a target, constantly tested for how far he could be pushed. Most of the time, he responded with some blistering smack talk of his own, and that would force his challengers to back down. But one day it all went a little too far, and a fight erupted.

Being larger and stronger than anyone else, Greg beat the snot out of one of his tormentors, then threw in a couple more punches as a message for everyone to leave him the hell alone. They both walked away from it, and it all appeared to be over—at first.

The kid Greg had beaten up, however, was part of one of those families that lived on the fringe of the school grounds, with older brothers, relatives, and friends who had turned to the life of gangs and thuggery. These older teenage kids were simply looking for trouble.

A few days later, a huge group of them jumped Greg on the school grounds; dozens of them, along with a number of black students, converged on the grassy area between the two main school buildings, the perfect place for an ambush. Between periods, they surrounded him there, trapped him, and fell upon him *en masse*. Greg had no hope. The fight drew a crowd, but there was nothing anyone could do. They beat on him, and beat on him, and beat on him, and all I could do was watch in shock and terror, wanting to but unable to help him. When his attackers finally scattered, Greg lay there in a crumpled heap, a horrid mass of blood and broken bones, broken teeth, broken eye socket. Terror and shock blasted through the crowd of stunned onlookers. Girls screamed and cried, boys like me scattered to hide. Who would those thugs come for next? I remember teachers crying, an ambulance coming, the police.

No one was ever charged.

It was many years before I spoke to Greg Perez again. He never came back to Nathan B. Young Junior High. I ran into him at my twenty-year high school alumni reunion and asked him about that beating. He tried to blow it off, but it was clear it had changed his life. It had taken him months to recover, but he would never regain his full health.

This bloodbath emboldened the black kids in school and the thugs in the surrounding neighborhood. For them, it was a badge of honor. Word spread like wildfire that an all-out riot would be next. They were coming for the white kids.

We were all sheep being led to the slaughter. Memories of six months of traction and body cast were fresh. I imagined Greg Perez's broken body covered in a plaster cast and resolved that would *never* happen to me. Every day, I went to school with an increasing sense of dread, my stomach twisted in knots. Would that day be my turn?

I don't know if we told our parents about the pending riot and they did nothing, or if we just didn't tell them. In retrospect, it seems hard to believe that the attack on Greg Perez didn't make its way to our parents' ears.

Our bus driver Polly, a short, middle-aged firecracker of a Southern woman, knew all too well what she was driving us into every day. She knew what had happened to Greg Perez, and she must have heard rumors about the coming riot. One morning, we all showed up at the bus stop like usual, nervous as we were, and boarded the bus. Polly drove us across town and pulled into the circular drive in front of the school. She apparently noticed an unusually large number of black kids in the area, kids who were too old to be hanging out at a middle school bus stop. Before she realized this, four or five of us had trickled off the bus, but then she hollered at us to get back on. As soon as we did, she slammed the bus doors and drove all of us back home again, dropping each one of us at our respective bus stops. She made sure to tell us this was for our safety and if our parents had any questions, to call her.

It was the weirdest way ever to get a day off from school, fraught with unanswered questions and unseen danger. Something must have triggered her instincts that morning, and she may well have saved some of our lives. Even though it was unheard of for a bus driver to take her passengers all the way back home—seventeen miles—I have no recollection of any reaction from the school, our parents, or police about this.

The result for us was literally fear for our lives, the kind of terror that keeps you up at night. Our parents weren't doing anything. The police had only shown up when Greg Perez had been beaten almost to death. No one was going to protect us—except ourselves. That night, dozens of boys got on the phone and devised plans to defend ourselves. The plan was simple: to arm ourselves with anything and everything we could. Switchblades, hunting knives, brass knuckles, nunchuks. My friend Billy brought a machete. I never saw one, but I don't doubt some of them brought guns. As my father kept an arsenal at home, acquiring weapons was easy for me. I chose things easy to conceal: brass knuckles and a switchblade. I considered taking a pistol, but instinctively I knew that a gun would be very, very bad. The nature of the weapons we brought meant that if a fight did break out, the results would be far worse than a simple beating. No one brings a machete or a switchblade to a fight just for show. People were going to die.

Can you imagine a handful of terrified seventh-graders, armed to the teeth, resolved to go into battle against a large number of much older teenage gang members? A showdown was coming. Nathan B. Young Junior High had become a war zone.

Rumors flew around school about when the riot was going to happen. What our attackers did not know was that we were going to be ready. I walked around every day with fists clenched and heart hammering, adrenaline shooting through my body, waiting to get jumped at any moment. Further rumors spread that the riot was going to happen on the P.E. field, which made sense to me, because all the thugs could be hiding on the perimeter and rush out there at the appointed time, do as much damage as they could, then scatter before any authorities could stop them. More rumors that the time was set spread like a brush fire. This confrontation was going to happen.

Throughout that day, I was on the verge of throwing up or passing out.

I don't remember exactly how many of us there were, somewhere between one or two dozen, but we banded together in a circle so that we could see them coming from any direction.

The rumors were true.

Suddenly we were surrounded by a mob, dozens of black seventh-graders mixed with neighborhood thugs, and they were coming at us, yelling and taunting and jeering.

As they approached, our circle tightened, all facing outward. We pulled our weapons. Self-preservation and the scream of "Hey Rube" flashed through my head. Now I understood how the carnies felt on the midway when they needed to band together. If there ever was a "Hey Rube" moment, it was now.

When they saw our array of knives, brass knuckles, clubs, the machete, they stopped in their tracks. Their jeers and taunts fell silent. We had never fought back as a group. Some of them tried to egg on others of their number, but none of them were willing to come into weapon range.

Shouts of "Pussies!" flew back and forth and someone in our crowd yelled, "We're going to kill you!"

They all hovered ten to twenty feet away.

My heart was in my throat, hammering. The metal of my brass knuckles was warm in one hand, slicked with sweat, switchblade in the other.

The thugs dispersed, rats slinking back into their burrows, and several of the black students, who moments before had been prepared to obliterate us, ran inside to the P.E. teachers and administration office.

It wasn't long before the adults came running out onto the field, and they all came looking for us and our weapons.

~

A sense of urgency took over. I needed to hide my knife and brass knuckles. At the age of 13, I was still cognizant enough to know this was bad. My heart pounded wildly as the situation swung from pending riot to an onslaught of angry teachers. I was in full-on panic and only managed to ditch the knife. The brass knuckles were still in my pocket. As the teachers and coaches swarmed the school grounds, one by one we were all dragged inside the school office, and interrogated.

Someone yelled at me, "Why would you do something like this, bringing weapons—brass knuckles!—to school?"

Considering the gauntlet of threats and intimidation I lived every single day, the question felt unbelievably asinine. Greg Perez had been beaten almost to death. The riot had been well publicized. I had stepped into *The Twilight Zone*.

When no acceptable answers were forthcoming, we were all told we were going to be expelled or suspended. Phone calls went out to all the parents by the dozens. I remember the caravan of cars pulling up to the school.

My father *never* came to school, not for parent-teacher conferences, not for PTA meetings, not for school events. But he came to school that day, utterly furious. He walked in as I sat there in the hallway outside Dean Ciccarello's office, awaiting my turn for the axe to fall, and he was stone silent, giving me the hard stare. I briefly told him what had happened. One by one, my cohorts and their parents were ushered into the dean's office. This was his first time coming to this school, in this black part of town, the first time he had seen the neighborhood and the student body. I could see in his eyes that he'd had no idea what was going on and how bad things really were. New school policy had dictated our future and the lack of safety, and he was pissed, mostly mad at himself for not being aware.

When my dad went into the dean's office and shut the door, I heard him go ballistic in full-on Italian style. "What the hell is going on here? I had no idea what I was getting my son into! Why would my son need to steal my switchblade and my brass knuckles to come to your miserable school! Was he that afraid for his life at this *shithole you call Young!* What kind of school do you run here that all these boys feel they have to bring weapons to defend themselves! And you're going to expel *them? I should beat your ass for allowing this to happen!"*

I couldn't believe what I was hearing. My fear drained away, replaced by pride at how my dad defended me. I had done the right thing to protect myself and my classmates. If I ever saw him more furious, I couldn't recall a time. His son's life was in jeopardy, and the school did nothing to protect him.

Through the door, I heard him go on, "You are *not* going to expel my son or any of these kids! My son is coming back to school tomorrow! And so is every single one of those boys! You *had better* get this fucking school under control or I will be back!" The threat in his voice was plain but fierce, from one Italian man to another. Old school.

When he came out, he slammed the office door behind him, took me by the shoulder, and led me out to the car. We went home. I spent the next day at home, wondering if I was going back to school, dreading it. The day after that, I went back to school. We all did.

As the dust of uneasiness and fear settled, a sense of calm tension remained. Both sides kept their distance. It was a bizarre sense of detente.

The internal conflict and confusion ate at me, along with sickening thoughts about the bloodbath that almost happened. Would I have stabbed someone? Shattered their face with my brass knuckles? Would I or any of my friends have been killed?

I was the kid who believed in Dr. King's "I Have a Dream" speech. But now, black kids had wanted to hurt me just because I was white. All along, altruism had told me the racism I saw around me was wrong, but now I didn't have a right answer. What was the right way to be a good human being? What was the right answer in the face of hate? How could I ever show compassion to a group of people who wanted to hurt me? The wounds cut deep and left scars in me, in everyone involved, as deep as the ones Greg Perez carried.

This incident multiplied my father's bigotry by a factor of ten. Whereas before, his prejudice had been abstract and amorphous, it was now concrete and burned cherry red. In his mind, blacks were all "thugs and lowlifes" now, and no doubt these beliefs were reflected and amplified by the company he kept.

~

As part of the federal mandate, starting my eighth-grade year, the students swapped schools. Black and white students went to Buchanan Junior High on Bearss Avenue, in the white part of town. A smaller percentage of black kids came to the white part of town, one might guess because they didn't want something like that riot to happen to them or they dropped out. Rather than fifty-fifty, the ratio became something like seventy-thirty.

Even in the eighth grade, however, things were never settled and amicable between us. The best that could be hoped for was maintaining that sense of detente.

Some days, the balance was broken.

One day, at the end of P.E. class, I was designated to collect the scattered volleyballs, and I found myself alone on the far end of the sports field.

Five black students came at me. The specter of Greg Perez sprang out of the shadows of my mind. The same switch that my dad exhibited on the man who introduced me to the word *fuck* must have triggered in me. Before they could gang up on me, I launched myself at the nearest one—his name was Reggie. I seized a handful of his afro, twisted my fingers tight, and went nuts on him, pummeling his face as hard and fast as I could, *boom, boom, boom, boom* until I saw a steady stream of blood. Survival instincts filled my head, and my body was on fire. It was me or them and I was not going down, not alone and not that way. The rest of them fled from the crazy white boy, and eventually Reggie got loose and ran, too.

As he scrambled away, I looked down at my fistful of dark, curly hair, my heart hammering, mouth dry, the sick euphoria of adrenaline-rush coursing through me.

I never told my parents about that attack on me. I couldn't even call it a fight, because the guy I grabbed didn't land a punch. I had gone berserk on him, frightening the rest of them off.

~

The tension lasted through junior high and well into high school. There were no more attacks on me, but the violence continued, even among the girls sometimes. I went into high school hoping it would be different, but fearing it wouldn't.

There was one place, though, where the tension subsided, redirected into common goals in a place where everyone was equal.

The football field.

My sophomore year of high school, I played tight end and on special teams for kick-off returns. Many of my classmates from junior high school, white and black, and I found ourselves on the football team together at Chamberlain High School. We found ourselves, adversaries for two terrible years, now having to work together, to be comrades.

One of the strange things that happened quickly was that those old animosities fell away during practice and games. In practice, we were too focused on the immediacy of drills and learning plays. Helmets and uniforms made us all look alike. On the football field, we could respect each other for having made a good play. We gave each other nicknames in a brotherly way made all the odder by what we had gone through in junior high. If we won a game, we would celebrate by having dinner together. Becoming friends seemed beyond the realm of possibility—our worlds were too far apart—but we could respect each other, and that became the first step.

The coaches certainly knew about what had happened to Greg Perez and the Bloodbath That Wasn't. Several new members of the football team had been involved in the riot on one side or the other. I can imagine the coaches must have discussed this in depth with the aim of preventing another such altercation.

I can't speak for the girls or the boys who did not play football, but maybe we, the football team, became the example. In the most public way, we worked together, strove for the same goals. Off the field, the schoolwide tension simmered, but it never reached the height it did on that day when a bunch of seventh-graders nearly killed each other.

As tenth, eleventh, and twelfth grade came and went, the camaraderie of the football field became the mortar that spackled over the wounds. By the time we graduated high school, some of us, black and white young men, had become close friends. Some of them remained close friends through my college years. Detente had turned to peace, and peace turned to amity and understanding. I cannot say the wounds were healed, at least for me, because the scars remain.

～

One of the things that still troubles me is how the aggression was so one-sided. Even in eighth grade, on the white side of town, I never witnessed white kids taunting the black kids. Maybe I just didn't notice it, but the white kids I knew simply didn't go looking for fights. And it was not just boys. The black girls were ruthless, and fights sometimes resulted in a white girl getting a terrible beating. It was never to the extent of Greg Perez, but it was still a horrible sight. The constant threat of aggression kept me on edge, and I imagine most of the other white kids as well. What troubles me is why. Because of my experiences with the Bejanos and the other carnies, I always wanted to be fair, to treat people equally, to believe we could all just get along, to judge someone not by the color of their skin but by the content of their character as Dr. King said, and part of me is angry that it became so difficult. Idealistic notions fall quickly to the wayside when physical danger comes calling, and then it falls to who's the meanest, the strongest, the most dangerous, and that saddens me. I can't forget the hostility that was directed at me, and it's made me guarded in ways I don't like to consider. I still feel a deep sense of regret, but that's how it was, how it had to be. I didn't know until years later about the abuse that the first black students in desegregated white schools suffered. It must have been a similar kind of hell. No one I knew talked about it. But I have no doubt my black classmates did. Was it all about righteous payback for centuries of awful history and oppression? Or was it simply territorial? Some terrible mix of both, amplified by mob mentality and exacerbated by extreme poverty? Hundreds of years of bad history distilled into poison, and one school full of children was made to drink it.

Our parents were informed of the new busing regulations, but they didn't ask questions. I still struggle with that fact. Most of the parents never attended the school open house. Whether they were too busy or too apathetic, I can't say. But I can say that no one had a clue what lay in store for us. No one questioned the danger or the ethics of busing their beloved children into the "other" side of town. Yet everyone knew to stay away from there. Nightly news reports were as full of crime reports from that side of town as they were of Mafia-related incidents and trials. I held that against my parents for a long time. They put me on a bus and sent me forty-five minutes away into a war zone filled with land mines. It felt so much like a betrayal, like being thrown to the wolves or abandoned to fend for ourselves. Our parents simply accepted the government mandate, unable to send us to private school.

Mandating school integration was a well-intentioned idea, a noble experiment, but whoever was responsible clearly had not anticipated the harsh reality of what would happen, what children would have to go through, or if they did suspect, they were willing to have *us* pay that price.

I suppose it's fair to say the experiment was ultimately a success, given the fact that many of us became good friends by the end of high school, but it took a very long time and the cost was so very high. An entire population of children was left with deep internal scars. There was no question that we were lab rats in a grand social experiment. The trouble with lab rats is that some of them have to die. For me and my classmates the cost was high—especially high for Greg Perez.

Chapter Twelve

A Good Fella

WHEN YOU THINK OF Tampa today, it's easy to visualize the sun and beaches, tourism, big business and industry as well as professional sports like the Tampa Bay Buccaneers or the Tampa Bay Lightning.

In the early seventies, it was still considered a small town, but it was a small town unlike any other in the United States. At that time, corruption in the government and law enforcement was deeply entrenched, tainted by decades of Mafia influence that stretched far and wide. Vendettas were the norm, splashed across the front pages of newspapers. Anyone who dared to cross the mob often paid a hefty price.

Such was the case in 1970 when Gaspar Ciaccio reneged on his gambling debts and became the subject of one of the most famous scenes in movie history. In the film *Goodfellas*, Ray Liotta plays Henry Hill, a New York hitman hired to come to Tampa and teach Gaspar Ciaccio a lesson, the old-fashioned Mafia way. Taken to Lowery Park Zoo as depicted in the movie, brutalized, and left to dangle over the alligator pits until he made good on the money he owed, Ciaccio managed to survive, settle his debts, and tell the story.

My father always had his ear to the ground, constantly feeling the pulse of Tampa, listening to the chatter. He often heard the word on the street long before it hit the papers and may well have known a hit on Ciaccio was coming.

Word of this incident hit the papers and exploded into the public consciousness. After this, everybody knew the mob was really in charge.

But this story is only the tip of the iceberg. Ciaccio's story is typical of how the Trafficante family and other mob bosses dealt with those who crossed the line or got in their way. Many people simply disappeared or took their beatings and went quietly home to hide.

The 1970s marked the beginning of the decline of the Mafia's influence in Tampa. Federal law enforcement decided enough was enough and turned their attention to organized crime in Florida. Sustained operations by local and federal law enforcement chipped away at the Mafia's empire, but the gangsters did not go quietly. Each Mafia figure taken down by the FBI sparked a hidden battle to fill that void. The fight for territory and influence was ongoing and pervasive.

Tampa cop Richard Cloud became a public figure, much like Eliot Ness and his Untouchables, as he formed a one-man army on a crusade to take down the Tampa Mafia in any way he could.

My dad had never forgotten his encounter with Henry and Fano Trafficante. He had been a young man full of hope and dreams, and they had scared him into putting them on hold. That stuck in his craw. But unfortunately, that encounter was only the beginning. My father's experiences and the way this spilled over onto my family dovetail in surprising ways with the backdrop of the 1970s Lounge Wars and Mafia decline.

By 1973, money poured into Lucky's from every direction. With my dad and Bert working in tandem, it was a fine-tuned machine. My father was happy, and Bert was ecstatic.

As Lucky's success grew, though, a constant threat loomed—what if they caught the eye of Trafficante again? There was no way to keep Lucky's operation small. Its success fed itself; word was spreading. In the years since the "meeting" with Henry and Fano Trafficante, things had changed; my father's mini-empire had grown, his clan had gotten bigger, and he had finally gotten a taste of real money and success. No one was going to take it from him. Couple all of that with the fact that my mother had been newly diagnosed with a debilitating illness, there was no way he was going to stop.

So, he applied his power and influence to prepare for the day the Trafficantes would come. He had thought through all kinds of scenarios, no matter how brutal. He took precautions against these scenarios, and he trained his staff well. If the gangsters came, he would be prepared—or so he thought.

~

In the days before Lucky's, I can remember my dad going before the board of Hillsborough County and the City of Tampa, trying to get zoning for a liquor license. His request was denied. I remember him being furious, stomping around the house, yelling, "They're stopping me! They're blackballing me!" I didn't know what blackballing meant. I just remember him being glued to a city commission meeting on television and sitting there cussing at the television. "The fix is in!" he growled.

When he acquired an interest in Lucky's, with its existing liquor license, that was his Holy Grail, and he was going to defend it with everything he had.

He told me this story, but I don't know exactly when it occurred:

Late one night just after Lucky's closed, three wise guys in nice suits came to the door. One of them was a man named Angelo. My father knew him.

"You know why we're here," Angelo said.

"You're gonna have to spell it out," my dad said.

"You were told to stop. You didn't stop. We know what you're doing here," Angelo said, conversationally. "You had your chance. So now we're here to stop you."

A few of my dad's friends were still in the bar, and they moved in behind him. The gangsters hadn't hit him from behind or shot him in the head. There was a certain code of honor in them coming to do their job and telling him directly, to his face.

"Like hell!" my dad snarled. "I'll kick all three of your asses here and now!"

"Come on now, don't make it complicated, Art," Angelo said. "Just let us do what we need to do. We don't want to go too far. I know you got kids. Just let us go back to Henry and tell him we taught you a lesson. Then just stop. Just stop, Art."

"Go fuck yourself. I let you beat me up now, word gets out on the street, I lose my reputation. I lose my business." With a bad enough beating, they could cripple him forever—physically *and* financially. He raised his fists. "So let's go. Right now."

They looked at him like he was crazy. They couldn't have been sure he didn't have a gun. He was pretty sure they did.

But the challenge hung between them, unanswered. Angelo

looked at him for a long time, then finally turned to the other two goons. "Let's go." They backed away slowly. "You're an idiot, you're crazy, Art. You know this ain't over. You know you're going to have to pay the price."

"You know where to find me!" he called back.

But the trouble was, they *did* know where to find us.

~

The early 1970s marked a sea change in Tampa government and law enforcement.

Until then, there was an unwritten rule in Tampa: people of Italian or Cuban heritage, whose families had lived there at least two generations, were above the law. Future cops and future criminals grew up together, just like their parents had, and their grandparents before them. All of them had migrated to Tampa to carve out a life for themselves. Jeopardizing those generations-long relationships was simply not done. It was another aspect of how the Mafia had been allowed to establish such widespread influence and success.

In 1967, a new mayor was elected, Dick Greco, the youngest mayor in the history of Tampa. Greco was a third-generation Italian-American from Ybor City. As soon as he took office, he shocked the Italian community by launching a new effort to clean up corruption in the city government and the police force—and that meant taking on the mob. Turning a blind eye to Mafia activities had been tradition for decades. An organized criminal enterprise like the Trafficantes' could not have existed without corrupt cops, corrupt prosecutors, and corrupt judges. To begin the effort of cleaning all that up, Greco hired a new police chief, James "Babe" Littleton, a man with a reputation as the most honest man in the Tampa Police Department.

Littleton was given carte blanche to do what had to be done to curtail organized crime, and that included cleaning up the police force. He promoted Richard Cloud to sergeant and put him in charge of the narcotics squad. Richard Cloud lived by the same code of honor and justice as Littleton. Cloud would root out corruption in the police force with the same dogged determination as he dismantled the Mafia's criminal apparatus.

Cloud brought two men, Ken Larsen and Bobby Pennington, into his anti-Mafia operations, put them undercover, and sent them to infiltrate the mob world.

For several years, Cloud compiled information on underworld figures, drug trafficking, and their biggest customers. In decades previous, those individuals would have simply been arrested, the charges dropped, or sentences truncated to a slap on the wrist. Cloud took a different approach. He was less interested in chipping away at the small-timers and more interested in taking down the big dogs, which required cases that were impervious to corrupt judges and prosecutors, volumes of indisputable evidence, and often, federal involvement. Because of his hard-nosed methods, he made a lot of enemies. He was the kind of cop that movies were written about—larger than life, willing to do whatever was necessary to stop the bad guys, including pissing off his fellow cops. The corrupt cops and their Mafia handlers despised him, the single biggest threat they had ever encountered to the Mafia's not-so-secret supremacy.

Cloud was famous for his unshakable honesty. He once

confiscated the television set his stepfather had just bought from a guy he worked with. It turned out that the television had been stolen in a burglary, so Cloud arrested the man who had sold the television, then went out, bought a new one of the exact same model, and gave it to his stepfather.

Tampa's lounges and bars were the conduits of the illicit narcotics trade. Between narcotics and bolita, so much money was at stake that criminal groups were constantly at war to defend or expand their territory. Cloud's arrests—and he always made it a point to testify in court against his collars—chewed away at the fringes of the various organizations, but he was always aiming for the big fish. He wanted them gone. He wanted the corrupt officials gone. In the 1970s, Tampa was still a relatively small city, less than three hundred thousand people, so the numbers of mafiosi were much smaller than cities like New York, where the Gambino crime family numbered roughly five hundred or in Chicago where the Syndicate numbered as many as two thousand. Nevertheless, the shadowy layers of connection between the Trafficantes and the other criminal organizations were complex and interwoven. It was this network that Cloud and others wanted to drag into the light.

My dad and Bert never allowed any narcotics trade, no drugs, ever, but no doubt they knew people who did. Cloud's efforts may have created the opening that my dad needed to establish the toehold that he did in the Tampa lounge scene. He was an annoyance out there on the outskirts, but the Trafficantes now had to contend with a concerted effort by law enforcement to put them away once and for all. For every thug and Mafia capo that was indicted, other criminal groups rushed in to exploit the fresh vulnerabilities, to seize a bigger chunk of the pie.

~

Pressures mounted for the Trafficante clan as Henry and others were indicted on federal racketeering charges in 1972. Indictments did not curtail their operations, however, and my father's actions at Lucky's had not gone unnoticed.

Maintaining a tight grip on Tampa Bay gambling operations, Henry Trafficante ordered an attack on my father. Four henchmen were summoned by the family to pay a visit to my father's bar and inflict as much pain and embarrassment as possible.

But my father's carefully constructed grapevine network bore fruit. One evening in the bar, he got a phone call telling him four guys were on their way. He knew this was serious, and he had little time to prepare. Most people would call the police for help but that's not the way it was done back then. Bar owners handled everything themselves and in their own way.

This happened to be a slow night. There were only a few patrons, my father, and his 25-year-old manager Madelyn. When the word came, he quietly approached each of his loyal customers, told them what was coming, and asked if they would stay and help. If they were not inclined, it was time for them to leave, for their own safety. All five men stayed, thus putting their own lives on the line, because no one knew how ugly it might get.

The fear and anticipation stretched as seconds ticked off the clock. And then the door opened and four burly men in suits walked into the bar and sat at one of the floor tables.

My dad walked slowly to the front door and locked the deadbolt. He then approached the table, as if to take their drink order, but then he said, "I heard you motherfuckers are here to teach me a lesson."

It was at that moment that every patron leaped off their barstools and my dad, and even Madelyn threw themselves at the thugs, swinging fists, barstools, pool cues, whatever they had in hand.

The numbers were roughly even, but the four men were practiced leg-breakers. On my dad's side were a young woman, a mailman, an iron worker, a plumber, and a pizza man. Smashed beer bottles, gouged eyes, thrown chairs, and Madelyn with a pool cue turned the bar into a chaos of spraying blood, broken bones, and shattered teeth. Fortunately, no one had a gun or a knife, or people would have died. Had the thugs not walked into an ambush, things would have gone much differently.

By the time the thugs stopped trying to get up, twelve interminable minutes had passed.

My father and his friends heaped the groggy thugs in a booth, piling them on top of each other to make sure they didn't try to get up, while somebody tied their hands behind their backs.

Somehow, my dad and his crew had prevailed. They took stock of their injuries. A couple needed stitches from seriously bleeding head wounds. Another had a broken arm. Several probably had slight concussions and eyes that would soon be blackened, but everybody was alive, and everybody would recover.

They dragged the thugs to their feet and tossed them outside onto the curb.

"Next time," my father told them, "tell your boss to bring a bigger army."

Then he shut the door, locked it behind him, and surveyed the wreckage: smashed tables and chairs, shattered bottles and glasses, broken pool cues.

They all looked at each other with bloody lips and swollen eyes, and without further words, began to clean up.

Madelyn and my father found broken teeth scattered across the floor.

"Can everybody still eat solid food?" he asked, and everyone nodded.

"That was me, I think," Madelyn said with a grim smile.

"Pool cue?" he said.

"Pool cue."

He put six or seven of the teeth in a paper bag, and then, a day or two later, sent them to Henry Trafficante via a runner with a note that read: "You motherfuckers intimidated me once, but you'll never do it again. Give these back to the pussies you sent to hurt me."

~

That morning, I woke up for school a little earlier than normal and shambled in the dark toward the bathroom to pee. As I opened the bathroom door and stood over the toilet, the slosh of water in the bathtub spun me around. Somehow, I managed not to pee all over the wall.

Sitting in the bathtub, chest-deep in red-tinged water, his face dark and swollen, his lip split, his forehead cut, was my father. Steam rose around him, filling the bathroom with hot moisture and the smell of blood. His knuckles looked like hamburger. He looked at me silently with his swollen, bloodshot eyes. Blood caked his hair, bruises darkened his torso.

Stunned, I don't know how long I stood there.

He moved with painful slowness, and I think he said something to me, but it didn't register.

Finally I managed to say, "What happened to you? Are you all right?"

"I'm all right. I'm in a little pain, but you should see the other guy." He tried to smile but even that seemed to hurt him.

I just stared at him, any thought of getting ready for school drained away. I wanted to stay home and help him, but I had no idea what to do.

Just then, my mother passed by the open doorway and spotted him out of the corner of her eye. She gasped, "Jesus Christ! Art!"

"I'm all right," he repeated.

She read what had happened in his cuts and bruises. "Tony, you get ready for school. I'll take care of your dad."

"I don't want to go to school!"

Still soaking naked in bloody water, my father growled, "You're going to school."

So I went to school without receiving any further explanation, but all that day, I could not get the image of him—broken and bloody in a bathtub—out of my head. The memory snuck back in every time I stopped actively thinking about something else. How surreal it was seeing my father that way, but most importantly, what the hell had happened to him? Anger crept into me at his machismo. *You should see the other guy.* I couldn't help but think things were worse than he was letting on. Those thugs were going to come back, or others would, and they would keep coming until my dad was dead. He didn't have much time left on this earth. I was going to be the man of the house much sooner than anyone imagined. It was inevitable.

That night, we all came home from school and were getting ready for dinner. My father was all bandaged up. His cuts were crusted over, his eye frightfully black. In the living room, my sister Debbie was playing piano, but she was wearing an odd hat I'd never seen before, a kind of wide-brimmed fedora often worn by people in the seventies. The hat followed her head movements with the slight delay of a hat that was far too big.

I asked my dad, "Where did she get that hat?"

"I gave it to her."

"Well, where did you get it?"

"I got it last night. One of the thugs...left it behind," he said proudly.

Over dinner, he finally told us all the story of what happened the night before. Debbie's eyes got wide and scared when she heard where the hat had really come from, but then she wore it all the more proudly. As I listened to him tell the story, I couldn't help but think that in most other households, they talked about baseball practice, homework, and upcoming weekend events. But not in our house. We got to hear about an all-out brawl, where people got their asses kicked. We heard how vendettas were made. To spare the girls, he left out most of the gritty details, but when I asked him later, he told me everything.

And then he went back to work the next day, still covered in bandages. He didn't make a big deal about it. He just went to work, and nothing was going to stop him.

~

On the surface, things calmed down for a while. Both sides had sent messages. Both sides had taken their corners. But this calm did not last long. One morning on our way out the door to walk to the bus stop, my sister Debbie and I noticed our German Shepherd, Champ, lying on the ground, not moving. I hurried up to him. Blood leaked from his mouth, and his body showed that kind of deflated motionlessness only exhibited by dead things.

Debbie began to cry.

"Maybe a snake bit him," I said. Like Skipper Road, Lutz had an ample supply of gators and venomous snakes.

Then, as I drew nearer, I saw the hand-scribbled note lying on his dead body. I don't remember what the note said, but Champ had been poisoned. I just stood there trying to control my panic. Someone had poisoned him, then watched him die, and then left a note. Debbie stood beside me, eyes wide, losing her composure second by second.

We ran back into the house to wake up my father. He ran outside and stared at the dead dog. I don't remember much after that, except having to go to school in a terrified fugue. Was someone going to grab me or Debbie walking to or from the bus? I had never forgotten my father's talk about kidnapping, and now I knew exactly what he was talking about.

One thing was for sure: my dad was back on the mob's hit list, and they knew where we lived.

My dad put the word on the street to get the names of who had done this. He was pissed, scared, and cautious all at the same time. He wasn't someone who rushed into a vendetta; he took his time to think it through. After several days, a name surfaced of the person who had come to the property and killed our dog. He wasn't part of the mob, just someone they'd hired to do their dirty work. People like this were always thugs and henchmen—just like the guys in the movies, lowlifes who would do anything for a hundred dollars or even just the thrill.

Such guys were easy to find in Tampa, and they terrified me the most. I could spot them a mile away. They would come in the bar often. If they were on your side or neutral, great. If not, watch out.

Now that my dad had a name, he sent two of his best guys to pay *that guy* a visit. Story has it that they broke every bone in his body and left him to suffer, just short of death, so he could live to tell the story to his boss.

But now it was time for my dad to call the police and let them know that he was in fear for his family's safety. He asked that a police car pass by our house regularly. By this time, he had made friends in the Hillsborough County Sheriff's Department.

Cops, both Tampa police and sheriff's deputies, like to drink too. Besides, no cop wants to see harm come to a wife and kids. So they agreed to patrol the area.

As long as I can remember, we had guns and weapons in the house, all encased in a locked gun cabinet custom-made for my father. I had been taught at a young age how to handle these weapons, load them, unload them, and clean them. I was proud of knowing how to do all that. It was a true rite of passage. I was also taught how to shoot and protect our family in the face of danger.

A short time after Champ's death, I was awakened one night by the sounds of our dogs barking. My father was an avid hunter and raised hunting dogs, a special mix of beagle and bloodhound, seven of them in total. They were kept in a large kennel about thirty yards from our house. The dogs were going crazy with barking. Had a rabbit gotten into the pen? Was a wild hog taunting them from the outside of their cage? The noise was tremendous. I got out of bed and went to the gun case for my gun of choice—the Browning semi-automatic 12-gauge shotgun. My favorite gun was the .410, but a 12-gauge packed a whole lot more punch. It was the gun I used when we went deer and wild boar hunting.

Always taking the proper precautions, always prepared for anything that could happen, I slowly loaded the weapon and stood silently in the center of our dark living room.

My mom and sisters were still sleeping, I didn't know how with the racket outside. Goosebumps crawled up the back of my neck and down my arms, and cold sweat trickled down my face. Memories of the blood trickling from Champ's mouth rose starkly in my mind.

We had a nice house, but it was on a dead-end dirt road over a hundred yards from the main street, deep in the orange groves, with a lake to its back. I felt like a sitting duck.

The passing minutes felt like hours as I stood frozen like a statue, shotgun loaded in my hands. I just waited and listened, staring at the front door. Something didn't feel right. I did not want to wake my sisters or my mom.

I thought I heard a voice, low and quiet, but I had been standing there so long I couldn't be sure it wasn't in my head. I thought I discerned two or three more voices. My heart was pounding like it wanted to burst out of my chest. Sweat soaked my hair, my skin, my T-shirt.

Then I saw the front doorknob move, twisting, jiggling softly, testing.

I couldn't believe this was happening. I was going to blow away the first intruder who came through that door.

A noise from right behind me spun me around, and I shudder

to think what *could* have happened. It was Debbie, standing there in the dark looking at me with wide eyes.

"What are you doing here!" I whispered.

"What are *you* doing?" she said, looking at the gun.

"Get to the back phone and call Dad. Somebody is trying to break in," I told her. There was another telephone in the back of the house. I returned my focus to the front door, and she hurried off to make the call.

The front door was locked, but I heard the sound of metal grating against metal, a knife or screwdriver trying to pry the latch sideways, an old trick for breaking into any door.

They would be in the house in less than a minute. Flashes of my father's lessons, shooting to kill, killing to protect, raced through my mind.

My finger was ready on the trigger. The safety was off. I would kill them to save my family and myself. My dad told me about the law. They had to be in the house before you shot. If you shot them on the doorstep, you had to drag them inside. I knew how many shells were in the gun. A dozen crazy, fearful scenarios shot through my mind, how the blood would spatter, whether I would get shot, whether they could take the gun away from me before I could shoot.

I stood there three feet inside the front door, shotgun leveled, vibrating with tension, mouth dry. But I couldn't take it anymore. From deep within me, I mustered the deepest, boldest voice I could and yelled with everything I had, "I've got a gun and I'm gonna blow your fucking head off!"

The door stopped jiggling. The place fell silent, terribly silent.

What should I do now? There was no script for this crazy shit.

My arms were trembling, and the shotgun got heavier. My whole body felt heavy, even my heart, pumping laboriously like my blood was syrup.

I don't know how long I stood there, but at some point I opened the door to the carport and ran outside. By this time, my fear was turning to rage that these thugs could provoke such terror in me, could threaten my family. I shouted at the top of my lungs, "You fucking cowards! Bastards! Come back and I'll blow your fucking head off!"

I stalked out into the front yard, still yelling taunts, even as I was thinking *I've gone mad. I've gone crazy. What the fuck am I doing* outside? *If they're in that swamp area, I'm a walking target.*

But it didn't matter. I was a man now. Fuck them. I was going to kill them on sight, inside the house or not.

Darkness enveloped our house. No streetlights, no yard lights, just the sable expanse of night sky. If not for the moon, I couldn't have seen a thing. In the blackness of the surrounding orange groves danced the sparks of thousands of fireflies. Suddenly I heard noises in the swamp bushes. I spun and raised the Browning and let fly. *Bam!* Orange sparks blasted out and disappeared like fireflies. The spent shell went spinning away in slow motion. *Bam!* The thunder of the shotgun reverberated like a war zone echo. My ears rang. The smoke drifted away into silence. Just silence. No more voices. Maybe it was a rabbit or an armadillo family, but there was no sign of any human intruders.

Relief dashed through me, but I stayed outside, my eyes feverishly searching the dark, for how long, I don't know. But my blasting had awakened my mom and Antoinette.

Light appeared in the kitchen window with three frantic

faces. Mom and my sisters were calling, "Tony! Come back inside!"

In a daze, I heard them and backed toward the house.

Then as I turned, a light flashed at the corner of our entry driveway, about fifty yards away, a car, lights heading straight at me, straight at the house.

I froze in the oncoming headlights, leveling my shotgun straight at them, finger on the trigger.

The car slowed, still coming straight at me, and I heard someone calling my name.

"Tony! It's me!"

Coming from the car window.

"Tony! It's me! It's your dad, it's your dad!"

Exhausted yet relieved, I let the muzzle of the shotgun sink toward the ground as my father approached me. I just stood there staring into the headlights, ready to crumble to my knees.

CHAPTER THIRTEEN

MURDER AND SEX TOYS

MY DAD MET ME in the driveway and eased the shotgun from my hands. He could see that I was noticeably shaken. We both looked around, and he listened intently as I told him what I had just done. Without passing judgment or asking questions, he took me into the house where my mother and sisters were waiting. Everyone was crying, and I was still trembling so badly I could barely stand. Our entire family sat in the family room comforting one another, and my father was determined to get to the bottom of this.

After an hour or so, we all managed to go back to bed. I must have passed out after the adrenaline rush dissipated.

At 6:00 a.m., the phone woke my father up. No doubt we were all on edge, and the slightest noise was bound to startle us. It was Madelyn, the manager at Lucky's, and he knew instantly from her voice that something was terribly wrong.

"What is it?" he said.

She swallowed hard and said, "Bert's dead."

"What do you mean, 'Bert's dead'? What happened?" A chill must have shot through him, a cloud of sinister possibilities.

"Somebody shot him, Art."

Sitting on the bed, he braced himself. "Tell me everything."

"After closing time, Bert left to go play pool at a bottle club. He was drunk, like usual. I don't know how it happened. But somebody shot him in the chest with a .357 magnum, right there in his wheelchair."

A bottle club is an after-hours bar where people are allowed to bring their own booze and continue drinking.

No doubt a storm of thoughts and emotions rushed through my dad's mind. Was there a killer coming for him, too? Had he left the bar before the hitman arrived? Did the killer intend harm to all of us? Why Bert? In the spaces between grief and fear, he must have been thinking about the future of his business. "When did this happen?"

"About an hour ago. Right there in the club. The police are looking for the killer."

Barely holding his composure, he told Madelyn, "I need you to do something for me. I need you to go the bottle club and receive the body. Identify him and take charge of the body. Bert doesn't have any relatives here, just a brother in Wisconsin who's a total bastard. I've never met him, but Bert told me plenty."

"Yeah, I heard some of that," she said.

"Anyhow, I need you to go take care of him until I get there or else the state will do it."

"And you're coming right now?"

"I'll be there in two or three hours, I can't leave my family right now. Tony's pretty shaken, and Cindy and the girls are scared."

"Okay."

~

It was a little before 8:00 a.m., and my dad was pacing the floor. I was getting ready for school, nearing the end of my horrific seventh-grade year at Nathan B. Young. I was still nervous about the intruders and the shotgun incident. Red-eyed and hard-faced, he moved like a twisted bundle of piano strings. He checked that all the guns in the house were loaded and made sure all the windows were locked.

I stood there watching him, my mother following him around in her walker. "What's going on, Art?"

"Bert's dead," he said, "murdered."

My mom went stiff and trembling at the same time, "Oh, my God!" She sank into a kitchen chair and started crying.

"Last night. He was in a bottle club and somebody shot him square in the chest."

As I listened to this, too young to know the fullness of everything happening with the Tampa Mafia, my first thought was that Bert had pissed someone off in a pool game, which could often get incredibly heated, and that person had pulled a gun. Knowing how belligerent Bert could be when he was drunk, I have often thought his last words might well have been, "You're not man enough, you pussy!" But by this point, Bert was practically family. His and Dory's engagement party had been epic. Bert had treated me like a grown-up, trusting me to handle his most expensive possessions. And now he was dead.

I stood frozen there, stunned, crying. In less than twenty-four hours, my emotions had been twisted into pretzels. My mom was sitting there, sobbing, white as clean linen, rocking back and forth. My dad looked back and forth between us, then he took me by the shoulder and sat me down at the table. Mom was sobbing, clutching her mouth.

The aftermath of my dad's storm of emotions was engraved on his face, like the wreckage left on shore after a hurricane. The worst had passed for now, but he had settled into a frenetic sense of resolve. There were important things to be done, and they had to be done *right now*. "Son," he said, "you been through a lot, but I need you to help me out."

Just then, the phone rang, and he got up and answered it. He listened intently for a few moments. Then his face went white as milk, and he hung up without saying a word.

My mother and I questioned him, but he wouldn't tell us what the caller said. Much later he told me what the caller had told him: "'Bert's dead. You're next. You and your whole family.'"

But when he sat down again, the fear on his face was clear. He took a long, deep breath, elbows on his knees as he leaned toward me. "You have to be a man now, Son. I need you to do something for me that's very big and very important."

I sat a little straighter and tried to swallow my fear. "What is it?"

"Dory is on her way over here. She's going to take you over to Bert's house. I need you to help her and get some things for me."

"Why me?"

He paused, considering how best to tell me. "I can't be seen going over there. I've got to stay here and protect your sisters and mom. Bert keeps a big stash of cash in his closet and a bunch of diamond jewelry in his dresser drawer." He sketched out a map with a piece of paper where I was to look for things. "I want you to go to Bert's house and grab all that stuff."

"But why? Isn't that Dory's now?"

"No, it belongs to me and Bert, and now that Bert's gone, I have to get it before Ralph finds it. His brother Ralph is no doubt on his way here right now to take over Bert's estate. Bert hated Ralph's guts, called him a 'greedy mother F'er.' Ralph's been estranged from the family for years, but there's nothing we can do about that now. Bert didn't have a will or any type of estate planning. As next of kin, Ralph will become the executor of his estate, and he will take *everything*."

All these words were foreign to me. Estate, will, hatred among family members. My head was spinning.

"That doesn't seem fair," I said, thinking of Dory.

"That money came from Lucky's. It belongs to me. Stuff it in a pillowcase and bring it back here. You hear me? Get in, get out, and get back here."

I nodded.

My sisters were standing in the kitchen doorway crying. Our entire house was melting into a puddle of grief and fear.

"None of you are going to school today," he said. The tone in his voice suggested this was not because we were sad.

My insides were vibrating, stuck between sadness for Bert, empathy for Dory, and my father's contagious fear. But his resolve was contagious as well. When Dory showed up a few minutes later, I went outside and got in her Cadillac without any further words.

I had never seen her so disheveled. She always looked like an elegant fashion model, blonde hair perfectly coiffed and make-up flawless. But today, she looked ragged, run over by a car. She gave me a wan smile, tinged with regret. Dory and Bert were an odd couple, Bert being who he was, but they adored each other. No amount of make-up could hide the pain on her face.

"Uh, I'm really sorry about Bert," I said. My heart was pounding, my chest aching. My limbs felt like lead.

"Thanks, kiddo," she said, dabbing at her eyes and nose with a tissue.

On the short drive to Bert's house, Dory held back tears as best she could. "We haven't even opened all the engagement presents yet."

This saddened me even more. Just a few short weeks ago, their house had been a place of joy and celebration. And now... What was going to happen to her?

We pulled up in front of Bert's house and hurried inside. Dad's mention of unwelcome eyes, coupled with what he had demanded of me, gave me prickles up the back of my neck. It was such a strange feeling going into someone's house like that, a dead man's house, a family friend's house, looking for buried treasure like I was some sort of pirate. My dad's request had been crystal clear, so I went straight to the bedroom, yanked a pillowcase off the bed, and headed for the closet.

The cash was in a strong box in the closet, and my dad had given me the combination to the lock. That he and Bert had trusted each other enough to share this information came home to me as soon as I opened the box and saw the piles of cash stacked up in there. I paused only a moment to think about how much money that could be before I grabbed a handful and stuffed it into the pillowcase. By the time I was finished, it struck me how heavy cash was. I lugged the pillowcase over my shoulder and headed for the dresser.

In the top drawer there was a rolled-up towel that, once unwrapped, contained piles of diamonds and diamond jewelry. Where it had come from, who it was for, and how much it was worth, I couldn't guess and didn't have time to ponder. I stuffed it all into the pillowcase. The glitter and sparkle of these shiny objects served as a distraction for why I was there in the first place.

Behind me, Dory sobbed quietly. She had lived here with Bert for several months. Was any of this hers? But she didn't argue with me, just stood there and quietly sobbed while I did what I was sent here to do.

By the time I was finished, she had composed herself and stared at me intently as if to gather the strength to tell me something, one of those pregnant pauses everyone experiences at least once. Slowly she said, "Tony, I need your help."

"Sure, Dory, what can I do?" I said.

"It's time for you to grow up." Words that I had heard many times lately. She swallowed hard, her face flushed. "You're going to see things you've never seen before. Can you hold this for me?" She handed me another pillowcase. I set down my burden, took her pillowcase, and held it open while she opened the next dresser drawer.

Inside that drawer were piles of things I had indeed never seen before. Dildos of every shape and size, vibrators, things that looked like stainless-steel rockets, bundles of silk and lace and leather, handcuffs swathed in pink fluff, and other things I couldn't identify. My eyes must have bugged out of my head. I couldn't help but imagine all the things she and Bert must have done with all this, and she must have known exactly what I was thinking, creating the most awkward moment of my life up till then.

Dory's flush deepened, tears streaming down her face. In her hand she held an enormous plastic penis, and it flopped around as she waved it like a wand, this beautiful, distraught woman, almost blubbering, "I'm sorry you have to see this, but I can't let anyone else see our personal stuff. I've got to get it out of here." I couldn't take my eyes off the thing as she plopped it in the pillowcase. She grabbed everything out of the drawer and threw it in, one by one by one. My mind was racing. What the hell was *that thing* for?

It dawned on me that because Bert was a paraplegic, his sexual private parts did not function. These devices represented the only way he could have sex with her. What must that have been like for him, to be in bed with a woman like that and be limited to using outside devices? It struck me then, how much they loved each other, that these objects became their sexual bridge. This was extremely personal, and it was a side of Bert hidden behind the irascible drunk.

It was embarrassing for me, but for her it must have been so tenfold, sweet soul that she was. I tried not to catch her eye, tried to look anywhere else than at the things in her hands, but we were only twenty inches apart. The bag got heavier and heavier.

Eventually Dory and I finished up and headed back to my house where my father was waiting. Between the drive to Bert's and the drive home, I had aged ten years. Emotions with which I hadn't the slightest clue how to deal turned my insides into a sick stew.

Back at home, I handed the heavy pillowcase to my father.

"Did anyone see you?" he said.

"I don't think so," I said. In that moment, his question felt cold and heartless. What I wanted was for him to ask me how *I* was. How did I feel? But at that age, I was a man. I had a job to do, so I did it.

The phone rang again.

He answered it, listened for two seconds, then slammed it down again.

"What is it?" I asked.

"Nothing," he said, picking up the pillowcase. "Go on to your room now. I have to deal with some things."

~

Ralph and his wife arrived about fifteen hours after Bert's death. Ralph did exactly as my dad predicted. He took over everything. They took over Bert's house, Bert's car, Bert's boat, and Bert's bank accounts. Bert was barely cold in the morgue when they moved their happy asses into Bert's house. They must have dropped everything in Wisconsin like a rotten potato and come running to Florida, given the speed with which they glommed onto Bert's wealth and possessions. They exhibited no sign of grief or mourning. But the worst was yet to come.

Dory and Bert had been living together for a while, so almost everything in the house belonged to both of them, but because the house was in Bert's name and engagement has no legal standing under Florida law, Dory had no rights to any of it. When the time came for Dory to enter the house and get her remaining personal belongings, they wouldn't let her take anything. They kicked her out of the house. Maybe in the back of her mind she knew this would happen and that's why she was so intent on removing her personal effects for no one else to see.

I remember driving to Bert's house several days later with my father to confront Ralph about Dory's welfare. She deserved some help, and she had a right to her possessions.

This was the first chance I had to see Ralph. It shocked me how much he resembled Bert, except that he walked on two legs. But Ralph had little of Bert's charm. Ralph had a slickness to him, like the worst kind of amalgam of used car salesman and televangelist. Even at that age, I could see the greed in his eyes, a substrate upon which he built his entire life.

A shouting match quickly ensued in the front yard, while I sat in the car, but it didn't last long. My father may have felt compassion for Dory, but beyond pleas for basic human decency, he quickly realized there was nothing he could do to change Ralph's mind. Ralph's wife called Dory a poisonous stream of vile epithets.

When he came back to the car, I said, "Bert was right about him."

Dad started the car. "He sure was."

"Can't we do anything?"

Dad put the car in gear, his face tight with suppressed anger. "Not much. I can't push him too far. He's my new business partner."

I was really proud of him when he gave Dory a sizable chunk of that money I'd brought home in the pillowcase, to help her get back on her feet. She accepted it tearfully. Dory stayed in contact with us for a year or so but slowly moved on with her life.

Everything about Ralph stuck like a burr in my dad's craw, but he had to play his hand very carefully. The wheels of calculation and planning were already in motion. Bert had been the answer to my father's liquor license problem, and it was now a chain that shackled him to Ralph.

Much of my father's recent success was tied to that liquor license and Lucky's Lounge. He wasn't about to let it go, even if he had to put up with Ralph.

Fortunately, before Bert died, he and my father completed their purchase of another liquor lounge and package store out on East Highway 92, near Plant City. The Penn Lounge was still in Hillsborough County, but roughly twenty miles from anything or anyone, far away from the core of Tampa, and therefore, far from the mob. This place was way out in cracker country, no Latinos, no blacks, no Italians. It was in the Penn Lounge that he saw his exit strategy. But first, we all had to face the aftermath of Bert's murder.

Bert's aging and frail parents asked my father to be a pallbearer at Bert's funeral in Wisconsin. He initially accepted the invitation, but when the time came for him to get on the plane, he canceled at the last minute because he was afraid to leave his family alone.

Instead, we all went to visit my aunt and uncle on their farm, deep in the woods of Pasco County. Fortunately, school had ended, so it was easy for him to say this was just a family visit. He played it up that we were all going to help out my aunt and uncle on their farm. They had pigs, chickens, and cows on their hundred-or-so acres. I sometimes missed all of our livestock from Skipper Road. My memories of this are vague, except that I knew this visit was a pretense. We were hiding out, lying low. We stayed for about a month, making it almost like summer camp.

Meanwhile, my father was trying to figure out who ordered the hit on Bert. He put the word out all over Tampa. It wasn't long before the police arrested the killer, a black man named Calvin Johnson. Plenty of eyewitnesses made the arrest incontrovertible, but his motive was never established. Johnson was not part of the pool circuit that took Bert to the bottle club that night, and there was no known association between them. Why would anyone kill a man in a wheelchair? Did Bert do something to provoke the attack? Was he simply the easier target? Was my father next? Were we all still in the gunsights? Calvin Johnson had the stench of hired assassin. But who hired him and why? Were the death-threat phone calls simply the Trafficantes taking advantage of the situation, or had they hired the gunman?

My father was not himself for a while after Bert's death. He was jumpy, rattled. He put out a reward across the Tampa area for any information, determined to protect his family. In a Mafia-riddled city like Tampa, people talk. The scuttlebutt that came back was that the mob was unhappy with Bert and Art. Bert and Art didn't play by the rules. Art had ignored the warning to stay the hell away from gambling. Art was blackballed. He would never have a liquor license. And next, Art was going down, too.

~

Meanwhile, Detective Richard Cloud had been hitting the mob hard over the last several years. His principal target was the young mobster, Joe Bedami Jr., a narcotics trafficker with tentacles in bars and lounges across the Tampa area. Cloud was also taking a special interest in the corruption so rife within the local government and the police force.

The FBI had been putting tremendous pressure on Tampa's criminal syndicates. In the late 1960s, the heat had driven Santo Trafficante Jr. to Miami, but that didn't mean he'd taken his operation with him. It remained as deeply rooted as ever.

Henry Trafficante was indicted on federal racketeering charges in 1972. He was convicted in 1975, but he would not go to prison until November 1977, after exhausting his legal recourse. The five years between arrest and imprisonment implies a certain lackadaisical approach to prosecuting Mafia figures, exactly what Cloud was fighting against. Henry Trafficante only served two years, because he was listed as a pallbearer at the funeral of one Armando Rios in December 1979.

Detective Cloud's investigations, with the help of undercover officers Ken Larsen and Bobby Pennington, rankled the Tampa cops most steeped in corruption. He had become the most powerful man in the Tampa Police Department, but he was breaking the code that police officers should protect each other at all costs. The code was to turn a blind eye toward "lapses in judgment." Calls for Cloud's suspension or firing came often and loudly. A lot of people admired him. A lot of people despised him. Some said it was only a matter of time before *his* corruption was revealed as well. But he took on the Italian Mafia and chased leads all the way to Colombian drug cartels.

In February 1975, Cloud's unpopularity came to a head when he and two other officers were accused of roughing up two suspects in a parking lot before taking them to jail. The charges were bogus, and Cloud was offered a lie detector test to clear his name. He refused, and that proved to be the excuse needed to fire him.

Cloud's firing caused a stir throughout Tampa, both among his detractors and his supporters. He had been working closely with the FBI for years, and they saw him as an invaluable asset, so they hired him as a special consultant on organized crime. Under federal jurisdiction now, he continued his crusade against the Tampa mob. Cloud made a practice of following mob figures and pulling them over at will. His heavy-handed questioning and passive harassment made him the most hated figure in law enforcement. Like him or not, he had his own special way of getting at the truth, and the mob grew tired of his intimidation tactics. Thanks to Tampa's top cop, the mob scene was turning into a pressure cooker with all sides caught in the middle. For the first time ever, the Tampa Mafia had been pushed to the verge of extinction, and they were not going down without a fight.

~

Bert's death didn't even make a ripple in the greater Tampa consciousness. I don't remember it being in the newspapers. He was just a Yankee cripple. He wasn't Latin, or Hispanic, or Italian, or even connected to Tampa.

Calvin Johnson's trial was equally uneventful. No motive was ever sufficiently established. No connections to the mob were established, but then again, no one in law enforcement ever bothered to look under those rocks. He did seven years in the state penitentiary for Bert's murder. Whether he became a rich man when he came out remains unknown.

Bert's murder and the resulting chaos erupted in a blinding flash, and my father was left to wonder what to do next, how to protect his family, and more immediately, what the hell to do about Ralph.

Ralph was not a good businessman, and his wife was just as greedy and detestable as he was, but also controlling and belligerent. She was even worse when she was drunk, and she was drunk a lot. They were a matched pair, those two. Given the number of times my dad and Ralph butted heads, I have no doubt my father would have loved to beat Ralph to a bloody pulp on numerous occasions, but he never did.

Some people would retreat from these problems, but that time hiding out had given my father the opportunity to compose his thoughts, to plan the way forward. So rather than retreating, he charged like a bull.

He made a deal with Ralph to take over the Penn Bar and leave Lucky's Lounge in Ralph's hands. Lucky's was still doing tremendous business. Ralph saw *all* the dollar signs. It took some convincing, because Ralph wanted it all, every last drop of Bert's wealth and property, so he had to get Bert's contractual business partner out of the picture. So, my father abandoned Lucky's to Ralph's care and took over ownership of the Penn Bar, miles from the City of Tampa out on Highway 92. It took roughly nine months to extricate himself from Ralph, an excruciating, aggravating process, but when it was finally over, he had exactly what he always wanted—a place of his own, *with* a liquor license.

When the ink was dry on the business deal and he was in sole ownership of the Penn Bar, he promptly renamed it Art's Lounge in big, neon letters. And then he managed a final *fuck you* to Ralph. My dad made the final order for a large shipment of liquor for Lucky's, about $20,000 worth, but at the last minute he changed the delivery address to the new Art's Lounge. The bill floated in space for a little while and finally came to rest on Ralph's desk. No doubt Ralph was furious, but there was nothing he could do except pay the bill or else lose his own ability to restock his liquor.

But my dad still had the mob to contend with. Bert was killed on June 21, 1975. No matter how many precautions my father took, it was never enough to help us feel safe.

In the face of relentless pressure from Tampa police and the FBI, Tampa's criminal organizations were coming unglued, struggling to hold on to power. A series of events would eventually lead to a grand showdown between the mob and law enforcement. Tampa cop Richard Cloud would find himself in the crosshairs of some of the most notorious gangsters Tampa had ever seen. One might say the waters around Tampa Bay were very dangerous back then. Bert's murder and the unforeseen events that were about to happen were almost certainly unrelated, but they help illustrate the ruthlessness of the Tampa Mafia. They were just two casualties among many, many more. And worse, my dad was still in their sights.

CHAPTER FOURTEEN

THE END OF INNOCENCE

BY THE END OF 1975, our nation was preparing to celebrate its 200th birthday. The bicentennial was upon us, and the federal government, state, and community leaders were planning festivals, parades, and celebrations across the entire country. Each night, the three major television networks led with heroic stories as the enthusiasm built across the land. But the summer of 1975 had been a dark and desperate time for me and my family, living in the aftermath of attacks on my father, Champ's killing, Bert's murder, and intruders in the dark lurking outside our home.

As a young teenager, I watched the lead-up and news coverage to the bicentennial. There was no escaping it. Our nation stood tall, awash in a wave of pride and patriotism, maybe looking for something to feel good about after Nixon's disgrace and the monstrous failure of the Vietnam War. Maybe we all wanted to just pull out the stops and throw the biggest party the world had ever seen.

In Tampa, however, the bicentennial was not the only news item in the press. No, we had our own headline-maker, and his name was Richard Cloud, a particularly polarizing figure who was easy game for the press. His shakedowns became infamous, his name, local legend. The public aftermath of his firing in March

1975 still reverberated through the halls of power and the media. People either loved him or despised him. His crusade continued unabated, however, as the FBI ramped up its efforts to root out the mob and its corruption. Cloud's techniques and undercover operations were revolutionary at the time, and he had kept his skin in the game by working as a private investigator and consultant for the Florida Department of Law Enforcement (FDLE).

While the investigations into the mob hung like a black cloud over Tampa, I did my best to ignore them and tried to get excited instead about the upcoming bicentennial. I wanted desperately to have fun with my friends and classmates. I wanted to be free of stress and anxiety. I wanted to be a typical teenager like all my friends, but the pressure of the nightclub business dogged me everywhere I went, a hungry, growling dog that couldn't be ignored.

Music was the one thing that truly helped. My love of and fascination with rock 'n' roll and disco had emerged over the last year or so and had taken off like a brush fire. We had a jukebox at our house—an old one from Dad's bar—and when I wasn't listening to the likes of Queen's "Bohemian Rhapsody" and Led Zeppelin's album *Physical Graffiti*, I had the radio playing every waking hour: Springsteen, Journey, Pink Floyd. I loved them all. I knew every artist and every song and most of their lyrics, and to this day, I can rattle off music trivia from the '60s, '70s, and '80s without missing a beat. In many ways, music was my escape.

And then there was my friend Tommy Dolan. When I was 14, he and I tore through the orange groves and secluded backwoods of the Lutz area on our motorcycles, lost in the thrill of the moment, memorizing every bump and swerve of the lakeshore and woods. Our tires made trails we knew like the backs of our hands. We built elaborate tree forts and secret hideouts and created a world that no one else could penetrate. I could imagine for a while that I was not surrounded on all sides by peril and darkness.

It was on one of these rides that Tommy introduced me to marijuana. "Colombian gold," he called it. It was the most potent weed on the market at the time. In our small world, pot was sold in plastic sandwich baggies and measured in fingers. Two fingers, three fingers, four fingers. If you had the money to spend, a full lid was like hitting the jackpot.

Not surprisingly, this Colombian drug connection was also a focus of Richard Cloud's and the FBI's ongoing investigations, but there was no shortage of pot or reefer around. If a kid wanted to score, it was as easy to find as milk in the grocery store. So, for a kid who lived with a cloud of fear hanging over his head, it proved to be the single most effective way to forget all that, just for a while.

But the pot didn't dampen my overwhelming anxiety. The older I got, the angrier I got at my dad for the danger he continued to expose us to. I ached over the plight of my mom and her failing health. I needed something to help me forget all that, and, at least for a while, the marijuana provided a bit of respite. As for me, I always made sure I had an ample stash on hand. Tommy also introduced me to hashish and THC powder, which looked like a crystalized version of baby powder and when it was smoked, had a hallucinogenic effect on the mind. It was the quickest, easiest way to escape. It also made me feel invincible, helped me stand tall and feel like a fighter. That, at least, was what I told myself.

Tommy was also a part of that facade. He was older and more experienced than me, and I looked up to him. He seemed to know so much about all the things I was desperate to learn, and most of it had to do with the underbelly of our sick society. We would lose entire days stoned out of our minds and drunk on cheap Boones Farm strawberry wine, but the pot and booze couldn't mask the darkness. It was always right there, hounding me, and all I had to do was look into it and let it grip me and I would be gone. At times, it felt as though I was falling into a deep well.

Something had to change. Bert's murder plunged the entire family into that darkness and fear. We tried spending some time at my aunt and uncle's farm, but that relief only lasted for a short while. When that hiatus ran its course, our family's pain and fear came back full force.

My mother and Dory came up with the brilliant idea of taking us to Disney World. Ironically, Orlando was only a 45-minute drive away, but we had never been there. As soon as the idea was raised, the eyes of my sisters—and probably mine, too—lit up like sparklers.

Mom and Dory seemed to know how important it was for all of us to get away, and they worked painstakingly to make the trip as perfect as possible. They arranged for us to stay at the Polynesian Village, while Dad stayed home to deal with Ralph and the bar transfer.

What better place than Disney World to distract us from the darkness that haunted our lives. Amid the singing and dancing, the myriad of great rides, and the ever-present Mickey and Goofy, I felt like a kid again. Maybe the world could be a happy, positive place. There was no Mafia at Disney World. There was no violence, no fear, no looking over my shoulder. Just being there lent a feeling of safety and security; it was like being on another planet. I remember walking around, touching everything, wide-eyed and giddy with the scent of a dozen different kinds of food—from hot dogs, donuts, and popcorn to ice cream in the shape of Mickey ears and one amazing restaurant after another. I must hand it to Disney; their magic worked wonders on all of us, even a jaded, increasingly cynical 14-year-old like me. My sisters simply sparkled with joy, and Mom's skin had a healthy glow for the first time in years.

By this time, her MS (multiple sclerosis) had crept its way throughout her body and limited her ability to stand, forcing her to use a walker. But a walker was no match for a sprawling theme park like Disney World, so we all took turns pushing her around the park in a wheelchair. No one minded. In some ways, as we made our way from Adventure Land and Space Mountain to Cinderella's Castle, seeing Mom's eyes beam with joy at every new discovery brought us all closer together. Even Dory, who had plenty of her own woes to forget, smiled and laughed and paid special attention to my mother. She seemed a different woman, if only for these few treasured days. She loved each one of us, but Bert's death had changed her life and cast her future into uncertainty.

Like all good things, our trip had to come to an end. It was time to return to Tampa. Back to reality. Back to days and nights of tension and vigilance. The news, not surprisingly, was still filled with Mafia arrests and indictments, car bombs and random shootings, headlines that suggested how bleak things were in the city of my youth; and those were just the incidents that made the news.

With all the law enforcement pressure, one might have thought that the mob would try to lay low for a while, but that's not what happened. For the first time ever, the Mafia underworld had been threatened, and the result was a kicked hornets' nest of gang violence, territorial jockeying, and power struggles.

Right around this time, a new figure was rising to power in the Trafficante crime family, an underboss named Frank Diecidue. Diecidue was part of a connected crime family that had worked for the Trafficantes for decades. Frank's father, Alfonso "Al" Diecidue, had been a highly ranked associate of Santo Trafficante Sr. and Jr. Frank "Daddy Frank" Diecidue operated gambling and loansharking rackets across the Tampa area, along with narcotics trafficking and arson. He was well-known around the bar scene because of his prominent front business, Dixie Amusements, a vending machine company that primarily dispensed cigarettes and assorted games in bars and lounges across Tampa. Dixie Amusements was an incredibly lucrative enterprise in and of itself, but Diecidue no doubt used this to keep tabs on activities in those establishments. Even though law enforcement kept pushing its way into Mafia activities, Frank Diecidue pushed back.

As the heat from law enforcement increased, Santo Trafficante Jr. took the opportunity to seek profit elsewhere and moved to Miami, leaving Diecidue to oversee his own crew and expand his operations and power. Emboldened by this new power, Diecidue moved into additional territories and flexed his muscle.

My dad was acquainted with Frank Diecidue through the vending machine business. Unlike Henry Trafficante, Diecidue never threatened my dad, so he held a cautious respect for the mobster. He thought Diecidue may have actually liked him or respected him, given that my dad was one of the few Italian bar owners who had stood tall against the relentless pressure of the mob's "invitation." The fact that Diecidue replaced Henry as the family's Number Two man, an outsider chosen over a brother, may indicate some serious internecine struggles in the organization.

My dad's refusal was highly unusual, as all Italian bar owners acquiesced at one time or another simply to avoid trouble. Frank knew my father wasn't from Tampa or connected through generations of Latin families. Good or bad, my father staked out his own territory and had thus far been allowed to live. Despite his constant vigilance and posse of supporters, he could have fallen to any number of assassination methods used by gangland figures around Tampa—car bombs and drive-by shotgun blasts were a mob favorite. He made it a practice to steer clear of the other Tampa crime syndicates, such as the Colombians and Jamaicans. Whether Diecidue was connected with Henry Trafficante in the attacks on my dad and my family, we never knew. As events unfolded, my dad's caution regarding Diecidue proved to be well-founded.

∼

On October 23, 1975, at about 9:50 a.m., Richard Cloud was home on a sunny Thursday morning. An olive-green and black Dodge Charger with two men inside pulled up outside his house on sleepy, residential Alva Street, both dressed in T-shirts and trousers. Stolen Hillsborough County license plates were affixed to the bumpers. A man got out and brought a cardboard box to the door, appearing to be making a delivery.

Cloud's two children were off to school. His wife Wanda had left for work about half an hour before. He was already busy making phone calls to colleagues about leads they were following, but he was expecting a phone call from a home builder. Two days before, he and Wanda had visited the Lutz area—the same area where our family lived—to look at a new house. He wasn't expecting a knock at the door.

The man with the cardboard box approached the door, knocked, and waited, slipping his hand into a hole in the box to take hold of the grip of the pistol inside, a Czechoslovakian .32-caliber semi-automatic pistol with a silencer.

When Cloud opened the door, the gunman opened fire. Cloud tried to fend off the gunman with a ceramic ashtray and a potted plant, fleeing deeper into the house, wounded and running for the telephone, but the gunman pursued him inside and finished him off. Cloud was shot four times.

Moments later, a roaring engine and squealing tires shattered the neighborhood silence. No one heard anything else.

Sensing something was terribly wrong at the Cloud residence, one of the neighbors came to investigate, saw the bullet holes in the screen door, and called the police. Cloud was pronounced dead at the scene, setting off a shock wave in the law enforcement community across the entire state.

His colleagues immediately called upon the FDLE and FBI to investigate the killing, fearing that the investigation would be drowned in the cesspit of Tampa's corruption. Cloud had been actively investigating several corrupt cops and their connections to the mob. Assassinating a police officer on his very doorstep, though, even a former one, was tantamount to a declaration of war.

The Richard Cloud murder case would not be swept under the rug. A grand jury was convened the following day. A number of underworld figures were dragged in and questioned, among them Henry and Santo Trafficante Jr., but it resulted in no solid leads. No one was talking. Quietly or not so quietly, the entire Tampa underworld exulted in Cloud's death. Even my dad had despised him, fearing that he might someday fall victim to one of Cloud's infamous shakedowns.

It wasn't until January 1976 that the case broke open. An annoyed landlord brought a man named Benjamin Foy Gilford to the attention of police. They soon discovered that Gilford was a convicted felon escaped from the Florida state prison. His jailbreak had been aided by his friend and criminal associate Marlow Haskew, a local thug with a significant rap sheet and several Mafia killings already under his belt. As soon as investigators discovered that Haskew owned an olive-green Charger, they zeroed in on the pair immediately.

Haskew quickly confessed to the shooting, admitting that it was a contract killing into which he'd brought his associate, Gilford, as the trigger man. Haskew sang like an operatic diva on the mob's activities, including the unremitting violence of the Lounge Wars that had been raging through Tampa for several years. In June 1976, while awaiting trial, trigger man Benjamin Foy Gilford was found dead in his cell, strangled by a bed sheet.

Haskew's confession and cooperation implicated several prominent mob figures, including Joe Bedami Jr., a narcotics trafficker who had been a target of Cloud's investigations for several years, and Frank Diecidue. The law enforcement dragnet had kept pulling up Diecidue's name, but they couldn't put together enough evidence to convict him—until Haskew's testimony.

Ultimately, Marlow Haskew turned state's witness in return for a life sentence, rather than the death penalty. The order to kill Dick Cloud had been passed down through several layers of plausible deniability that likely went all the way to the top of the mob organization. Everyone knew Diecidue was the Trafficantes' Number Two man, so it's possible the order to put Cloud in the ground came all the way from the top.

A low-level lackey named Anthony Antone was the man convicted of hiring Haskew and Gilford to kill Richard Cloud, on the orders of Victor Acosta, who gave Antone $10,000 to finance the job. Victor Acosta disappeared as soon as the indictments came down, skipping town allegedly with help from the head of the Tampa Police Department's criminal intelligence section, Jack De La Lana.

Anthony Antone's conviction, however, was only the tip of the spear, sparking a massive series of racketeering and conspiracy indictments. It was Frank Diecidue who had passed down the hit order through Victor Acosta and Anthony Antone before it finally landed in the hands of Haskew and Gilford. As the slow gears of justice continued to grind, Frank Diecidue was convicted of conspiracy to murder not only Richard Cloud, but also several of his business rivals who had been trying to cut into his vending machine operation. He had taken the opportunity to try to eliminate the competition.

Anthony Antone was executed by the State of Florida in January 1984.

In December 1976, Diecidue was handed a forty-year prison sentence, but in a shocking (or not so shocking) turnaround, in 1979 his conviction was overturned on a technicality, after which he was free to resume his position as the Number Two man in the Trafficante mob.

Victor Acosta surfaced in Coney Island, New York, in January 1978, having managed to evade capture for almost two years. He was charged with first-degree murder by the State of Florida and with conspiracy to commit murder by federal prosecutors. Less than twenty-four hours after being indicted and jailed, he was found barely alive in his cell. He died soon afterward. His guard admitted bringing him sleeping pills, and an autopsy revealed the presence of the drug in his system. His death was ruled a suicide.

~

For months, the citizens of Tampa Bay were exposed to wall-to-wall news coverage of the Richard Cloud assassination. This unprecedented act changed the dynamics of the Tampa mob and law enforcement.

For me, standing in my living room literally poised to kill someone with a shotgun had a way of dispelling any tattered remnants of childhood. I had risen to the occasion, baptized by fire. Not only was I a man now, I was starting to look like a man as well.

I was no longer "cute little Tony." The women who hung around Art's Lounge began to take notice of me in new ways, and I began to notice them in new ways. I came to understand the role they played in the nightclub, in the lounges. Their make-up was bright, their smiles ready, and their hair perfect, usually worn high in the up-do fashionable in the 1970s. They wore micro-shorts and mini-skirts and low-cut blouses revealing plenty of cleavage. Their friendliness to men, and sometimes to me, made it clear they were professionals, or at least, they were lonely women looking for a fling or a wealthy husband. They evoked such a strange mix of emotions in me. On one hand, they were so much older than me, it was all kind of silly. On the other hand, great swaths of exposed womanly flesh in all the right shapes, meant to be ogled, set my teenage hormones on fire.

This was also the time when Tampa gave birth to its now famous reputation as the Strip Capital of the World. The bar business was so competitive that each bar had to have its own gimmick. Liquor, pool hustling, package stores, and gambling were the usual permutations, but in the 1970s emerged the strip club. The conservative uproar was immense and the laws just as hypocritical as the regulations around liquor, but these emerging clubs put full nudity on display.

No other bar personifies this business strategy better than Diamond Lil's, a liquor lounge that famously took on the City of Tampa to allow both nudity and liquor under the same roof. The case made history and set in motion a controversy that lasted for years. Since my father knew all the bar owners around Tampa, he would sometimes visit his competition, including these strip clubs, and trade liquor or loan money. I was at an age where I could tag along, and the eyefuls of stunning women turned my teenage testosterone into a nuclear bomb. I had already been exposed to Dory's secret drawer of sexual playfulness, but the things I saw in those places gave me the greatest teenage boy bragging rights ever. I knew more about the female anatomy than all my male friends put together and could expound upon it in great detail. The stories I told riveted them, and being that kind of fount of all knowledge made me feel even more like a man.

So, women and sex were simply in the air in the Tampa lounge scene, and Art's Lounge had its own set of regular female professionals. My dad let them all ply their trade. I grew to know the hookers as working women and for the most part, kept my testosterone in check. When I was in the bar, my dad watched my interactions with these women. In some ways it was a test, to see how I would handle myself around them. He admonished me to maintain my dignity and to never succumb to the sleaze. This was all part of his efforts to groom me for a future in the bar business. He'd seen enough bar owners and customers lose themselves in that realm, only to self-destruct, that he knew it was a very slippery slope. Even at that age, I seemed to sense this instinctively. Maybe it was all this tremendous exposure to women, nudity, and illicit sex that dampened its power over me at a young age. The first few times I was the target of their flirtations, I probably amused them with my stunned awkwardness, but over time, I learned that it was all a game, a primal ritual, a dance. I eventually learned the steps. By the time I was 18, I came to enjoy putting them back on their heels with my own repartee, watching them scramble for something to say, like they had so often done to me.

The land on which Art's Lounge sat included a ten-room motel, mainly frequented by long-haul truckers, but he also rented the rooms by the hour. No doubt the truckers found the ready supply of hookers in the adjacent lounge to be a significant draw. When my dad asked me to handle the keys to the motel, it was the rare occasion that I would rent a room for a full night.

~

By the time Art's Lounge was firmly established, I was 15 years old. The new location was on the east side of Tampa, near Seffner, about eighteen miles away from the dog track. There were no more partners, no partner conflicts, no shared profits, just my dad, complete with his own lounge, his own package store, and his own liquor license, with his years of accumulated management skills, contacts, and customer base.

Art's Lounge was so profitable in other ways that he scaled back the bookmaking operation; the distance for the runners had become prohibitive. The package liquor store proved to be a cash cow. Tampa had an ancient law on the books that prohibited the sale of liquor on Sundays. Long known for being a part of the Bible belt, Tampa's conservative base and numerous churches insisted that law be kept in force to protect its citizens from drunken behavior on Sunday. Realizing the golden opportunity before him, my father began to sell a bottle of Sunday booze here and there to his regular customers. Just like in the days of Prohibition, if somebody wants to drink, they'll find a way to drink. Word spread quickly among my dad's customers that they could score a bottle on Sunday. No matter that he jacked the price up three times the normal amount; his clientele was happy to pay it. What started as a few select customers grew into hundreds of loyal customers each and every Sunday. The bar sat in the middle of a big chunk of property, surrounded by a circular drive that led to the motels at the rear. At peak times during the height of this period, there were dozens of cars lined up pointing to the back entrance where discreet hand-offs occurred. Not surprisingly, the busiest hours were noon to 1:00 p.m., at the exact time church let out. So, the same Bible-thumping parishioners who supported the lock-down of Sunday liquor sales were the first in line to get theirs. Try wrapping your head around that one. As months went by, I often worried that the lines of cars stretching into the main road would bring unwanted attention from the police. But I kept my mouth shut for the time being.

Much of my dad's posse followed him to Art's Lounge, but he quickly collected new clientele. This area of Tampa was the home of the hardworking, union hall people, and farmers and migrants who all liked to drink. Their way of life was *work hard, drink hard*.

Over time, my father developed a close personal relationship with the local beat cops and Hillsborough County Sheriff's Department. Policemen liked to drink, too, maybe more than most, truth be told. Art's Lounge became a frequent watering hole for both sheriff's deputies and Tampa police detectives, off duty of course. They liked that my dad had resisted joining the mob and that he worked hard and played by their rules, at least mostly. They turned a blind eye to his gambling operations, pool games, women, and most importantly, liquor sales on Sunday—as long as he never dealt in narcotics. That was a deal-breaker for police back then. A few vices were acceptable—indulging them was how the mob had flourished as long as it had—but never illegal drugs.

Throughout my childhood, my father would come home from work, put his big wallet, fat with cash, on the counter alongside his snub-nose .38 revolver. It was almost as common as a set of keys. We knew not to touch it, but we knew why it was there. When it was gone, it was in his pocket. When he was working the bar, he kept it under the counter within easy reach, and if things ever got tense or rough, he would put it in his pants.

One night in the new Art's Lounge, Madelyn was working, and there were a couple dozen patrons in the bar. One of them was my cousin Buddy Martoglio. Buddy was a traditional Italian, short, stocky, and loyal, married with four kids. Like most of the Scarpo family, he worked hard and drank hard. Buddy and my father have been close confidants for decades, even to this day, and it was his presence that turned this incident into a family legend, like the time they all pulled their guns in church.

A man came into the bar and caught my dad's eye instantly. My dad was well practiced at recognizing thugs, men who came in looking for trouble. So, when somebody he had not seen before came in, sat down and ordered a drink, his attention was instantly focused. The man had a cold, belligerent look in his eye and in his manner, as if he were working himself up to something and needed booze for a boost. Before long, he started hassling one of the other patrons, smack talking. Dad was always his own bouncer, and he had long had a reputation as one of the most brutal bouncers around, fists of steel. He came around the bar to put a stop to the altercation brewing. Instantly, as if the thug had been waiting for this moment, he whipped out a switchblade with masterful speed and put it to my dad's throat.

In the Old West, my dad could have been a gunfighter. Just as quickly as the thug pulled his knife, Dad simultaneously pulled his .38 and put the muzzle to the man's forehead.

And there they stood like two mannequins, both rigidly frozen but determined.

Chairs tumbled and crashed as patrons scrambled in all directions. Madelyn stood behind the bar, frozen, hands over her mouth. Buddy leaped off his barstool but froze two steps away from the confrontation. He knew that if he took another step closer, one or both of them were going to die.

The two men were shouting at each other, over each other, "Put it down! Put it down!"

"I'll fucking kill you!"

"I'll blow your fucking head off!"

"I cut your fucking throat!"

"You're fucking dead!"

The thug was sweating profusely, knowing that even if he cut my dad's throat, he'd be dead instantly.

For interminable seconds, they yelled at each other, "Put it down!"

"No, *you* put it down, motherfucker!"

"You first!" The thug was still cocky, a puffed-up junk-yard dog.

"All I have to do is squeeze the trigger."

The cold certainty of my dad's voice must have popped the balloon of the thug's courage. After what seemed like an eternity of shouting, the thug eased back and dropped the knife on the floor.

With a sudden force of vengeance, my dad grabbed him by the throat, his finger tightening, drawing back the double-action hammer. The instant stretched into a moment of decision. His first instinct was to shoot to kill, but a misfired bullet could easily kill one of his friends and customers. In that instant, he restrained the vengeance and released the trigger, allowing the hammer to ease back. As the blood rushed to my father's head and his temper exploded, he wound up and clubbed the thug with the butt of the pistol. Buddy and several other friends seized the thug and tackled him. My father descended upon him with fists and the butt of the revolver. They beat the man to a bloody, groaning pulp.

As my dad stood over him, he still wanted to kill him, he told me later. This thug, probably hired to do a job like Richard Cloud's killers, had just come into *his* place of business and threatened him. His pride and ego roared up and tightened his finger on the trigger. He wanted to blow this lowlife's brains out and send a message back to the bastards who hired him, Diecidue, Trafficante, whoever it had been. But all he could think of was that if he pulled the trigger, if he killed someone in his bar, he would carry that burden for the rest of his life. He would never be able to let that go.

So he stepped back, looking at the bloody mess that lay on the floor, and yelled, "Who sent you? Why are you here?"

But the man couldn't or wouldn't answer.

My dad turned to Buddy and said, "Get him out of here."

Buddy and the other man dragged the thug outside and tossed him in a heap on the sidewalk.

In those days, that's how bar fights always ended: the losers outside in a bleeding heap on the curb, to crawl away to the hospital or wherever they slunk off to. The cops were never called. The cops never showed up. Florida rains came and washed the blood from the concrete, oblivious to dark stains and bad memories.

As Americans celebrated the bicentennial and the spirit of patriotism spread across the land, my father was left wondering who ordered these hits. Why did they keep coming? Was it a long-standing vendetta? Had he made that much of an impact on the mob, or were they just pissed he had survived and was making it on his own? One thing was certain: this had to end, no matter what. His partner had been brutally murdered, and now the assassins had become more brazen than ever. What was next? A car bomb? A shotgun in the parking lot? The kidnapping of one of his children? It was time for a summit. It was time for reconciliation. Too much was at stake.

With the backing of law enforcement and the confidence of his own clan, my father felt stronger than ever that this matter could be resolved once and for all. He summoned one of his runners to deliver a message to Frank Diecidue.

"Art Scarpo wants to meet. Name your place and time."

CHAPTER FIFTEEN

RITES OF PASSAGE

MY LIFE WAS A storm in 1976, surrounded by war zones. My junior high school was a war zone, fraught with fear and the threat of violence. My father's business was a war zone, under attack by ruthless mobsters. Even my family home had become a war zone, like a jungle outpost constantly on alert, tiptoeing in the dark with eyes and ears always open. It was no longer a place of comfort and refuge. How many nights did we all lie awake in bed, plagued by the fear that tonight might be another night someone was going to try to sneak in and kill us all? Life was like walking barefoot on piano wires.

There are times in life when you realize you're under great stress, but you don't realize the extent of it until it has passed, and retrospect offers some perspective. Would I have done some of the things I did if life had been less crazy? How much of it was typical teenager stuff, fueled by assurance of my own immortality, and how much of it was me trying to cope with darkness I saw everywhere? I still don't know. What I did know is that no one understood my world.

My mother's illness had progressed from a limp, to a cane, to a walker. She had CT scans and spinal taps and whole batteries of tests, everything medicine could muster in the 1970s. The trouble was, nobody really knew what MS was, much less how to treat it. This disease was eating away at her, chewing off bits of her life and dignity, but at the speed of a turtle. She could still cook, do housework, and use a walker, but watching her go through this, every day, left my life tainted by sadness and helplessness. None of my friends knew what was happening, what kind of world I was living in at home. No one knew about the bar business, about the gambling, the prostitution, the mob threats. I kept all that quiet, because my father had told me to, in no uncertain terms. When he said "quiet," he meant quiet. Nobody talked about it, not me or my sisters, to anyone.

In spite of all that, all the fears, all the grief, all the anger, I wanted so badly to be just a regular kid. I managed a B-average in school and found great pleasure in playing football. I also joined FFA, the Future Farmers of America.

As I've mentioned, the football field became the place where the hostile factions of black and white classmates began to build bridges, but because there were so many overlapping spheres of violence and fear in my life, it was impossible to discern which was causing me the most emotional turmoil on any given day. It was all just a poisonous, seething mess.

Nevertheless, I made my own bright spots where I could.

Ironically, FFA was one of the most intensive classes I ever took. The teacher, Mr. Satin, expected each of us to get an A+, and I think it was his pressure, in part, that led me to excel in the class. I learned so much from him. He called out laziness and lack of attention and encouraged us to do better. At our house on Skipper Road, my early years had included a crash course in animal care, with all the animals we kept around, plus the gardening my mother used to do back when she was still able to do it, but FFA gave me all sorts of great tips for an enterprise that came to me as a bolt of inspiration.

Mr. Satin's favorite field was horticulture, and he taught us how to grow tomatoes, peppers, onions, all sorts of vegetables and crops. He would have been horrified if he knew how I would use this knowledge. Then again, it was the seventies; maybe he wouldn't have been surprised at all.

The summer of 1975 was the year Tommy introduced me to marijuana, and I spent most of the rest of that summer stoned, as well as weekends after school started.

A funny thing back then, the clusters of Colombian Gold were full of seeds. If I wasn't careful to remove them before I rolled the joint, they would pop or explode when I was inhaling, which was startling even when I was high as a kite. One day, after a week of learning how to grow tomato plants in FFA, one of those mini-explosions blew a hole in my mind.

With that bizarre yet over-simplistic, sometimes-nonsensical intensity that comes only from being stoned, I realized that I never had to *buy* marijuana ever again. These were *seeds! Seeds grow!* And *seeds* turn into *plants!*

An aside to this epiphany, a strange thing, was that Catholicism became my savior, slowing my slide into dissipation. We were this close-knit Italian family, with extended family regularly visiting for parties and celebrations. The infamous backyard soirees on Skipper Road continued when we moved to Lutz, but because we lived on a lake now, every gathering became a grand event. The greater Scarpo family could be a bit of a rough bunch, dabbling at things that many, including the law, considered out of bounds. But there was this facade of Catholicism covering it all. My mother took us to Mass every Sunday, where I would see all my aunts and cousins, but almost none of the men in the family. Over the years, I went to catechism. I went to Confraternity of Christian Doctrine classes, CCD. I received all my sacraments. I had sat dutifully and reverently for Sister Dorothy Barbara's lessons. My sisters and I received our first communions, and the babies of the family were baptized. But I was a man myself now, watching all the men in my family break the rules and pay only lip service to the church. How much did the women know? Either they knew about everything and condoned it, or they turned a blind eye. The women were the ones who made sure all the children made it to church, but the older I got, the more I could peek behind the curtain and recognize the hypocrisy. My father had stopped telling my mother about the goings-on at the bar. Instead, he was telling me, showing me the ropes.

✦ I remember sitting in church at the baptism of one of my cousins' new baby, looking around at all the men in the family, including my dad, and thinking about how everyone around me was doing very bad stuff. It was like a scene out of *The Godfather*. No one had forgotten the pulling of the guns in church, and I had no doubt on this day most of the men in my family were probably packing, including my dad. And it made me angry. Baptism is supposed to be a beautiful thing, welcoming a new life into the Kingdom of God, and the men of my family were carrying weapons. The hypocrisy became one of the many things I was angry about.

For me, assuaging that anger, staving off the darkness, required chemical intervention.

So, at the ripe old age of 15, in spite of my upbringing in the Catholic Church, in spite of the religious education I'd received from Sister Dorothy Barbara, I launched my experiment, my first entrepreneurial venture: I was going to try growing Colombian Gold for myself. What I didn't use, I could sell. That it was illegal only barely crossed my mind. Illegal stuff went on all around me, untouched by the arm of the law. Why should it be any different for me?

Step One was study and experimentation. What I didn't learn in FFA, I studied in the *Encyclopedia Britannica*. I took the seeds from some of the pot that I bought and treated them like tomato seeds, carefully germinating, watching, planting, and then tending to them like a prized school project in an FFA state competition. I planted my seedlings in plain sight, out in the back corners of the swamp that adjoined the lakes. I put into practice the lessons about weeding and watering, although the soil was so rich I didn't need to fertilize. Back in the swamp among cypress groves and Spanish moss, I grew a crop of Colombian Gold that stretched ten feet tall, blending perfectly with the surrounding forest. Back in FFA, we would talk about tomatoes and pepper plants and I'd be smirking, thinking, "Yeah, screw that. I've got a whole crop of ten-foot pot plants that's the envy of any Colombian drug lord." Had they been legal, they would have won any state fair competition, but alas, legalization of medical marijuana in Florida would not occur until 2016.

The lakes formed their own little communities, each surrounded by a handful of houses, but they were all close enough that we could get acquainted with people on other lakes. My friends Tommy and Bobby both lived on different lakes than ours. It was such a beautiful setting. Our lake glimmered in the sun, sometimes mirror-calm, sometimes rippling from the touch of a breeze. Majestic cypress trees lined the banks, dripping with Spanish moss and overflowing with brightly colored birds. The water teemed with fish—and also with alligators and water moccasins. I loved the smell of it when I walked outside in the morning, lush and wet and alive. It was perfect for fishing, boating, and water-skiing, activities my friends and I pursued at every opportunity, anything that would serve as a temporary distraction from the lurking darkness, like frosting concealing a rotten cake.

Our lake had five houses on it. Our next-door neighbor was a wonderful old woman named Goldie Vogel. Her blonde hair had gone mostly gray, and she kept it short and serviceable. Long before we moved in, she had been the private live-in nurse for a wealthy man, and ultimately married him. When he passed away, she inherited everything, his entire fortune. When I heard about Goldie's history, I couldn't help but think about the contrast between her life and Dory's, the capriciousness of chance. Goldie had come to Florida from Kentucky.

"I brung the hillbilly with me!" she would say in her strong accent, but clearly, with a degree in nursing, she was an educated woman.

Thanks to her nursing, she understood my mother's illness, which was a real blessing. She was so kind to my mother, sometimes helping around our house with cooking or little jobs. Since we had moved to Lutz, Goldie assumed some of the role that Priscilla had played. My mother accepted Goldie's help and kindness with grace. We still invited the Bejanos for visits occasionally, but we never went back to Skipper Road.

Goldie's property was full of goats and rabbits and chickens roaming everywhere, with a sprawling garden. Her favorite pastimes were to cook and bake in true country style. Her pies with their perfect, flaky crusts would have won competitions at any county fair anywhere, blueberry, apple, peach, and because we lived in Florida, key lime pie.

One of her favorite dishes to cook, one that she was known for around the area, was chicken and dumplings. She would start by going out to the chicken coop, clubbing two chickens, grabbing them by the head, one in each hand, and she would spin them around like helicopter blades until their heads popped off, and they would spin away and plop to the ground in their gruesome dance of twitching limbs and spraying blood. Of course, I had seen this before on Skipper Road—we had always butchered our own animals out there—but it always horrified me, and this barbaric spectacle felt strangely out of place in our idyllic, lake shore community, like it was the kind of thing that should stay in the backwoods. Then she would proceed to butcher them right there in front of us. I remember my sisters watching this once with stricken, horrified looks. They had been too young to take part in the butchering activities on Skipper Road.

As far as I could tell, Goldie's second husband had no family, but from a prior marriage she had a swarm of children and grandchildren who came to visit her often. Her place was always a bustling hub of activity. Several of her grandchildren were about my age, and we bonded quickly over boating, water-skiing, and motorcycles. At weekly barbeques and cook-outs, it was always loud and boisterous, a mix of Scarpos and neighbors. We would play and swim, and I would always wonder if Goldie's grandchildren could see the darkness I was carefully hiding.

Goldie's son Bill lived with her on the property in a separate single-wide trailer. Bill was tall and thin, a few years on either side of forty, with weathered, leathery skin and sad eyes that were bloodshot all the time. I never saw him without a beer in his hand, even though he claimed to be a "recovering alcoholic," having gone through detox and rehab. But even then, I was pretty sure that being a recovering alcoholic meant you had stopped drinking. Nevertheless, he was a kind, sensitive soul who treated us all well. Everyone called him Uncle Bill. He usually put on a brave face, but I sensed a sadness in him that went all the way to the bone. His trailer was situated at the water's edge, maybe fifty yards from our front door. I would often see him outside, sitting in a lawn chair, head hanging. The only way I could tell he was awake was if he waved at me. I remember seeing him cry sometimes, the reasons for which only he understood. Perhaps because of this, he would occasionally get staggeringly drunk, shit-faced drunk, and wander the area, sometimes passing out such that Goldie would have to come and collect him, making excuses for him as she went, as some parents do when they have a child with problems. For my own part, I pitied him and the depths into which alcoholism could drag someone.

My dad embraced Goldie and Uncle Bill. No doubt the travails of Bill's life were familiar to my dad; he probably saw the same ritual being enacted at the bar every day. Had Uncle Bill been a mean or belligerent drunk, we may have treated them differently, but they were both kind, sweet souls.

But we lived in a veritable playground. With Bobby, Tommy, and Goldie's brood of grandchildren, we formed this wild gang of kids with a thirst for adrenaline that rivaled champion cliff jumpers. My mother was in no shape to see what I was doing, and my dad worked the bar every day. The only instructions we ever got were to be home by dinnertime. Then again, I'm not sure it would have mattered if our parents had said anything, drunk as we were on our own immortality.

We climbed the great cypress trees that grew right up to the water's edge, striving to climb higher and higher into thinner and thinner branches. We carried hammers, nails, and boards with us into the trees to build makeshift steps into the upper reaches. Place a board, tack it down, place a board, tack it down, up and up and up until we were five or six stories in the air. From there, we'd edge out onto a branch and shimmy way out to the end with nothing to hold on to, inch by inch; crouched over staring out at the vast acres of orange groves and the lake below, I'd take a deep breath, say a quick prayer and...

Leap out as far as I could reach, hoping to clear the shoreline and...

Splash!

From that height, we hit the water with the force of a cannon-ball. We didn't think about the fact that if we fell backwards off those branches, we would have landed on the cypress knees, the exposed roots reaching out away from the trunk. Landing on one of those would have meant certain death, but we were immortal, after all. So we flung ourselves into the abyss, hooting and yelling like howler monkeys, feeling light as a feather, every nerve-ending screaming with life, to be swallowed by the dark water. Then we would bob to the surface and paddle toward the bank, impatient to climb back up and do it again.

All that splashing and commotion tended to drive the alligators away. But I loved sometimes bringing the commotion to them. The lakes and marshes around the area were crawling with gators of every size. Having had my fair share of encounters with them on Skipper Road, and now that I was a man, at least in my own mind, they didn't frighten me anymore.

Drenched in Florida sun and steeped to the gills in my home-grown weed, we would all load into our speedboat and go gator-skiing. The lake was big enough that we could push the boat up to thirty or forty miles per hour. One of my equally stoned buddies would drive the boat while I was skiing along behind, and he would head toward the area where the gators lived and nested. They were always there, always in the water, floating motionless like logs. As we approached, I would cut my slalom ski to the outside of the boat and zip toward them at ridiculous speed. I could just see their eyes sticking up out of the water, and that was my target. I aimed straight for the head and cut across them with a huge splash and wave that scattered them in all directions. Laughing my ass off, we would circle the lake, giving them just enough time to compose themselves, then we would come around and do it again. It never occurred to me what might happen if I hit a big alligator, lost a ski, and went down squarely among them, or if it might happen to any of my friends. I was invincible, jousting with dinosaurs.

These modern-day dinosaurs became a kind of primordial punching bag for me. There were so many of them that they were easy targets, and they were so dangerous that I didn't feel bad about any childish cruelties I inflicted on them. In fact, alligators became a strange form of bonding between me and my dad, because I had entered, by incremental degrees, full-on rebellious teenager mode.

Hunting gators was an activity we could still do together without my simmering anger toward him rearing its ugly head.

Every weekend at our house, there was Sunday dinner. My mother, whether from her wheelchair or her walker, would make us an enormous meal. Heaping piles of spaghetti and marinara, meatballs, steak, lasagna, seafood, crusty Italian bread. My sisters would clean up afterward, and my dad would look at me and say, "Go get your gun."

I would grab my trusty .410 shotgun, my father would grab one of his many rifles, and the two of us would go sit on our dock and wait for the alligators to come by.

Our house was situated at the southern end of an oval-shaped lake, not far from where the alligators crossed from east to west on their nightly trek. At sunset, with rose-streamered dusk reflecting on the lake, slow-moving pairs of eyes would drift across the surface of the water about thirty to fifty yards from us.

The first time we did this, we sat on the end of the dock in the silence, our stomachs full of spaghetti feast.

I asked him, "What are we doing?"

"We're going to shoot alligators."

I nodded sagely, then asked, "What if we get one?"

He pointed to the flat-bottomed, aluminum johnboat moored to our dock.

"And then what?" I asked.

"We clean it and eat it."

There's a lot of meat on an alligator—they're pretty much a low-slung block of solid muscle—and my mom's fried alligator tail was one of my favorite foods.

So we waited for one to come close enough to get an easy shot. "Aim for right between the eyes," he said.

I'd gone hunting with him before, so I knew the ropes, but in this case the prey was going to come to us.

Several gators passed by at a range that made the shot less certain. At fifty yards, my .410 would hardly scratch an alligator's thick hide. We let those go on past. But then we saw a good one coming, maybe a five-footer, and we both took aim and fired. I don't know who fired first, but the alligator instantly rolled onto its side, two stumpy legs twitching in the air.

I let out a whoop and we ran to the johnboat. A couple of minutes later, we oared up beside the dead alligator. My dad shipped the oars. "Grab its tail and drag it in the boat," he told me.

I reached down to pull at the gator's tail, never having felt the thick muscularity of a fresh alligator's tail before. The sheer power contained in that appendage awed me. I lugged the thing up into the boat, and that's when things went further south than Florida.

The alligator is a prehistoric reptile with a very small brain, a thick skull, and a thick hide over that. The alligator I thought was dead lurched in my grip, its jaws springing open, its powerful tail almost throwing me out of the boat. Our shots had only knocked it out. I flung myself away and nearly went over the side of the boat.

My dad reacted instantly, raising one of the oars and crashing it down over the gator's head. He didn't dare shoot it again or he'd risk shooting a hole in the boat. The first tremendous blow knocked the gator stiff as a board, then he hit it again, and it fell limp and started to spasm.

We both stared at the thing for a long moment before my father said, "Okay, it's dead now."

But by that time, I think my heart had burst out of my chest and fled over the horizon.

Despite all the wild, daredevil shenanigans, despite my steadfast assertion of manhood, there were times when I was terrified, but I didn't dare show this fear around my father. I just had to go with the flow.

Besides shooting alligators from the dock, he also liked to take hunting and fishing expeditions into the swamp—deep, deep in the swamp.

"That's where you find the best fish," he would tell me to shut down my complaints. The truth was that he loved the back country, the undeveloped areas.

He would rouse me out of bed at 5:30 a.m., load our gear into the johnboat with its little troll motor—this was not the speedboat we used for water-skiing—and take off into the dark reaches of Florida back creeks, where the water was black and impenetrable and all you could see was leafy branches hanging over the water, festooned with Spanish moss. We had to duck under it all just to make progress.

We stopped the boat at a good fishing spot, well-shaded where the bluegill and brim liked to congregate, and I stood up in the boat to drop the anchor. The branches were so close my head came up among them, and I found myself face to face with a water moccasin as thick as my arm. Its head was the size of my fist. We just looked at each other for a split second of mutual shock, before my reflexes took over and I swatted the branch away.

But the snake fell into the boat with us and lay coiling and writhing, its light-colored underside twisting around the dark, mottled scales of its back.

Without even blinking, my dad pushed me out of the way, grabbed a paddle, and used it to flip the snake out of the boat.

"We're fine," he said as the disgruntled pit viper swam away. "We're fine."

He moved on from the encounter as if nothing had happened and proceeded to fill our stringer with fish. It was a while, however, before I managed any real fishing that day. Every branch had become a water moccasin poised to drop around my neck.

～

Not all formative experiences are positive ones, and I brought a fair amount of trouble down on my own head.

My marijuana mini-plantation took off like Jack's beanstalk. Before long I had so much high-quality weed, I didn't know what to do with it all. I spent so much time stoned, and I made sure my friends all had as much as they wanted. Several of Dad's bar posse even came to me for their weed. Along the way, I made some serious cash, which I kept in a coffee can in my closet. By the time I was 15, I had enough money for pretty much anything a teenage boy wanted.

But my sisters and my mom knew. They could smell it on me, on my clothes, and they saw me stoned all the time. They confronted me about it several times. They would yell at me. I would get indignant and defensive and blow them off.

Most surprising was that they didn't tell my dad. Maybe they didn't because they knew what he would do to me. Remember that rule he had about no illegal drugs, no narcotics around the bar. It wouldn't have mattered that I thought I was man, he would have striped my ass with his belt and put me back in that body cast.

It was many years later, while on a trip to my dad's hunting and fishing camp in North Florida, that several of his friends from the bar came along for the weekend, and everybody got drunk, sitting around the fire waxing stories and tall tales as they had in the past. Someone burst into compliments for me about how good my weed was, a sentiment that was seconded by several people around the circle. I froze, poked the fire quietly with a stick, and my dad just stared at me, his face a brittle mask of surprise and God knew what else. He didn't get outright angry, or yell at me, but soon after he told me that he and his friends stumbled upon my hidden weed farm while walking through the swamp. All of my precious plants had been chopped down to the stump, uprooted, gone.

I found out much later that he had given all the weed to his friends at the bar and they joked about it for some time. And that was the abrupt end of my marijuana venture. For several years, I had enjoyed my farming experiment but now it was gone. I counted myself lucky to have survived it, knowing my dad's rule about drugs and narcotics, but there was another time where he did not hold back the discipline.

That was when he found out I was also not only drinking heavily but stealing it from the house. I had cracked the seals on a bunch of expensive whiskey decanters. How I thought I would never get caught, I can't imagine, but as soon as my dad discovered this, he gave me one of the three worst whippings I ever got. It was so epic, frankly, that it ended my drinking spree forever, not to mention the shame that I had to endure.

But that rebellious streak went pretty deep, and not just against my family, but against the society I was coming to see as a pretty sick place.

The first time I got caught for petty theft, I was 13. We were on a shopping excursion to Maas Brothers, a prominent Tampa department store, with relatives visiting from Ohio. One of my cousins dared me to steal something. The gauntlet had been thrown down, and the potential consequences never once crossed my mind. I saw an eight-track tape I wanted, *Led Zeppelin IV*. Someone must have seen me stuff it in my pants, or maybe they spotted the weird rectangular bulge in my pants, but a security guard grabbed me on my way out the door. The police were called, and there I stood with my family and my relatives from Ohio showering me with incredulous disapproval as the police threatened to cuff me and take me to juvenile detention. Thankfully, they let my family take me home, but both the law and my father came down on me harder than I had imagined. As soon as we got home, I was still sick with humiliation when he whipped the pants off me. And then I had to go to juvenile court over an $8.99 eight-track tape.

He lectured me all the way to the courthouse that day. "When you go into court, remember, you have your name. You have to walk out with your name."

Everything was about "protecting your name," because that's all we really had in this world, he told me. As he spoke, on and on, I could see his pride in the name he had built for himself, and now I was jeopardizing that. I had brought shame upon our family. The law could go pound sand, but the thought of shaming my family made me sick to my stomach.

It was with this experience that the humiliation took root and grew into something positive, but I wasn't yet finished being a rebel without a clue.

There was a convenience store that we frequented that had a rack of refrigerator magnets with funny or snarky or inane aphorisms on them, stuff like, "Keep on Truckin'," a smiley-face "Have a nice day!" and "Ass, Gas, or Grass. Nobody rides for free." Bumper sticker stuff. They were maybe 49 or 99 cents back then. Every time I went in there, I would steal one of those magnets.

About the time I had collected $20-25 worth of them, the store owner called my dad and told him, "Your son has been stealing here for a long time. I don't want him in here anymore."

When my dad turned to me with this knowledge, the look of disgust, disappointment, and humiliation on his face was worse than any beating he could have given me. He didn't say anything, but he did give me a tremendous whipping, and I was forced to take the magnets back and apologize to the store owner. It was the look on his face that stayed with me, not the whipping. I couldn't tell if my father's expression had said, "How could you do this?" or if it was saying, "How could you get caught?" I still don't know. But the outcome was the same. I had humiliated myself and brought shame upon my family. I had jeopardized our name.

That was the final humiliation that formed into something I would carry around forever. From that moment on, anytime a friend of mine was doing something wrong or illegal, or I saw a man getting ready to cheat on his wife or his girlfriend, or anybody around me was on the verge of doing something corrupt, I would get physically queasy. It was like a corruption sensor in my stomach. Whenever I got too close to something bad, the wave of nausea would hit me, and it all grew out of the humiliation I had brought upon myself and my family. It didn't fully take hold for a few more years, because I was still growing weed, or maybe I was still able, in my teenage narcissism, to turn a blind eye to my own shortcomings. Nowadays, much later in life, it's a feeling I use almost like a divining rod or a metal detector. If I get this bad feeling in my gut, I change course or back away from whatever happens to be going on around me.

Whenever I visited the bar and interacted with the people there, this feeling hit me hard and often. People in bars can be fun, hilarious, gregarious, or they can be broken, sleazy, and mean. It's like there's no middle of the road; alcohol polarizes people's personalities toward these extremes.

Some people just had a darkness in them, I would come to realize, just like I did, and they often hid it so effectively it was shocking when it emerged.

~

My friend Tommy lived on one of the adjacent lakes with his mother, two sisters, and step-father. His sister Kathy was my age. She reminded me of Sissy Spacek in *Carrie*. I sometimes wondered if I was the only boy who ever talked to her, because she was not one of the popular kids, always awkward and reticent. We had the same bus stop, and spent time together waiting for the bus. Both of Tommy's parents were divers with Hillsborough County Underwater Rescue, and his stepfather was in law enforcement.

Tommy was the first boy I met in our new Lutz neighborhood. He was two years older than me, six inches taller than me, with long, stringy blond hair and a lanky, wiry build. He was one of those people who had trouble sitting still, constantly fidgeting, and constantly chain-smoking cigarettes. He had introduced me to marijuana and to drinking alcohol and wasted no opportunity to do the same to other kids around us. He reveled in his role as the great teenage sage, the worldly one among our crowd. He would puff up with self-importance and expound upon many fields of forbidden lore, from sex to drugs to liquor, all the taboos our parents would have frowned upon. He fancied himself a ladies' man, extolling his many sexual experiences, but even I could tell it was all talk. He was just too dorky.

What worried me about him was that he'd sometimes show up with the kind of bruises that only come from beatings. I never saw it personally, but his stepfather abused him terribly. In private moments, when it was just him and me, way up in a cypress tree, he would tell me about this, all these terrible things that his stepfather said and did to him, someone who was supposed to *rescue* people, help people, and uphold the law. But it wasn't just his stepfather. His mother, he said, was angry all the time and took everything out on him because he was the oldest, and the only boy. Both of his parents were heavy drinkers, and as soon as the drinking started, bickering soon exploded into fighting. I shared with him some of my concerns and apprehensions about my own life, but I kept all that vague; I never went into detail, because I had been ordered not to. Of course, he knew about Bert's murder, but I never told him about our dead-of-night intruders, or seeing my dad bloody and naked in our bathtub, or the killing of our dog.

One day in the fall of 1975, Tommy called to invite me to a sleepover. It seemed a little strange, as I had rarely been to his house, and sometimes it also felt weird that he was this older boy who seemed to like hanging out with younger kids. Something didn't feel right about that. He was another of those clueless rebels like I was, so a lot of the neighborhood kids kept him at arm's length. I may even have been trying to emulate him in the way that boys do when they're looking for someone to look up to.

Maybe he sensed my hesitation, so he said, "Come on, it'll be fun. The family's gonna be gone. Got some other people coming over, too. We'll smoke weed and stay up late and watch the late movie."

The late movie was often shows like *Kolchak: The Night Stalker* and weird old horror movies, and I just loved that, so I said, "Sure."

So, I packed up my toothbrush and pajamas and sleeping bag and rode my motorcycle over to Tommy's house.

I pulled up outside just as the sun was going down. The single-story, ranch-style house looked strangely deserted, with only one light inside to indicate anyone might be home. Tommy's motorcycle was parked along the side under the carport, with no sign of his parents' car.

When I went inside, Tommy welcomed me with a casual, "Hey."

There was a strange smell in the house I couldn't identify, something sour that made me wrinkle my nose. It seemed important to me all of a sudden that he and I not be the only ones here. "So, who else is coming over?"

"Looks like it's just us," he said with a shrug.

That queasiness settled into my stomach.

He said, "You bring the weed?"

I nodded and patted my pocket, which contained a plastic bag of my finest Colombian Gold.

We kicked back, lit up, and settled in front of the television. I had brought enough weed for several people, but Tommy and I proceeded to smoke it all. Joint after joint, we toked up. It was the most stoned I have ever been. I was floating in the clouds.

Everything we said and did was in slow motion and the sights and sounds of my surroundings moved in and out of focus. All I could think of was food; the munchies had set in. But even that couldn't erase the unease I was feeling, that queasiness in my gut.

It was like the air in the place was alive somehow and crawling all over me, keeping me on a knife's edge when I should have been blitzed out, like there was someone watching us.

I asked him, "So where are your parents?"

"Working."

"What about your sisters?"

"Sleeping over someplace else."

Why had he invited me over, when he'd never done that before? Was it because he wanted to score some weed? Was something troubling him?

George Carlin came on late night after the local news, launching into his now infamous "Seven Words You Can't Say on Television" routine. I remember being so shocked that the words weren't censored, because I had never heard any of them on television before. It didn't matter that they were well-seasoned tidbits from my own vocabulary, but it felt wrong hearing them on television. In that fixated way that happens only when stoned, I wondered if this was some sort of mistake. Were they left uncensored on purpose? Had someone missed it? What had happened? Was someone going to get in trouble for that? Any other time, I would have found Carlin's routine hilarious, but tonight it didn't feel funny at all.

Outside, crickets and tree frogs sang night songs. Bats flitted across the stars, hunting mosquitoes. Gators floated quiescent in dark, still waters. Inside, I found myself glancing around the room and noticed an adjacent room filled with objects. Metal things hanging from the wall. I could barely bring them into focus from my recliner.

Then abruptly out of the silence between us, Tommy lifted his head from his veil of marijuana smoke. "Hey, do you want to see some cool stuff?"

Chapter Sixteen

Summer of Death

I LOOKED AT TOMMY warily. "What kind of stuff?"

"You know. Stuff." He hauled his inebriated body out of the couch's embrace. "You know my parents are cops, right?"

I was too stoned to be sure, but I said, "I think so."

"They got a second job, too," he said. "They're both divers for Hillsborough County Underwater Rescue."

"What the hell is that?"

"They're the ones who go down to get the dead bodies when someone drowns or gets dumped in the river."

"Oh, *hell* no." This sounded gruesome to me. I hadn't forgotten my close encounter with a dead body on Skipper Road. Did undiscovered corpses still lie at the bottom of the Cone Brothers pits?

"Do you want to see?"

"See what? You're not keeping any dead bodies around, are you?"

"Do you want to see or not?"

"I'm not sure what you're talking about but yeah, I guess, sure." I was too stoned to refuse.

Gesturing me to follow him, he got up and walked into the nearby family room, about twenty feet away from where we'd been lounging on a couch. The walls were lined with shelves full of books and strange knick-knacks. I was too glassy-eyed to register everything all at once. Some of the books were photo albums, others were of the occult. He took a photo album down and flipped it open.

Even through the fog of THC, the photos would be etched into my memory forever. Pictures so vivid that once seen they could never be unseen.

"What the hell are you showing me?" I said, recoiling, my throat suddenly tight.

"My mom and step-dad take pictures of all the bodies they find. It's evidence, and they always keep a copy of the photos for themselves."

Why the hell would anyone keep pictures of dead bodies?

He stared at the celluloid horrors with fascination.

I had never seen death before, only the suggestion and glimpse of it at the Cone Brothers pits. Not even my own brush with death had brought home to me what it *looked like*. The photos laid bare before me depicted human bodies in every imaginable state of decomposition. Bloated, putrescent, flesh falling away from bones or eaten away by scavengers or fish, burst entrails writhing with maggots, bodies where the flesh had turned into rainbows of deep bruise and rigor mortis, white-filmed eyes half-open and staring at nothing, fingers nibbled to the bone. And the color, an awful shade of purple that I would never forget.

Tommy was telling me about what happens to a corpse in the water, but I wasn't listening.

"Oh, my God, what the hell are you showing me?" I yelled. My skin itself felt cinched tight around me. Acidic spit filled my mouth like I was going to throw up. I rubbed the skin of my forearms to hold back the crawling sensation.

"Settle down, man, they're just pictures." He kept flipping through page after page of human decay.

Some of the bodies had clearly been the victims of foul play, not drowning victims. Stab wounds. Gunshot wounds. Innocuous little entry wounds and great, gaping exit wounds.

"We got all kinds of cool stuff," he said.

Bit by bit, the imagery in the room around me made it through the fog around my consciousness and stuck in my mind like a spear. I had just stepped into a horror movie. I had just walked into a space of pure evil. It dashed over me like ice-water, freezing me to the spot.

There was a wooden altar set with black candles. On the altar were a ceremonial dagger and chalice that looked made of pewter, carved with demonic imagery. On the walls were mounted several kinds of swords, bizarre prints with images of Hell, goat-headed demons, Satan himself.

"Check it out," he said, grabbing the dagger and handing it to me. "Pretty cool, huh."

The dagger looked sharp and well-polished, the blade shaped like a fang or a talon, with satanic imagery on the grip.

Barely able to breathe, I shook my head. I had just stepped into Satan's living room. Worse, it had been here all along, and I hadn't seen it. Nobody had seen it.

He shrugged and put the dagger back.

"Tommy!" I said. "What the hell is this room we're in? What is this?"

"Well, our family is a little different than most. While most people believe in God and Jesus, we are believers in witchcraft and the occult. My mom and dad worship the Devil. My mom thinks she's a witch," he said defensively.

My heart was pounding out of my chest. I had never heard of such a thing in my life. Yes, the notion of Heaven and Hell was always taught to me, but knowing that Tommy was involved in this was too much. It felt like the Dark Knight in the flesh had just walked into the room. This was *The Exorcist* and *The Omen* all rolled into a sick ball made real before my eyes. The Catholic Church had taught me about the power of the Devil, about evil. And suddenly I was in the midst of pure evil.

I don't know why I didn't run screaming out of there. Maybe because I was so stoned, or in shock, or both, it felt more like a nightmare, like my feet were mired in thick tar.

Eventually, even in his own inebriated state, Tommy must have sensed that I was not responding well to the "cool stuff" he wanted to show me, so he shut the photo albums and put the dagger away.

We walked back in the TV room as if nothing had happened, just another everyday occurrence in the life of my friend. He found nothing abnormal or unusual about the experience and seemed happy to share it all with me. A small, wild, frenzied part of my brain was screaming at me to get out of there, but there was a strange inertia that I can't explain. Was I so afraid of offending Tommy that I would put my own life at risk? As I lay there in the recliner, eyes wide open and staring at the ceiling, constantly aware of Tommy in the room, aware of his every movement, my senses were supercharged. Was he going to sneak up on me in the middle of the night and cut my throat with that dagger? Were his parents going to burst in, tie me up, and sacrifice me to their dark master?

Was I going to go to Hell now just because I was in this unholy place? Would Satan's influence take hold of me and turn me into one of them?

Endless hours of endless spirals of endless, terrified thoughts.

I didn't sleep a wink the whole night, and I scrambled out of there at the crack of dawn, probably still high, racing my motorcycle back home.

My mom could tell something was bothering me when I came home that morning. She asked me what was wrong.

I told her, "I can't be friends with Tommy anymore."

Such a decisive statement alarmed her immediately. "What happened? Are you all right?"

"Nothing bad happened to me, but... I think...I think they're not really good people."

"What do you mean?"

Then it came out of me in an explosion. "They're Satan worshipers, Mom!"

She stared at me for a long moment, trying to tell if I was joking, but from my physical state it must have been obvious that I wasn't. "What happened?"

Then I told her about the macabre photo albums, the satanic paraphernalia, how Tommy seemed on board with all this, like he was part of it. She crossed herself and listened with an unsteady hand over her mouth. When I was finished, I said, "It was the most evil thing I have ever seen."

"Well, you just stay away from him now," she said. "Stay away from the girls, too. Who knows what goes on in that household?"

For weeks after that, nightmares of bloated corpses and satanic imagery kept me awake.

A few days later, Tommy came over to invite me to go riding motorcycles. I told him I was busy. He tried again a few days later. I told him I was not feeling well. I found excuses to be elsewhere or busy when Tommy wanted to hang out with me. It was all I could do to look at him whenever we were on the school bus together. Here were the three kids of that family, Tommy and his two sisters, and they looked perfectly normal on the surface. What evils had they enacted? What evils had they been subjected to?

Weeks turned into months of distancing myself from Tommy. On the school bus, I sat far away from them. The two girls were most hurt by this, because they didn't understand what had happened or what I had seen. Tommy seemed unsurprised and never mentioned it again.

~

My discovery at Tommy's home was not an isolated incident. It seemed as if all the dark underbelly of the world had gravitated to the Tampa area in the mid-1970s—the Mafia, narcotics trafficking, the profusion of strip clubs, assassinations, and now Satanism and witchcraft. By witchcraft, I do not mean the pagan religion known as Wicca; I mean the dark, dangerous, meetings-with-Lucifer-in-the-woods, sign-of-the-Beast, Aleister Crowley-and-black-magic kind of witchcraft. In the '70s, stories of satanic cults swept the nation, along with stories of UFOs, Bigfoot, and cattle mutilations. Most of the cult stories were hoaxes or the product of fevered, over-active minds. But in Tampa, there was a real-life, self-proclaimed warlock leading Dark Masses.

Lewis Van Dercar, sometimes called the Wizard of Zephyrhills, claimed to be a Prince of the Royal Order of Warlocks and Witches. He was an unusual man living in an eccentric mansion in Zephyrhills, a community about fifteen miles north of Tampa, five to seven miles from where I lived. Van Dercar became infamous around this time for his bizarre lifestyle, for his menagerie of exotic animals, including a Rhesus monkey, for the abundance of freakish, apocalyptic statuary that populated his acreage, and for his immense parties that were said to include demonic rites, orgies, and ritual sacrifice. The *South Florida Sun-Sentinel* profiled him in a newspaper article in December 1987, in which he claimed to possess a mysterious, plant-derived substance called "aquafleur" that granted him extended long life. His house was often the subject of juvenile dares, with kids sneaking onto the property. Van Dercar was Florida's most famous warlock. Whether or not he was a real warlock or an eccentric charlatan, he played up his persona with practiced showmanship, not unlike the evil flip-side of a televangelist. He became a thing of legend. Wild stories about him circulated through schools and grapevines, getting wilder with every telling.

Van Dercar's warlock persona and transgressive practices were part of a wave of societal rebellion that dovetailed with the anti-establishment mood of young people of the time. They were looking for ways to stick their thumbs in the eye of staid, starched-collar conservatism, the people who'd gotten tens of thousands of American boys killed in Vietnam, the people who'd gotten Nixon elected and still supported him in the face of concrete evidence that he was, in fact, a liar and a crook. Kids were flocking to musicians and bands like Ozzy Osbourne, KISS, Black Sabbath, and AC/DC, as rebellion for its own sake. These bands were singing about Hell and damnation, biting the heads off bats and chickens, and putting out albums that were wildly transgressive for the time. By today's standards, they seem tame and even a little quaint, but in the mid-1970s, the Religious Defenders of Impressionable Youth were up in arms over album covers dripping with blood, sex, and demonic imagery. Rock 'n' roll was The Devil's Music, they said. This was also during the ridiculous backmasking scare, where people were spinning their Beatles albums backwards, claiming to hear messages from Satan, and then burning records.

How Tommy and his family fit into Van Dercar's sphere of legend and rumor, I never knew, but several months after my sleepover at Tommy's house, I was told things that indicated the Dolan family was part of a larger cult. Even though I had embraced my rebellious teenager identity and was doing everything I could think of to flout authority, I could not venture into the realm of demonic evil even for fun. My Catholic upbringing was too ingrained, my fear of the Devil far too real.

One night when I was 15 years old, friends of mine got word that the Wizard of Zephyrhills was having one of his dark parties. Young people from all over the area flocked to these parties for the drugs, booze, and free-for-all atmosphere. By this time, some of my friends were old enough to drive, so five of us piled into a car and headed for Zephyrhills. The things I had seen in Tommy's house were still fresh in my mind. My friends were treating this witchcraft stuff as a silly joke, but to me, it meant death and damnation. I sat in the car quietly the whole way there, putting up as brave a front as I could. My guts were vibrating as we pulled up outside this strange house with its concrete wall concealing the property and its Gothic, wrought-iron front gate. There were cars parked everywhere, and I could hear the strange, grinding music in the distance, like something from a horror movie.

As we got out and approached the gate, I glimpsed the gargoyles and other statues inside, and my unsettled stomach kicked into full queasiness. I stopped in my tracks. "Uh, I don't think I can go in."

My friends looked back at me like I was a fool. "Oh, come on, man. Don't be a pussy."

This was a moment where curiosity and peer pressure won out over deep-seated terror.

I took a deep breath and followed them. Immediately inside the wall was a collection of the wildest statuary I have ever seen, dozens and dozens of gargoyles, busts, demons, mythical creatures, phalluses, some of them half-hidden in bushes and trees.

His house was as bizarre as his statues, a huge dome emerging from palms, pine, and cypress trees like a giant mushroom, with the statue of some demonic winged creature on the roof.

The music got louder and louder as we approached the house. There were hundreds of people around, moving among the statuary, in and out of the house, people of wide age range, from teenagers to gray-haired adults, many of them wearing dark, full-length robes and hoods. White face make-up and black eyeliner gave them a ghostly pallor. My insides were doing somersaults.

The inside of the house was like a set from an old horror movie, dim and candle-lit. A suit of armor stood in one corner. A massive chandelier hung from the dome above, antique rifles and swords on the walls, more of that strange statuary, a huge stone staircase to the second floor. The place was crammed with people, and the smells of alcohol and weed were thick in the air.

I didn't see any ritual sacrifice or orgies, but the demonic imagery was everywhere. People were drinking while others were chanting and most of them were getting high. If there were harder drugs around, I didn't see those. I mostly kept to myself that night, afraid to talk to anyone, and I had never been so relieved as when my friends decided to go.

My family had no idea when we moved into Lutz that we were moving into a place where a cesspit of real evil lurked beneath the surface of a veritable paradise. We went from the murdered corpses of the Cone Brothers pits, from the strangeness of carnie folk, to Satanists and witchcraft in Lutz. The irony of it struck deep.

~

By the spring of 1976, the horrors of Tommy's house had faded. I was hanging out with other kids and trying to forget what I had seen, what I was coming to believe about the people around me—that "normal" society was a paper-thin veneer over a bottomless swamp.

But then one day Tommy showed up at our front door asking if he could talk to me.

I came to the door and saw immediately that he was distraught, a loose collection of pieces held tenuously together by sheer force of will.

Choking back tears, he said, "My step-dad is dead."

I stared at him for a long moment.

"Blew his brains out in the bedroom," he continued. "Mom found him on their waterbed, bullet in his head and blood everywhere. They just took his body away."

"Oh, my God!" said Antoinette, who happened to be behind

me, curious about what Tommy was doing around after so long. She hurried off to tell the rest of my family.

"It...it...," he stammered, "it wasn't like the pictures. It stunk."

"Oh, God, man," I said, "I'm so sorry." The storm of conflicting emotions all but destroyed my capacity for speech. The first thing that came to my mind was the satanic family room, the evil in that house.

He sniffed once and rubbed his bloodshot eyes. "Just wanted to tell you." He turned to go back to his motorcycle in the driveway.

In that moment, my heart went out to him. He was just a kid who'd witnessed a terrible tragedy, a former friend who'd been abused in ways I couldn't even imagine, by a man who'd just killed himself in the family's home. What could Tommy have been feeling right then? Just the need for a friend?

"Hey," I said, "when is the funeral?"

He sniffed again. "I can let you know. They took Mom to the hospital, too."

"What for? Is she okay?"

He shook his head. "She's not hurt. But it's not good."

"What about your sisters?"

"They're okay. I've got to go clean up the blood and stuff."

Not knowing what else I could possibly say, I blurted, "Want to go boating sometime? Maybe we can ride cycles?"

He paused and half-glanced at me. "Maybe," he said. "Sure." The slump of his shoulders made him look like he was carrying elephants on his back.

Tommy's mother was hospitalized for a nervous breakdown. He and his sisters were on their own for several weeks. My sympathy for the family's tragic plight led me to start hanging out with him again. Whenever he invited me into their house, I found reasons not to go inside, but we went back to getting high and riding motorcycles. But even in the midst of these distractions, his heart was not in it. He was sullen and taciturn. Even as the school year ended and his mother returned from the mental hospital, he was not himself. Depression sank deep into him and took root.

But the tragedies of Tommy's family were not the only horrors of that summer.

~

On another day in the spring of 1976, my mom was baking something, and she ran out of flour or sugar. She sent me next door to Goldie's house to borrow some. I knocked on Goldie's door, but I didn't get an answer. So I headed over to Uncle Bill's trailer to see if he was home.

When I knocked on Bill's door, it swung open a crack, not having been properly latched.

I pushed it open a little more and called inside, "Uncle Bill?"

No answer, but I thought I heard some breathing. The air smelled of booze, like it always did around him. I peeked further inside.

A pair of feet were hanging off the side of the couch—but they were wearing women's high heels. The weirdness of this drew me inside. There lay Uncle Bill on the couch, stone drunk and passed out, wearing pantyhose and a floral print dress, a feather boa, and high heels.

"Jesus, what is this?" I exclaimed.

Bill did not move.

I stared at him for a long time, this skinny, withered man, lying there with his mouth open, red with lipstick, cheeks rouged.

Then I left, shaking my head, confused. I didn't know what cross-dressing was. I didn't know what a transvestite was. I had never even heard of such a thing. All I knew was that I couldn't tell anybody. My dad loved Uncle Bill. How could I tell him what I had seen?

I hurried back home and told my mom there was nobody home at Goldie's or Uncle Bill's house.

I told only my sisters what I'd seen. They agreed with me that this was really strange, and the three of us began to distance ourselves whenever we encountered him. No one noticed the difference in our treatment of him, because everyone took Uncle Bill with a grain of salt anyway. I never told anyone else what I had seen. I couldn't make sense of it.

In July, on a Saturday when my parents made us do chores around the house—all the vacuuming, dusting, cleaning, mowing the yard, and such—my sisters and I were finishing up our work. When the work was done, the extended Scarpo family would come for a visit, and we would get to swim and play all day long by the lake. The reins were let loose.

Several of us kids were gathering to commence the festivities, including Debbie and her best friend Nina, and one of Goldie's granddaughters, Patty, who walked with a cane because she'd had polio when she was very young.

I happened to spot something at the edge of the water. Moving closer, I could see it was a big clump of feathers gathering against the sand. An eerie feeling washed over me, a sense of uncanniness, cold fingers crawling up my spine. I stepped closer for a better look and realized the feathers were the same color as Goldie's chickens. Maybe an alligator had gotten one of them, or maybe Goldie was making chicken and dumplings, and these feathers were freshly plucked. But the unease wouldn't go away.

"Maybe we shouldn't go swimming today," I muttered, but no one heard me, or if they did, they didn't respond.

After all, the lake was infested with alligators and we played the odds with them weekly, always winning.

Looking out over the lake, I spotted our float, a small, inner tube-sized mini-raft, way out in the middle, past Goldie's house. I recognized it instantly, because my dad had gotten it from one of his liquor distributors.

"Shit," I said. "I love that float. Why is it over there?"

Patty said, "Uncle Bill took it with him."

"Uncle Bill took it to do what?"

"He bet me that he could swim across the lake," she said.

"Yeah, but our raft is over there," I said. The wind had taken it farther away. "I don't see Uncle Bill anywhere." Then I sighed and said, "Let's go get it."

I got in the johnboat, the same one we used to hunt gators. Debbie and Nina jumped in with me, and I paddled out to retrieve the float. As I crossed the lake, a haunted feeling came over me, forcing my hands to push the oar ever more slowly, as if holding myself back from reaching my destination.

The farther we went, though, the closer we got to the float, the more the sense of unease increased. Something wasn't right. Terribly, terribly not right.

As we paddled up beside the float, I spotted something in the water beside it. A body, floating face-down, arms stretched out.

Was this a prank? But then Debbie and Nina screamed, and they kept screaming. The air left my lungs. I couldn't breathe.

The T-shirt was one of Uncle Bill's.

The girls' screaming brought a crowd of people out of Goldie's house to the shore. I could see them all in the distance. Her house was always full of family on weekends.

All I could do was stare at him. Should I try to pull him into the boat? He was a grown man, heavier than me. Would that tip the little boat and dump us all in the water, flipping my sister and her best friend onto a corpse? I looked around for gators; I didn't see any, but you could never be sure. Was he dead? This part of the lake was near an area where alligators nested on the shore, and nesting alligators were not to be trifled with. Had a gator gotten him? Were his legs gone? Was the alligator still hovering around, possibly under his body waiting for dessert?

People were coming out of my house now, too, a hundred yards away, and from other houses around the lake. My mom was down by the water with her walker.

I couldn't touch the body. I didn't dare to.

The roar of a power boat engine rose from across the lake and sped in our direction. It was one of the other families that lived on the lake, the former sheriff of Hillsborough County, Mickey Newberger. Mickey and his two sons came racing toward us and slid up next to the body. They hooked Bill's arms and dragged him to the shoreline just a few yards away, and that's when I saw his face.

It was like one of Tommy's photos come to life, the most grotesque thing I've ever seen. Mouth gaping, eyes open and glazed, the colors like a yellow and purple bruise.

My heart was pounding out of my chest. The girls were sobbing, half-panicked.

"He's dead!" Debbie cried. "He's dead!"

Then from across the water, I heard cries of alarm. Goldie was running toward my house. My mom was on the dock yelling out to us. People were gathering around her, my cousins and Goldie's grandchildren.

Mickey and his sons tried to administer CPR over and over. I sat there in the boat watching every jolt to his body, hoping and praying that Bill would move or flinch, that the breath of life could fill his lungs, but all I saw was gallons of water pouring out of his mouth. He was gone. His lifeless body lay on the muddy lake shore, limp and masked in a grotesque shade of purple.

Not knowing what else I could do, I paddled back to our dock. My arms felt like chunks of wood, and my stomach was writhing like a nest of baby water moccasins. On the dock, my mother appeared beside herself with shock and fear, people were clinging to her to comfort her, including Goldie. She looked like she was on the verge of passing out. Others were yelling questions out at us.

As we neared the dock, relief spread on everyone's faces.

"Oh, thank God you're okay!" my mom yelled as we pulled up to the dock. She hobbled closer, and tears of relief poured down her face as she grabbed us and held on tight.

But then the looks of confusion spread around the crowd. They had all thought one of us had drowned or fallen victim to an alligator. I could barely look at Goldie.

Everyone was repeating, "What happened? What's going on?"

I walked up to Goldie with tears pouring down my face. I could barely get the words out. "It's Uncle Bill. He's dead."

I had never seen a human being fall apart like I saw Goldie that day. It was like all the life left her and she collapsed against my mother like a balloon with air let out. The mix of emotions that crossed her face was crushing shock and grief, and maybe a wisp of knowledge that this day had finally come. Among the crowd were several of Goldie's family, and the shock of my revelation stole their breath, too. Patty was in shock, as she was the one that took Uncle Bill's bet that he could swim across the lake.

About six months later, Goldie moved away. She couldn't bear to live on the same property where she had lost so much, first a husband, then a son. My family stayed in contact with Goldie for a few years after that. Some of Goldie's family, her grandchildren who had become my friends, still visited occasionally. My parents became godparents to one of Goldie's grandchildren. But, like so many things, like the Bejanos, we faded away from each other.

Goldie's departure opened the door for a new set of neighbors to come in and change my life yet again.

~

In the fall of 1976, about eight months after Tommy's stepfather committed suicide, I was visiting my Aunt Rose on the farm in Land O' Lakes, another lake community north of Lutz. Tommy rode his motorcycle over to our house to ask me if I wanted to go to a movie with him. His mother was out of the mental hospital, but she was never the same. His sisters Kathy and Rebecca had mostly withdrawn inside themselves, seldom speaking to anyone on the bus rides to school. I couldn't bring myself to ask them about all the satanic paraphernalia in their house. Were they still Satanists?

When my mom told Tommy I wasn't home, he left and sped back home in the darkness.

Twenty yards from his driveway, a neighbor's dog darted out in front of him. He slammed on the brakes but hit the dog and went flying over the handlebars. The landing broke his neck, and he died instantly.

When I heard the news, I felt the crawling presence of real evil at work in the world. It could have been stupid happenstance, but the signs seemed to be everywhere. Was the Devil taking his due? Or was it just the ignominious, senseless death of a troubled teenage boy from a troubled family?

At Tommy's funeral, I couldn't help thinking of him as my friend, however strange that sounded after what he had showed me. Could I have done anything differently that would have helped him? I was too young to help him or to help his sisters, but I may have missed an opportunity to make a difference. The entire family was a strange, traumatized wreck, devoured by evil. But on the surface, they had been the perfect family. Both parents were cops. They lived in a nice house on a beautiful lake. But underneath lay profound disquiet and darkness. My Catholic upbringing had inculcated in me understanding of the struggle between good and evil. I told myself that Tommy's family had chosen evil, and they had paid the ultimate price.

How was I supposed to pretend anything was normal after this? How was I supposed to be a normal teenager with a life full of witches and warlocks, corpses, alligators, Mafia thugs, racial violence, and cross-dressing alcoholics? In a world of abuse, when bad things happen all around us, we look for signs and patterns, we use intuition to guide us, and I saw evil everywhere I looked. I wanted *out* of it. I wanted so badly to be normal.

CHAPTER SEVENTEEN

MAFIA RESOLUTION

AS LONG AS THE Italian Mafia has existed, its crime families have dominated the local communities where they took root. Tampa was no exception. The Trafficante crime family with all its leaders, soldiers, and small-time thugs, from Santo Trafficante Sr. to Santo Jr. and on down to the present day, squeezed Tampa Bay in its grip for over a half a century, leaving a swath of corpses, shattered lives, and corruption behind them. All that power and influence reached its pinnacle in the early 1970s, but with the assassination of Richard Cloud it began to fracture, and the FBI was jamming every chisel they could into the cracks.

This fracturing couldn't have come at a better time for my father and my family. Since 1967 we had endured the wrath of the Trafficante organization and lived our lives in fear. The interesting thing about criminal organizations, they rise slowly and accrue power through fear and intimidation, slowly infiltrating businesses, law enforcement, and government. Inevitably, they become so powerful that they can no longer operate under the radar of law enforcement and public tolerance. At that point, law enforcement must act, as it did with Al Capone's Chicago Syndicate, as it did in Tampa with the Trafficante family. The way law enforcement brings down widespread criminal organizations is to chew away at the fringes of the organization, starting with thugs and small fish, taking bigger and bigger bites, until they get their teeth into a major figure, like Al Capone or John Gotti. Little by little, the organization is crippled and splintered to the point it can no longer function at its previous strength and capacity. The slow slippage becomes an unstoppable avalanche as more indictments roll in, prompting plea bargains in exchange for testimony against bigger and bigger fish, a downward spiral. In the case of the Trafficante family, Cloud's assassination opened up the Number Two man, Frank Diecidue, to indictment and ultimately conviction and prison.

Frank Diecidue (a.k.a. "The Underboss" as the FBI had come to call him), along with several others, was indicted for conspiracy to murder Richard Cloud, and the trial took place over six weeks in October and November of 1976, a year after Cloud's assassination, during which time Diecidue was free on bond. There was no telling how the trial was going to go. On one hand, the FDLE and the FBI had built iron-clad cases against these mob figures, exposing just how corrupt the Tampa halls of power were. On the other hand, working against them at every turn were people like Chief of Police Charles Otero, who had replaced the man who hired Cloud to clean up the city and who publicly stated, over and over again, that there was no organized crime in Tampa. One of Otero's close friends was Tampa PD's criminal intelligence section chief, Jack De La Lana, who hid one of the Cloud conspirators, Victor Acosta, and transported him out of the city when the indictments came down. It was with the collusion of people like Otero and De La Lana that the Mafia had thrived for decades. There was so much at stake, it didn't matter how iron-clad the prosecutors' case was; the outcome could still be a coin flip.

By late 1976, my dad had made Art's Lounge into the biggest bar in the East Tampa-Brandon area, the go-to establishment for check-cashing and Sunday package liquor sales. Art's Lounge had become a multi-million-dollar operation almost overnight.

The clientele who frequented Art's Lounge were hardworking people, union people mostly, white Southerners. Union members came from out of town for their union jobs. They needed hotels. They drank heavily. But more than anything, a traveling union man needed a place to cash a check for his entertainment and expenses. There were, of course, no ATMs in those days. So my father opened a check-cashing service out of Art's Lounge. His fee for cashing a check was 1 percent of the amount, plus a bottle of liquor or a case of beer. It was a service that his customers jumped at. As word of this spread, he became his own little bank, cashing millions of dollars' worth of checks, a gush of revolving money. One percent was a modest cut—credit cards nowadays charge 3 percent or more—but the extra bottle of booze made sure the profits flowed.

As I've mentioned, cops were union members, too, and they appreciated the fact that my dad didn't allow narcotics anywhere near his place. Miles away in Tampa, the lounges were the centers of Mafia narcotics trafficking. Out on the eastern perimeter of Hillsborough County, my dad indulged people's vices, but no narcotics. Art's Lounge was far away from Tampa proper, but Hillsborough County politicians and officials were unbelievably corrupt. Thanks to decades of mob influence, everyone was on the take, and everyone was *used to* things being that way. That, however, was coming to an end amid the aftershocks of Cloud's investigations and murder.

Nevertheless, my father still worried for his family's safety. He'd built a posse of his own, but one could never have too much muscle. So, he ingratiated himself to a new group of potential allies—the Hillsborough County Sheriff's Department, under the leadership of Sheriff Malcolm Beard. Beard was a larger-than-life figure, practically a force of nature in that good ole boy way unique to the South, but he was not the hard-charging bull of raw honesty that Cloud was. When my dad donated a huge quantity of booze to the police union Christmas party, Sheriff Beard was suitably grateful. More of such donations followed, further cementing the mutual back-scratching arrangement.

Before long, my father began to sell liquor on Sunday, under the watchful eye of the Hillsborough County Sheriff's Department. Customers could drive around the back of Art's Lounge, where the stockroom and package store were—out of public view—and pull up under an old, filling-station-style roof complete with the *ding-ding* drive-thru hose, and pay triple the normal cost for their bottle of Jack Daniels.

By this time, I was working at the bar on Sunday mornings, cleaning up and doing odd jobs like raking up pine needles from the parking lot, but I was unaware of his machinations. I saw this endless succession of cars driving around the back, heard the distinctive *ding-ding* over and over, knew that Sunday liquor sales were illegal, and saw the stacks of cash in his office.

It was a random Sunday like many others when my father asked me to climb on top of the roof and sweep the leaves from the gutters. It was a spectacular view. I could see the traffic in all directions, as well as the parade of vehicles that wrapped around the building and spilled out onto the main road. I chuckled to myself, but then I spotted two squad cars across the street, not more than forty yards away. In the grocery-store parking lot next door were two more police cars. On the other side, at Burger Box, were two more squad cars.

There was a raid coming!

I ran to the roof's edge and yelled and whistled down to my father right below, as quietly as I could. "Dad. Dad!"

He finally stepped away from the head car in the line and poked his head out. "Jesus, Tony, what is it?"

"Police!" I hissed, pointing in all directions.

"And?"

"There's six of them out there right now! The *liquor!*"

"Stop."

"But, Dad—!"

"You need to stop."

"You're not listening to me! They're going to bust you!"

"Shut up!"

"Dad!"

"Tony! I said, zip it. You think I don't know they're out there? They're *watching out* for me."

It took a moment for this to sink in. "You mean like, guards."

"That's what I mean."

"Oh."

He had procured his own personal security force—equipped with badges. He supplied the police union hall with booze; they supplied him protection from the mob.

I couldn't help laughing at myself, then at the hypocrisy. Of course, that's what the police were doing, protecting us while we sold liquor on Sunday in blatant violation of state liquor laws.

But, given the corruption so prevalent in the local law enforcement agencies—it was, after all, a kind of corruption that brought them onto our side—he wasn't sure if even that was enough. Even with the Sheriff's Department protecting us, the fear persisted. Something had to be done.

So word was sent to Frank Diecidue that my father wanted to meet. The relentless pressure of gangland attacks and intimidation against his business and his family had reached a boiling point, and he had too much to lose.

In October, during Diecidue's trial while he was free on bond, my father met him in a nondescript coffee shop on Nebraska Avenue. My dad was accompanied by two of his best men, as was Diecidue. My dad had called the meeting because he believed Diecidue to be a man who held to the Old-World code of honor. With the heat of a murder trial and the blizzard of racketeering charges eating away at the Trafficante organization, this might be the opportunity my dad needed to end the hostilities.

Once they both arrived at the coffee shop, the two men made their way to a back corner table. The henchmen took their strategic positions around the coffee shop and outside.

There they were, two men. One a survivor, a man who had beaten the odds, a man that had accumulated wealth and power with the help of his own loyal posse; the other, an almost broken man, forever trapped in his role as the Number Two man behind Santo Trafficante Jr., on trial for several counts of conspiracy to commit murder.

Frank Diecidue had the full head of dark, slicked-back hair

typical of Italian men, wearing an expensive tailored suit and polished Italian shoes, prominent gold rings, gold watch, gold chains. But Diecidue looked tired to the core, like he hadn't slept in weeks. He stood to go to prison for the rest of his life, maybe even die in Florida's electric chair. On the previous few occasions when my dad had met him, he seemed hale and confident, a man with the world at his feet. But now, ten tons of bricks had fallen on his head.

My dad did not know whether Diecidue was involved in the threats and attacks against us. Was it all a long-standing vendetta from the days when Henry Trafficante had been Tampa's gambling czar, or had Santo Jr. always hated my dad for embracing the people of cracker country and betraying his Italian heritage? Was it Diecidue who ordered the attacks against my dad? He didn't think so, but he couldn't be certain. His instincts told him that Diecidue was not behind the attacks, but he couldn't count on that. Cut the head off a snake and it could still bite you. But if he played his cards right, he could ensure that he would be left alone—and most importantly, that his family would be safe.

As the two men sat there in silence for a long time in Old World Italian fashion, each took the measure of the other.

Finally, my dad said, "I'm grateful for you sitting down with me, Frank, really grateful for listening to what I have to say."

Diecidue nodded vaguely, then said, "Where you come from, Art?"

"Pennsylvania. But my dad was from Bari. Came to America with nothing."

"That's the Old Country, all right," Diecidue said. Bari's history went back more than three thousand years. "My *padre* came from Cianciana, south of Palermo." A true Sicilian. "You know, I gotta hand it to you, Art. You done pretty well for yourself, all on your own. Everybody knows about you."

My dad straightened a little at that. "Thanks, Frank." He was having difficulty reconciling the amiable man before him with the one who had ordered the murders of not only Richard Cloud, but also two of his business competitors. But he did not dare bring that up. "It wasn't no picnic, Frank, but we're here."

Rats can only thrive in the shadows. Shine a bright light on them, they scatter. Day by day, month by month, Cloud's investigation had peeled back the mob's concealment of shadow and mystery, exposing them to the light, even though many of Tampa's top officials, most prominently Police Chief Otero and Sheriff Malcolm Beard, refused to acknowledge it in public. With Cloud's death, the media had taken up the torch. Journalists had started digging.

"Well, Art," Frank said, "none of this is no picnic, right? We gotta do what we gotta do."

My dad nodded.

"So why?" Diecidue said. "Why'd we have to go through all this to get here? All you had to do was say 'yes' to Henry and Fano."

"When I was a kid, maybe ten years old," Art said, realizing this was the time for candor, the time to put all his chips on the table, "there was a guy back in Pennsylvania, an Italian gangster, tried to force my father into doing a job for him. My father said no. They tried to intimidate him. They came and killed all of our chickens, over a hundred of them, just to scare us, all because he said no to a bully. You never say 'yes' to a bully, he drove that into our heads."

Diecidue nodded, twisting one of his gold and diamond rings. "How's the family?" Diecidue said. With a certain inflection, those words could be a deadly threat, but today they seemed to be spoken with genuine concern. "Your wife, she's sick, right? What's it called, multiple sclars or something?"

My dad stared at him. "It's called Multiple Sclerosis. You know about that?"

"Everybody knows she's sick, Art." He said it so nonchalantly. "What!"

"I read up on it a little. That's gotta be a terrible thing, watching your wife go through that, does bad things to the whole family." He wiped an unexpected tear. "Family is everything." How many of his own family had he seen die? Mobsters who lived to a ripe old age were the exception, not the rule. One thing about Italian families is the deep devotion to one another, love, loyalty, and closeness, built and cemented by spaghetti dinners every Sunday, family birthdays, christenings, holidays. The mother is the center of life in Italian culture, the matriarch of a family, exemplified by the Virgin Mary and other female saints. It could be no less true for a mafioso; family blood was what bound their entire enterprise together. "Taking care of her has got be expensive and hard."

My dad nodded, still unable to fully process the idea that the Trafficante mob and God-knew-who-else knew about my mother's illness. "Enough tests to choke a cow. We don't have no insurance. And there ain't no cure. She can barely stand nowadays, legs don't work, gets around in a walker or a wheelchair. Arms won't work for much longer. She tries, but...some days there ain't much strength left for trying. It's changed her. It's changed *me*. She's gonna die by inches, like cancer that takes years to kill you."

"That's got to be hard on the kids, am I right? Watching their mama go through that."

"The girls, they try real hard, filling their mama's shoes, helping out around the house, but they're still just kids." A lump was forming in his throat. Could he really be having a conversation like this with a man on trial for murder?

"Little Tony, though," Diecidue said, "he's growing up to be a man."

"I'm working on that."

"Chip off the old block, that kid." Diecidue sighed. "Family's everything. Sometimes a guy gets a raw deal. Life's hard enough as it is. But you're still around."

"I'm still around," my dad said. Then he took a deep breath. "Frank, I'm asking you this one time. I asked for this meeting because I think you're a stand-up guy. Everybody in the bar business looks up to you. I'm asking you, hasn't my family been through enough? I mean, you got a lot on your plate these days. Hassling a small-timer like me, that ain't worth your time. You got bigger fish to fry. I'm not hardly doing any bookmaking anymore."

Diecidue leaned back in his chair. "You asking me to back down? Are you asking me to get people to lay off?"

"That's what I'm asking." Asking so directly had put a needle-sharp point on the question in a culture where little was ever spoken openly or directly. Euphemism, innuendo, body language, those were the ingrained ways of communication.

In the silence, my dad studied Diecidue's face, employing years of experience as a poker player with carefully honed instincts as a judge of people. A well of emotion was hidden behind the mobster's face. Were there traces of regret there? Remnants of the overweening pride that came with his position? Recognition that the Trafficantes were too overstretched to keep hounding one cantankerous bar owner? Despair over his impending fate? Diecidue sucked his teeth, toyed with one of his rings. Then he said, "Okay, Art. If there's one thing I've learned about you is that you're a tough son of a bitch. You can take one hell of a beating and never back down. Now, your old partner Bert, that's another story."

My dad recoiled in his seat at the mention of Bert's name. What did Frank mean by that? Did he order the hit on Bert? Within seconds of him showering my dad with accolades he was done. Just like that.

"Art, we put you through enough. You don't bother us, we don't bother you. You win. No more."

My dad couldn't believe what he had just heard.

Diecidue said, "The past is the past. Your operation ain't hurting ours. You're way out there in cracker country. The boss don't think you're really Italian anymore, hanging out with all those redneck cracker sons-a-bitches." He shrugged and sniffed. "I beg to differ."

To restrain the urge to bounce in his chair, my dad stood abruptly, gaining the attention of the nearby henchmen. "Thanks, Frank. I won't forget it." He extended his hand. "You're a good man."

Diecidue stood up and shook it.

～

In November 1976, Frank Diecidue was convicted of firearms possession, racketeering, and three counts of conspiracy to commit murder, and sentenced to forty years in prison. Much of the Trafficante organization was in prison or under investigation or indictment. Santo Trafficante Jr. had largely moved his operations to Miami. Anthony Antone, the man who'd hired Haskew and Gilford to kill Richard Cloud, was executed in 1984. Gilford died in jail, the day before he was to be sentenced. Haskew was given a thirty-five-year sentence. In 1979, a federal appeals court over-turned Diecidue's conviction on a technicality, and he was released.

After Diecidue was released from prison, he resumed his role as the Number Two man in the Trafficante mob. A sort of strange bond, maybe even friendship, formed between him and my dad, perhaps based on that meeting in 1976. Diecidue would occasion-ally visit Art's Lounge and sit at the bar among the crackers and rednecks. He would have a drink, be kind, and shoot the shit like everyone else. Maybe Frank Diecidue had come to believe he had gotten a second chance.

From that meeting forward, my father felt like the victor. He had beaten the Trafficantes. But he never told us about what had happened; he told me none of this until decades later. There was no specific moment where my father came to us and said, "It's over." All we knew was that he smiled more, laughed more. A great weight had been lifted from his face. It happened so slowly, I didn't even notice it until months had passed and I realized that some-thing had changed. The sense of pervasive fear had evaporated. The bar business was still a dangerous game sometimes, but he didn't have to contend with the mob anymore.

In 1987, Santo Trafficante Jr. died. Vincent LoScalzo moved in and assumed control of an organization vastly diminished from its heyday. Frank Diecidue remained its underboss until he died in 1994. When LoScalzo took over, little was left of the Trafficante dominance; the Five Families of New York had moved in and es-tablished operations in several Florida cities, including Tampa and

Miami. Most of the Tampa old guard were in jail, retired, or else "retired" by the ambitious, ruthless young mobsters who had come up behind them.

Vincent LoScalzo was the son of a Trafficante family soldier, a Sicilian who had come to Tampa via the LoScalzo crime family of New Orleans. By the time I was an adult in the early 1990s, LoScalzo and I knew each other by reputation. He played up his role of mob boss in the media, but whether he still held any power in the Tampa underworld is debatable.

He owned a jazz club called Brothers Lounge, a sophisticated hot spot renowned for its live music. It was a club I frequented, the kind of place where one dressed to the nines to get in the door. He always gave me a polite nod. Its subdued lighting and live music made it one of my favorite places to bring dates or groups of friends from time to time. Vincent and I never spoke of the past, what had gone down between my father's organization and his. There was only casual respect and acknowledgment.

That is, until New Year's Eve 1991. I brought my girlfriend and two other couples to have dinner and dance the night away. The house was packed, and there was a large cover charge that included dinner.

Later in the evening, a commotion at the door grabbed my attention. Vincent stood at the door, barring entry to five drunk, unruly young men. They wanted in, and they wanted in very loudly. The altercation was on the verge of getting rough, and Vincent was alone at the door. All the men working for him seemed to be occupied elsewhere. The argument was a powder keg with a fuse lit. That's when he caught my eye, and gave me the look, the little nod, one Italian man to another. He needed help. I had acquired my dad's sense of impending violence, and I knew this was about to explode. I had my girlfriend with me. It was New Year's Eve. No one wanted a bunch of idiots to trash the place. My friends had no idea who Vincent was, or of the history between my family and his, but I gave both of them the Scarpo look that said, *Don't question, just follow me.*

We got up and joined Vincent at the door. The five guys tried to push their way in. We formed a wall of trash-talking muscle behind Vincent that got their attention instantly, a barrier made of posturing and confidence. The minute I took my stance and tightened my facial muscles with a fierce stare, it was clear that I meant business. There was no yelling; our voices were clear and direct.

"Cross this line and you guys will pay the price," I said matter-of-factly.

The beating would have been quick and unmerciful. As soon as they saw it in our faces, their enthusiasm for barging in waned. They gave us sullen looks and threw trash talk back at us, but only as they were walking away. They disappeared without further incident.

We stood there for a moment as the rest of the club's attention moved past the incident.

Vincent turned to me, "I know who you are. I know your family. Your father's a good man, a stand-up guy, always has been. Thank you for helping me."

"It was nothing, really," I said.

"Your money's no good here tonight," Vincent said. "All of you. New Year's Eve is on me."

I stared. My friends beamed with appreciation.

"You come to my club anytime," he said.

And then, as if nothing had happened at all, my friends and I returned to our seats, offering a brief explanation to our girl-friends, and proceeded to dance the night away.

In that moment, something shifted that I never expected. Here we were, just two Italians who were once adversaries, almost like veterans who had been on opposite sides of a war that was long over. We never talked about the incident after that. It was just a wink, a nod, a handshake.

Just like that, in less than a minute, twenty-four years of bad blood, fear, and violence dissipated. It was over in the blink of an eye.

CHAPTER EIGHTEEN

THE PERFECT NEIGHBORS

IT WAS ABOUT six months after Uncle Bill died that Goldie Vogel sold her house and moved away. She was never the same after what happened to him; she needed to be closer to her children and grandchildren and moved back to Kentucky. After the house sat vacant for a short while, a lovely couple bought the property and moved in. They were Lily and A.J. Howard, a sophisticated Southern couple in their sixties.

Where Goldie had been brashly "hillbilly," Lily Howard was the epitome of the cultured Southern belle, always meticulously groomed, with a perfect coif of blonde hair. She was a classy lady of a kind I'd never seen before. She was so different from the female customers at Art's Lounge, or anywhere among the blue-collar Florida crackers of Hillsborough County. She had that Savannah-style accent that suggested Old Southern Gentry.

A.J. Howard was a male version of that image. Tall, fit, white-haired, sophisticated, a true Southern gentleman in immaculately pressed suits, with more of a Charleston accent. He was exactly who you might expect to be sitting on a plantation veranda sipping a mint julep.

Both of the Howards were realtors, well off enough to employ a full-time housekeeper, which was unheard of in those parts. They hosted dinner parties with lavish quantities of Southern cooking.

Lily took an instant liking to my mother and came by to visit almost every day. This was a real blessing, because my mother's illness isolated her more and more. She couldn't drive anymore. Goldie had become her closest friend, but now Goldie was gone. Priscilla was far away out on Skipper Road. Lily often brought us food, or freshly baked cakes, and always with her brilliant, beautiful smile. She and my mom would sit and talk for hours, they would bake together, and I loved seeing that. We lived so far from anything that it was difficult for my mom to make new friends.

A.J. was the hardworking type, always on the go, making deals, moving and shaking. He and my father hit it off quickly. My father was happy to have a man living next door, someone to look out for our family when he wasn't around, which was mainly due to the long hours at the bar. Our Mafia travails were over, but Art's Lounge was doing a tremendous business. My dad was cashing great sums of payroll checks, so, situated as we were on a dead-end road far from anywhere, we were still the target of a few intruders and attempted thefts.

My father and A.J. often went fishing on the lake. On one of these excursions, he told A.J., "Listen, I work at night. I work till three or four in the morning. Please, please always keep an eye out for my children. Please keep an eye out for my wife. If anything happens, I've got to be able to know that I can call you."

A.J. said, "I keep a double-barreled shotgun by the front door."

This was an affluent area, an idyllic place, but we were living far out in the woods. A couple of times A.J. came running over with his double-barreled shotgun in the middle of the night to run off intruders. He was a man who valued his privacy and his property, and he wasn't shy about chasing off people who clearly weren't supposed to be there.

The Howards had two children, a son and daughter, both of whom were married with children of their own. They loved our little slice of paradise there by the lake, the fishing, the barbeques, as much as Goldie's family had. We got to know some of them, but they were different from Goldie's country hillbilly clan.

~

But even as one dark chapter closed with Uncle Bill's death and Goldie's departure, even as we were enjoying getting to know our new neighbors and slowly putting the mob threats behind us, another dark abyss opened under my feet, something for which I was utterly unprepared.

Tommy's death still lay like a specter over the community, over the kids who lived there, and especially me, but none of us talked about it. Whether or not I could admit it to myself, he had been my friend. His mother and sisters continued living in their house on a neighboring lake. Whether they continued their satanic practices after Tommy's stepfather died, and who else might have been in their group, I had no idea. But I still saw Tommy's sisters every day, as we rode the school bus together.

The succession of traumatic hits had left its mark on them. Their stepfather's suicide, their mother's temporary commitment to a mental institution, their brother's death. It was like a pall of evil remained over that family, and the two girls couldn't escape it. They became even more withdrawn, almost wasting away, their eyes haunted by things I couldn't imagine.

Until one day.

Kathy and I were walking to the school bus stop on a cool, dewy morning in the early part of 1977. I don't remember where Rebecca might have been, maybe taking a different bus to a different school.

But something was on Kathy's mind. Today, she was walking *with* me, like she wanted to say something, but couldn't bring herself to do it. With each step, the pressure inside her seemed to build until it sucked at her feet like tar.

I paused and looked back at her. "Are you okay?"

"Tony," she gulped, "I have to tell you something. I have to tell somebody."

Something in her tone sent a chill crawling over me, just like that night I was in their house.

"Something happened to me," she said, her voice choked like there was a hand around her throat.

For me, it was like seeing a rogue wave rising from the swells, growing inexorably higher, bearing down on me; knowing there was nowhere to run, knowing it was going to flatten me into the sand and then wash me out to sea.

She looked almost feverish, her gaze darting around, her fists squeezing the straps of her school bag. "They did things to me," she said. "My stepfather. My brother. My mom... She...she knew. I was the youngest. It was all part of the rituals. They tied me up. They cut me and did things with the blood. They... Tommy, he..."

I swallowed hard, knowing what must be coming, wishing not to hear it.

She took a deep breath as if to compose herself for just long enough to keep speaking. "They raped me. My stepfather. My brother. Both of them at different times. Over and over. They made me go on the pill so I wouldn't get pregnant. They put...things in me." Tears streamed down her face, and strings of spittle stretched between her teeth.

The image of Tommy raping his sister while she was tied up, while the rest of them, these mysterious figures from *my community,* in their satanic robes, were chanting and carrying on, made me sick to my stomach. It was so difficult to think about in those terms—it still is. But it wasn't sex. It was rape.

A vast hole opened underneath me, and I fell into helplessness so deep I didn't know what to do or say. My mouth filled with the taste of bile.

"They did it to Rebecca, too," she said, "but I...got it the most."

I stared at her for a long time, and she looked back at me utterly helpless, utterly desperate for someone to *hear* her. My mouth was moving, but I couldn't make words come out.

Her voice rose, pleading, then fell to a half-whisper. "You've been to our house. You've seen their...stuff. You believe me, don't you?"

It wasn't my proudest moment, and it became one of those failures that stuck with me to this day, the kind that ripples through the rest of one's life. What had spurred her to choose me to confide in? Some lingering shreds of loyalty to Tommy remained in me. Could he have been capable of incest with his own sisters? I didn't know what to believe. How could the boy I thought I knew do something like this? I had already seen so much that the average person simply would not believe. There had been so much death, so much darkness. I wanted to run from this terrible knowledge. But I also wanted to help her, and I hadn't the slightest idea how.

As I stared at her, frozen, wanting to help her, comfort her, anything, I had a flash of insight that this poor girl was so irrevocably broken it would be like hugging a mannequin made from shards of glass.

Finally, I said, "Kathy, I don't know what to say to you. I have no idea what to say to you. I'm so sorry. I think you need to talk to someone."

But she *was* talking to someone: me!

As soon as I said that, the light of desperation in her eyes simply went out. A steel door ten feet thick came down behind her eyes and she shouldered past me, clutching her bag to her chest. I just didn't know what to do. In fact, there was so much about that family that scared me to death, I was frozen by fear. They were Satanists. I had no idea who else might be in their group. Members of the police force? Other powerful people?

Only now as an adult can I fathom what it cost her to say those words to me. I tried calling after her, but it was as if I had become a ghost to her.

I could barely function at school that day, plagued by images of what those people had done to her—what Tommy had done to her. What could I do to help her? I had no clue. Law enforcement had a long-standing habit of turning a blind eye to so many things. It was such a crazy story, would they even believe her? If I went to the police, would someone come after *me*?

When I got home, my mom immediately saw how upset I was. She asked me what was wrong, but I just went to my room and shut the door. I sat down on my bed, legs shaking, sick to my stomach. I couldn't be sure what was even real, what was "normal." Evil, real evil, was all around me, hidden behind carefully constructed facades of normalcy. It was too horrible, and I couldn't help her.

Her stepfather was dead. So was Tommy. I simply couldn't wrap my mind around the enormity of what had happened to her. Even now, as an adult, I find it difficult and I am haunted by the fact that I could not help in some way. I eventually realized that I should have just listened; that was all anyone could do for her.

Through two more years of high school, Kathy never, ever, spoke to me again. It was many years before I told a soul what she had told me. What must her life have been like in the years that followed? How might her pitch-black secrets have eaten away at her mind and spirit? Had she managed to overcome them and rebuild her life? Was she even still alive? How many other girls who had suffered this kind of abuse were out in the world, walking ghosts patched together by habit, drugs, and sheer force of will?

These were questions without resolution, and that was the hardest part.

～

Lily Howard and my mother became close friends. In the months since the Howards had moved in, I'd learned a lot about class and respect from Lily. She was a beautiful woman, and I admired her, looked up to her.

About nine months after they moved in, I happened to be home one day when Lily burst in, distraught, her normally perfect make-up ruined by tears.

My mother welcomed her with immediate concern, and they sat together at the kitchen table. I hung back and listened.

"I'm leaving A.J.," Lily said, barely controlling her sobs.

"What?" Mom said.

"Divorce. And don't ask me if we're going to work it out."

"Why? What happened?"

Lily clutched her hand over her mouth. Then with all the self-control she could muster she said, "I'm so sorry, Cindy. I'm afraid we're never going to see each other again. And I love you and I love your family. You've been so good to...so good to me."

"Oh, you can always come back and visit."

She gave my mother a wan, tearful smile. "Of course."

But something told me that she was never coming back. The Howards were the perfect couple, the ideal. Something here didn't make sense.

"But what happened, Lily?" Mom said.

Lily took a long, deep, shuddering breath. "Oh, dear Lord, that collection, those tapes!" Then she shook her head vehemently. "I can't even say the words, Cindy. I'm so sorry. It's just over."

Mom just held Lily's hand for a long time and let her cry.

"All these years, you think you know someone!" she sobbed.

She wasn't just whistling Dixie, as the saying goes.

After about forty minutes, Lily made her way to the door, and said tearful goodbyes to Mom, and to each of us kids. Then she left, and we never saw her again. Usually when a couple was getting divorced in those days, it was the man who moved out. The fact that she left so quickly created a bizarre mystery for all of us.

My dad came home soon afterward, and Mom told him everything. He just stood there scratching his head sadly, bewildered. I could see the same wheels turning in his head that were turning in mine. His keen intuition was telling him something was wrong. But men didn't talk about such things. This was the Howards' private family business.

So Lily was gone. We didn't see A.J. much after that, and the drama at the Howard residence dropped out of my attention for a while.

With the Mafia terror fading, we all began to enjoy the spoils of my dad's success. We had nice things, we took trips, we threw great parties for family and friends. The Scarpo rowdiness was mellowing only slightly with age. At school, I had settled in with a good group of friends from good families. I was playing football, getting involved in my high school, academics, science, and excelling at my classes. I became one of the popular kids. I started driving.

What I appreciated about that group of friends was how we all pushed each other to succeed, to be our best. We wanted to look our best, to talk our best, and to use our minds to their full potential. But even through all this, I never quite trusted it. I had seen too much. But that didn't mean excellence wasn't worth pursuing. Maybe the pursuit of it helped me keep the darkness at bay, because so much of what I had seen—drunkards and philanderers and hustlers—was the result of people's inability simply to manage life or to manage their own weaknesses.

Today, I believe it was my group of high school friends, those amazing guys and girls, who helped keep me from despairing in the face of all the darkness I had seen. Their support, and my pride, I suppose. But let's not give the impression that we were the uptight, starched-underwear kind of kids. We drank, smoked, partied, but the world was our oyster. Most of us went to college together, stood up at each other's weddings, and remain friends to this day. I embraced all those distractions and began to have tons of *real fun.* Stress had weighed so heavily on me for so long, the sudden realization of its absence was like a breath of fresh air, like

I'd been living in a coal mine for years without knowing it until I emerged into the sun. Dates and girlfriends came and went like tides of teenage hormones. I still got into trouble. I knew where the boundaries were, and I pushed them at every opportunity, but I always returned to the center.

Over the weeks and months after Lily left, mystery swirled next door at A.J.'s house. Our house shared a pie-shaped driveway with his, and people came and went at all hours of the day and night. He was still friendly to us when we saw him, but he made no attempt to socialize. He just kept to himself. Yet there was always activity over there. Curiosity tugged at me, but I was preoccupied with my own teenage life. A few times I saw young people about my age coming and going in those cars, and some of the girls were just stunningly beautiful.

When my sisters or I asked about all the activity over there, Dad said, "Stay away from there. No need to bother him." Something in his voice, a tension, suggested that he knew more than he was letting on, but I just shrugged and concerned myself with school, friends, and a girlfriend. As a newly minted driver, I was enjoying the freedom of getting away from our dead-end road, paradise even though it was.

Sometime in early 1978, I went for a stroll down to the lake. It was one of those days where I just wanted to be alone and reflect, probably about school or girls or upcoming things to do with my friends. Just beyond A.J.'s house lay the area where the alligators congregated and nested. The breeze was cool, carrying the scents of orange groves and the lake itself. The surface of the lake was like gently rippling glass. Seagull calls echoed in the distance. It was the kind of peaceful that people dream about, an idyllic, pastoral moment.

I noticed a girl come out of A.J.'s house and sit down against a tree to read a book. I had seen cars full of people coming and going, but never a person alone. She was pretty, with long blonde hair, and hippie-style in her clothing. Maybe she was A.J.'s niece or something.

I walked over to her to say hello, and she gave me a cute smile. Closer now, I could see she was a year or two older than me. Dressed in short-shorts with long, tanned legs, bra-less in a tank top, the loveliness of her body seized my attention instantly.

"You live here?" she said, pointing at my house.

I nodded, and we introduced ourselves. We made chit-chat for a few minutes, then I asked her how she was related to A.J.

"Oh, we're not related," she said.

My eyebrows went up. "Are you living here with A.J.?"

She nodded. "And with Paul, and with Jackie, and with Sharon, and—"

"And you all live here?" I said, taken aback. All the comings and goings were starting to make sense.

She nodded slowly, wrapping her arms around her shins and rocking slightly.

"Where are you from?" I asked.

"Nowhere, really. My parents are jerks. Haven't seen them in two years."

"Oh, wow, I'm sorry. Where have you been living since then, before here, I mean?"

She shrugged. "Here and there. A while back, I ran into A.J. He offered me a place to stay for a while until I figure things out."

"That's nice of him," I said, sitting down beside her, but something was crawling in the back of my mind, an off-ness to the situation. Was there something about the land that attracted strangeness? The trailer that once belonged to Uncle Bill was right over there.

Then she told me about having to get out of her house, away from her parents, without saying why. I could imagine what terrible things she might have experienced, but what surprised me was that she was so upbeat about everything. She was happy to be here, and her smile just lit up her face. Whatever darkness life had given her, she had left it behind. My mind wandered in and out of her story, because I was sitting there feeling this powerful attraction to her, thinking about how pretty she was, and at the same time feeling sorry for this fellow human being who'd gotten such a raw deal. Even though I had no idea how to respond to what she was telling me about her life, the longer she talked, the more comfortable she became with me. I just listened.

In a lull, I asked her, "What has it been like, I mean, not going to school, not having a family?"

Her eyes teared up instantly, and her voice choked. "I try to read a lot. I miss my friends." Then sobs welled up, and she cried for a few moments. I wanted to put my arm around her, but she quickly composed herself, wiping her tears and her nose. "I'm going to get my diploma though. I'm studying."

"So how long have you been staying with A.J.?" I said.

At the mention of his name, her face darkened slightly. "A few weeks. It's strictly a temporary gig, you know? Sometime soon, I'll be moving on."

"That's nice of him to let you stay here for free," I said.

Her face darkened more. "Nothing's free. For any of us."

I had seen enough that any youthful naiveté was long since

dispelled, but I put two and two together in that moment. All those young people coming and going. Susan was not alone in "staying with A.J." Could something like this be the reason Lily had left in such a hurry? Could A.J. have a dirty side to him, just like Tommy's family had? What secrets did he hide?

"Hey," she said, her face brightening, "want to go horseback riding?" A.J. kept four beautiful horses in the back of his property, where Goldie had kept her chickens.

"Sure!" I hadn't been horseback riding since leaving Skipper Road, and I was grateful for the change in subject.

So, we saddled up two of A.J.'s horses and went for a ride in the orange groves that surrounded the area. Sadly, most of those trees died in an arctic cold snap in 1981, but in my teenage years, they were lush and green, and the smell of orange blossoms still takes me back to that time.

Because Susan was older than me with such a different background, our conversation was unlike what I was used to having with my friends. She was worldlier, a little careworn, but her spirit still glowed, unlike Kathy's, which had been utterly snuffed by the time she confided in me. Susan led me to an area of the lake where I rarely went, an area she clearly knew, where we dismounted the horses. With a predetermined look in her eyes, she unrolled a blanket on the ground and said, "Tony, why don't you come sit down by me?"

The blood rushed to my head, and just like that I was in a scene from a movie, out there surrounded by trees and the raw nature of the land. Orange groves could hide more than marijuana crops, it seemed.

$\sim$

One might assume that a real romance struck up between Susan and me after that, but she clearly wasn't interested in any sort of steady relationship. This mystified me a little, as we had had such a nice day together, but I soon found out why.

A few days later, I went over there to see if she was around. I knocked on the door, and a different young woman answered, just as beautiful as Susan.

I stuttered a little, "Uh, I'm Tony. I live next door. Is Susan around?"

She grinned and snapped her gum. "Yeah, sure. I've seen you around." She stepped aside and let me in. "Keep your voice down, though. They're shooting." She was wearing a silk bathrobe that came down to about mid-thigh. One glance up and down at the sheer fabric made it pretty clear she wasn't wearing anything else.

I hadn't heard any gunshots. "Shooting?"

She gestured me to follow her and took me back to what had been one of the guest bedrooms when Goldie was living there. The door was open, and I could see two naked people, a man and a woman, both a couple of years older than me, getting up off the rumpled bed. Obviously, I had just missed something a great deal more exciting. Bright lights shone down on the scene. A cameraman was checking his equipment. A microphone hung from a boom above the bed.

The realization struck me like walking into a vivid dream.

There was a pornography studio forty yards from my house.

From where I stood, I could have hit the wall of my bedroom with a rock. The teenage boy fraught with raging sex drive part of me had just hit the mother lode—this had to be the best-kept secret in the world—but deep down, queasiness was burbling.

The two naked people put on bathrobes. I recognized their faces from having seen them around.

The cameraman gave me half a glance then went back to what he was doing. "Y'all take five."

Suddenly Susan was next to me, wearing a bathrobe herself, looking a little rumpled. "Hey Tony!" She smelled of sweat and gin. She took me by the arm and led me toward the kitchen. "Want a drink?"

Not knowing what to say or do, I followed along. "Uh, sure."

The house smelled of marijuana and cigarette smoke. As we walked through the house, I saw five or six girls about Susan's age, maybe as old as 21, and two or three guys of the same age range. On the dining room table, there was a bag of pot, some rolling papers, and a Zippo lighter. There was a slab of mirror covered in a pile of cocaine the size of my fist. There were half-empty bottles of liquor and beer. The guys and girls were just circulating around the house as if it were a normal day at home. Two of the girls looked me up and down with flirtatious grins. A long-haired hippie-looking guy gave me a nod and a "Hey."

They lit joints and cigarettes, poured themselves liquor. Susan handed me a glass of gin and lemonade. They all just lay around talking, like my friends and I did, shooting the shit, talking about going out dancing that night. They looked at me as if I might be the new kid on the block.

The cameraman called from the bedroom. "Bill! Jackie! You're on. Sharon, I need you for make-up."

A skinny guy with long straight hair, wearing a set of workout shorts, headed toward the cameraman's voice, followed by a brunette who was higher than the moon.

I couldn't help but wonder how many of these people had already had sex today—or just finished for that matter?

I sipped the astringent gin, hoping it might overcome the flounder flopping around in my belly.

"Let's go outside where we can talk," Susan said. "They have to have quiet on the set."

"Uh, okay."

We passed what had been the house's family room, and I saw that it now had a huge screen and a projector, one of the big ones that had the three different color lenses. The walls were lined with video tapes. VHS had only been introduced in the U.S. the year before, and my family had a VCR now, but I could not have conceived anyone having a collection of this size. Nearly all of it was pornography.

"Son of a bitch," I breathed.

Susan hooked my arm and took me outside. We went down to the lake and sat with our drinks.

"Are all of those people...do they all have stories like yours?" I said.

She nodded. "I don't know where A.J. finds them all, but yeah. A.J. Howard's Home for Wayward Teens."

"And he makes you do this? Do you like it?" A tinge of juvenile jealousy found its way into my tone, quickly quelled by the nonchalance of her shrug.

"There are worse things," she said. "It's better than being on the street. I mean, sex and drugs and rock-n-roll, right? Living the dream, right?" She laughed, a little bitterly.

"But does he force you?"

"He's nice for a couple of weeks, but then he makes stronger and stronger suggestions, you know?"

So A.J. was some sort of world-class sexual deviant. "No won-der Lily left him."

"Who?"

"His wife."

"Oh. Never heard of her."

Inside, I could hear Billy and Jackie having sex. How could I not have noticed this before?

Later, I went home with my head in a whirl, like a spinning yin-yang pattern of wanting to dive in headfirst with this bevy of beautiful girls next door and at the same time seeing A.J., a man I thought I knew, prove himself to be not only a pervert himself but a purveyor of perversion. I never told a soul about this, not my sisters, not my mom, not my dad, not my friends. It was my little secret.

Susan and I continued to see each other occasionally, when the mood struck. We became what today would be called "friends with benefits."

One day, I was over there visiting her when A.J. came home. He looked as he always did, the quintessential Southern gentleman in a light-colored, well-pressed suit.

"I see you've met my roommates," he said nonchalantly.

"Yes, sir, I have."

I was looking around for the nearest exit, feeling like a fox caught in the henhouse, but there was no anger in his voice, only a kind of blasé cordiality.

"Have you met all of them?" he said.

"Well, I think so," I said. "They're pretty, aren't they?"

"They're beautiful, yes, yes. Well, I wanted to make sure you met them." Then he looked at me squarely. "But this must be our little secret." Across the room, a girl I hadn't seen before was reading a magazine, an absolutely stunning Latina. "You may have any of them you like, any time. But not her." The girl with the magazine was his. "And this is not something I want your mother or your father to know about, do you understand? This is *my* world. You can play in my world all you want, just don't expose my world, do you understand?" A hard edge appeared in his voice, something I had not heard from him before.

"I understand," I said.

He smiled and nodded. "Good boy."

I took Susan's hand and led her outside to get away from the creeping sensation A.J. had evoked in me.

Susan and I sat by the water and talked, but then she fell silent for a while, gazing across the glassy surface of the lake without seeing it.

Then she said, "I think I need to get out of here."

I wasn't surprised to hear her say this.

"It was fun for a little while, like falling into this hedonistic pit and just wallowing in it for a while. Plus it was nice to be off the streets, having enough to eat and all that." She had rounded a little, filled out now that I paid closer attention, but there was a shadow gathering behind her eyes, the kind of thing that all the positivity in the world couldn't keep down. "But I've seen some weird shit. Done some things I'm not proud of." She sighed. "I was talking to one of the other girls about feeling exploited, she's like, 'Yeah, absolutely.' I didn't know if it was just me being uptight." She kept looking over her shoulder to see if anyone might be within earshot.

"He doesn't pay us anything, just gives us 'play money' sometimes for us to go out. He buys us nice clothes, takes us out to dinner to his favorite restaurant, Red Lobster."

But then the haunted look in her eyes darkened, making her face seem gray and gaunt. "I have to get out of here, Tony." She was barely keeping her desperation in check. Emotion was welling out of her like blood from a stab wound. "He's trying to make me Girl Number One, just for him." She shuddered and rubbed the goosebumps on her arms and legs. "I can't do it. He's too old and creepy."

Once again, just like with Kathy, I didn't know what to say. I just stared at her, feeling helpless. I didn't know how to help her. I couldn't be her therapist. And the selfish part of me didn't want her to go.

Then she gave me a smile filled with a young girl's innocence. "That's why I like hanging out with you, Tony."

~

Susan lived with A.J. for less than a year, and she and I continued our casual relationship. Meanwhile, I went on with my life. I stayed focused on high school and got my first job, as a busboy at an Italian restaurant named Mama Mia's. I saw all sorts of crazy things happening in A.J.'s house, much of it being filmed for distribution.

Anytime A.J.'s name was mentioned in our house, my dad would admonish me and my sisters to "stay the hell away from there."

And then, Susan disappeared. I went to see her one day, and I was told, "She's gone. Took off."

I received a letter from her a couple of days later telling me that she had saved up some money and gotten on a bus to Miami. As usual, she offered few details other than to say she was happy to close the book on that part of her life. It was time to get her GED and get on with the real world. We corresponded for a while after that, but eventually that ceased. I never saw her again.

A couple of months after Susan left, I came home one day from working at the bar and spotted two helicopters circling what looked like our house. The closer I got to home, the more alarmed I became. Had the mob come back?

But then, as I pulled down the driveway we shared with A.J.'s property, I realized it wasn't our house they were circling. Circling A.J.'s house were ribbons of yellow police tape. Flashing lights and police cars were everywhere, both local police and unmarked cars that had to be the feds.

Police officers were escorting girls out of A.J.'s house and loading them into a paddy wagon. By this time, A.J.'s "wards" were almost all girls, with maybe only one or two guys. I got out of the car and stared. I never knew what happened to any of them. I couldn't help comparing their plight to Kathy's. Seeing them arrested angered and saddened me. They had done nothing wrong except to fall under the influence of a corrupt man who exploited their desperation and naiveté. Just like Kathy, they had been trapped.

I ran in the house and found my mother in her wheelchair and my sisters all watching this spectacle.

Debbie said, "What the hell is going on over there?"

"I don't know," I said. "I don't have any idea." But I knew exactly what was happening. "This is crazy with the helicopters!"

We watched them take A.J. away in handcuffs. He didn't glance even once toward our house. Fear that the police would come over and ask us questions turned my insides to jelly. I didn't want to look A.J. in the eye, and I did not want to be put on the spot. I knew too much, and I didn't want anything to do with this terrible situation. Just like that, he was taken away by a police cruiser. He went to prison for a long time. Since he was already a man in his sixties, I don't know if he ever got out.

All the activity at A.J.'s house ceased and fell silent.

During A.J.'s trial, I found out from my dad that A.J. had owned an old-time theater in Sulphur Springs just a few blocks from the dog track and what had been the Springs Tap, as well as several other porn theaters around the Tampa area. It was in these theaters that he showed his films. He must have decided that it was cheaper to exploit runaways and make his own movies than to license original films from porn studios in California. All he had to do was find some young, naïve, troubled people, buy food and drugs for them, and give them a roof to sleep under. He had either left the real estate business or was using it as a front for his pornography operation.

It turned out that my dad had known all along what was going on at A.J.'s house. They used to go fishing together, but one day A.J. had shown him his bevy of beauties, offering them to him like a pimp. My dad flew into protection mode.

He said, "I have two teenage daughters. If you ever cross this property line again, if you ever so much as look at my girls, look at my wife, talk to my wife, talk to my daughters, I'll kill you."

My dad didn't make such threats lightly. A.J. stayed away from them, but he had no problem introducing me to his sick world, knowing that my father would make good on his threat.

My dad told me about this encounter after A.J.'s arrest, and I didn't have the courage that day to tell him everything I knew. I eventually came clean, and that was when he told me the story of how A.J. had made the same offer to my dad as he made to me: "Take your pick, except for that one."

By the time I graduated high school, I had no idea what was real. Everybody seemed to wear a carefully crafted facade covering untold depths of dark, quirky secrets. Was my science teacher a cross-dresser? That girl over there was hot enough to be a porn star. How many of the people I saw on the street were high, or tripping, or cranked up on cocaine? Was that banker a Satanist? Did that priest abuse altar boys, or that Baptist minister frequent male prostitutes?

It was like every single person around me was living a lie, putting up false fronts, wearing masks. How could I go through life trusting anyone?

Chapter Nineteen

The Dance

AS IS THE CUSTOM with Italian families where the young men are groomed to one day take over the family business, my father started showing me the ropes of the bar business in earnest when I was 17, planning for me to take over his empire someday. By the time I graduated high school, it had indeed become a mini-empire, complete with a small, well-armed militia. He believed I was capable, smart enough, charming enough, tough enough. But at the same time, he had been buying savings bonds for me since I was born because he wanted me to be the first Scarpo to go away to college, the first to represent the Scarpo family as a formally educated person. He wanted to be able to say *he* had done that. However, it was always *his* plan that the moment I graduated, I would return to Tampa, where I would train and take over his business.

I had been cleaning up around the bar on weekends for several years. In the Old West, I might have been something like the spittoon jockey, as he had once been at Tony's Tavern back in Spangler. It was my job to do the cleaning: toilets, floors, pool tables and shuffleboards, the bar. As far as my dad was concerned, 17 was the perfect age, because the legal drinking age at that time was 18. It was also the minimum legal age for working in a bar.

But when I was 17, he peeled back the curtain and stopped trying to shield me from things. It was time to plunge into the nitty gritty, the nuances. For example, when I turned 17, he gave me the job of ferrying sacks of cash back and forth from the bank. Cashing all those payroll checks required having a lot of currency on hand. Often, I was shadowed by one or two members of his posse in a different vehicle. Eventually I started carrying a .38 in my pocket, knowing I had to make it from the parking lot to the door of the bank or the bar. Just like when I was holding that shotgun in my living room, I had to be hypervigilant, ready to shoot anyone coming for that bag of cash. That's just how it was.

I had always been an observant child and teenager, very self-aware. Two things fascinated me: watching people interact and making money. I had already learned a few entrepreneurial ropes with my prior weed business. Most kids my age were preoccupied with playing sports, dating, partying, school, traveling; in short, being kids. But maybe it was my experiences that led me to think beyond those things. I still enjoyed those things, but by 17 I was more interested in digging deeper. I wanted to *know* things: how the world worked, how people worked, how they fit together. My parents often remarked that I was the kid who asked too many bizarre questions.

But here's something I understood early: knowledge is power. Knowledge grants confidence, it lets you build something from nothing. And one of the many things I inherited from my dad was a love of making money.

Making money was a game—a dance.

Moreover, it was a game that applied to many aspects of life. Making money was not unlike dating and sex. Many of the dance steps were similar.

My dad's personal history as a tradesman also rubbed off on me. He'd been an electrician when I was a baby and during that time had taken his first steps into the bar business. When I was old enough to get my work permit at 16, he put me on a path to learn trades. He saw it as a backup plan if I didn't make it in college. So, for about two years, I apprenticed with various tradesmen around the area. Of course, he knew them all, and they knew me. I learned to be a plumber, an electrician, a roofer, a drywall hanger, a millwright, and yes, a ditch digger. I met some down-to-earth, hardworking people and had great respect for them. All of these were various degrees and types of hard, physical labor, all honorable trades that paid well, but none of them spoke to me as something I wanted to do for the rest of my life. As I had other options, I wanted to explore them.

By the time I was 17, though, I had already been exposed to the pool hustling, the primal want for sex, the brutality of violence, the best *and* worst of human behavior. It was like I was living in two different worlds. My high school friends had no conception of what I had been exposed to, what I had *done*. Their jaws would have fallen off had they known. They had no clue that on Fridays I would come home from school, where everything was normal teenage stuff, and enter the world of booze, cigarette smoke, gambling, hustling, and women.

But, like I said, I was a teenager. I worked hard, but I played harder, and the bar business offered some unique ways to play. In many ways, it was like an extended party that happened every night, and almost everything you touched made money, and people were happy to pay it.

Every bar has an individual character to it, an atmosphere that's a combination of decor, location, clientele, but most importantly the attitude of the people who run the place. This atmosphere is part of what draws people. It was my dad's unique combination of excitement, enthusiasm, and hustle that made his bars so popular. People wanted to be part of it.

By this time his customers, his posse, had been around for almost twenty years. They were like my uncles and aunts. I knew their kids. Whether they were drunk or sober, I had to deal with them, learning how to handle drunks, how to talk them down, or talk them up. Everyone had a point of no return, when they had had too much to drink and they became the person hidden underneath the veneer. I had to get to know both versions of that person, where the point of no return was, and how to handle them after they crossed it.

The bar business is not for introverts. I watched my dad handle people. He was always walking the bar and talking, joking, leading the conversation. I learned the exact same thing. In many ways it was like being a therapist. Much of it was just knowing how to listen. Everyone had a story, a drama they were living through on any given night, and they came because they needed someone to tell it to, someone to have a beer with while they told it, and someone to tell them everything would work out all right.

I was wide-eyed and open-minded to all that surrounded me. So it was no surprise that heavy rock 'n' roll and unique movies filled my mind. What excited me and so many other people in 1975 was The Who's rock opera *Tommy*, so strange and unique and over-the-top. But it sparked a new craze in the latter half of the 1970s—pinball. It became the rage in arcades all over the country, but also in bars and lounges. After I saw *Tommy* in the theater, I wanted to become a pinball wizard

Art's Lounge always had at least one pinball machine, sometimes two or three. The pinball machines were a magnet for people drawn to the flashing lights and sounds. Both my dad and I became experts at the game, and we quickly learned the nuances of each machine. Just like individual pool tables, pinball machines had their own personalities, their individual quirks, their unique *TILT* thresholds. The pinball machines were places for conversation, commotion, and excitement—but also for betting. Along with learning the skills, I quickly learned the hustle. First, start by building excitement around the machine, gathering some onlookers, and then slipping in a few $20 bets on scores, bonuses, or achievements, going double or nothing here and there. I was already a novelty attraction, a young pinball wizard, but I was among a crowd of people who'd just cashed their payroll checks. They were there to booze it up, to play the ladies, to immerse themselves in that atmosphere of revelry, and we were there to help them do it. The dance of the pinball machine's flashing lights and sounds grabbed their attention. The dance of the little steel ball as it spun and bounced at the stroke of the flippers held their attention. It became almost a spectator sport, with a little competition thrown in, and they loved it, even if they lost a little money. A little money from them, here and there, added up to a lot of money for me.

However, I felt like I was on a railroad track headed for the bar business. It was a one-way ticket, no getting off. It had been decided, it was inevitable, but that darkness—so pervasive, like the world's normalcy was just a bandage over a deep gash—still lurked in everyone behind a couple of shot glasses. I didn't like being around drunk people. I didn't like what alcohol exposed in so many of them. But I didn't know how to get off that railroad track.

Even though I wasn't sure I wanted to be in the bar business, I still watched and learned the dance. This was the University of Real Life. It offered the best education on people, their habits and raw emotions. I was determined to succeed and understand the intricacies of human behavior.

One of the most fundamental dance steps I learned from my dad came from the way he handled whiskey and beer salesmen. These salesmen in their ill-fitting suits and comb-overs would visit weekly to take orders for Budweiser and Jack Daniels. Their sales relationships lasted for years. The first time I witnessed one of these meetings shocked me.

The back room of the bar, where my dad was meeting with one of these salesmen, erupted in shouting.

"Goddamn, you're a cheap sumbitch!"

"I said, I'll take ten cases of J.D., but you're gonna throw in two more."

"You want me to throw in my wife, too? I can't do that!"

"Get the fuck outta here!"

Even though my dad had taken on the deep Southern accent, he was still Italian. Grandiose, passionate hand gestures filled the space between the two men.

"Come on, I can get a better deal at the Circle K, you smelly bastard!" The insults were *usually* good-natured.

"I wouldn't pay that much if every bottle was gold-plated!"

"Fuck you, no way!"

It was like watching shrewd Arab traders haggle over the best price for a camel. The salesmen knew my dad was a high-volume trader; his business meant a lot. It's entirely likely no one sold more Jack Daniels and Budweiser in Hillsborough County than my dad, so it was often a standoff, a verbal wrestling match, a game of chicken over who would get the best deal.

"Look, you can throw in three extra cases or you get in your car, get the hell out and I won't shove a potato up your tailpipe."

It was a game he always won, because they loved his money. Every sliver of advantage he could get over his suppliers, whether it was price terms or extras or anything to sweeten the deal, made him more money. And so it went, on and on, week after week for years. Sometimes the yelling would rise like a storm, then subside.

"How's the family?"

"Good. Wife's busting my balls. How're the kids?"

"Kids are great."

"Tony's a chip off the old block."

"Been hunting lately?"

"Yeah, shot a ten-point buck last weekend."

Then the pause of niceness would disappear in another storm of shouting and fighting, a sparring match with money, booze, terms, and sales as the weapons. Liquor was powerful, profitable, and how much money the business made was dictated by how the liquor was bought. The battle raged on until each side was happy, and it always ended in a handshake.

When the deal was finally made, my dad would leave the room to go cut a check. Sometimes he would leave them sitting alone in the room while he went off to do something else for a while. Then he would come back in. "Are you still fucking here? What are you here for?"

"Come on, Art, for Chrissakes, why you put me through this shit?"

Then my dad would hand him the check, and they would shake hands.

"See ya next week, Art!"

While I was shocked at first at the way my dad treated these guys, I was even more startled that they kept coming back for it, thinking they must be gluttons for punishment—until I realized that they loved the bizarre dance as much as he did. Beer salesmen on Mondays—Budweiser, Miller, Schlitz, and Pabst in those days, long before Coors made it to Florida—and liquor salesmen on Wednesdays, peddling Wild Turkey, Jack Daniels, and vodka. At that time, the only vodkas around were Smirnoff and some rotgut shit named Skull. These salesmen appeared like clockwork, and he abused them all, but if he truly didn't like them, the humor disappeared and he was just brutal. If a newbie salesman came in, my dad would eat him alive and send him scrabbling out like a kicked puppy. Before long, the distribution companies knew better than to send in the newbies.

The first time I saw this, I thought *What a jerk! My dad was such an asshole to him, this guy who's been coming in here for fifteen years.* It sounded like the poor salesman was just getting beaten up, but after he left, my dad looked at me and cracked a smile.

"That's how you do business, Tony. That's how you do business."

What I initially took as anger was really an unusual level of mutual respect. It was a strange combination of laughter, seriousness, and loyalty.

This was my first introduction to negotiation—hard, brass-knuckles negotiation—a process that's the backbone of any good business.

My dad applied this kind of negotiation—one might call it slam dancing—to everything he ever bought and sold. He didn't do this at the grocery store or shopping at Sears, but if it involved two-way negotiation, there was no tougher customer. Cars, boats, chickens, hunting dogs, lawn mowers, property...anything. I used to wonder why he went to such lengths, because it seemed so exhausting, but as I got older and recognized it for the dance that it was, the game, it became fun, a *usually* good-natured competition over who could get the better deal. Who was the sharpest? Much like war, victory always went to the one who *cared* more. If you decide to dance but you miss a step, shame on you—you're going to lose that day.

My dad won far more battles than he lost, and when it came to settling debts and cashing checks, he *always* won. Always.

Whenever he lent someone money, he kept collateral, whether it was the title to a pickup or the deed on property. He never made personal loans, ever. It sometimes happened that he became the new owner of whatever that collateral was, and he never hesitated to collect it.

But when someone owed him money, he had a nose like a wolf for sniffing out financial catastrophe. If someone couldn't pay, he didn't break legs or faces like mob loan sharks; he would generally inquire as to the reasons behind the delay but if he determined that the borrower would likely stiff him, he could be scary and relentless as hell.

If he was about to be cheated, however, the gloves came off.

Sometime in 1979, at the height of our check-cashing operation, my father was cashing over a million dollars a month in payroll checks for various companies. One company in particular ran a fairly large trucking operation and employed many people. The employees often came in on Friday nights, payday, to cash their checks. On Friday evenings, the banks were closed, so my dad was essentially fronting his customers the money from their paychecks until he could deposit them on Monday. If a check bounced, we would not discover this until Wednesday or Thursday.

One particular week, $12,000 worth of payroll checks from this trucking company bounced all at once, the equivalent of about $45,000 in today's dollars.

Normally, if a check bounced, my dad started with a phone call to the owners informing them that their check had bounced. But when that many checks bounced all at once, we knew we had a big problem. My dad made a couple of phone calls to the owner, but the guy didn't answer the phone and he didn't return the messages.

My dad had a bad feeling that this guy—we'll call him Earl— was up to no good.

So, we loaded up on the following Friday morning, my dad and I and his snub-nose .38, and headed out to pay a visit to the owner of this trucking company.

I had a vague understanding that Dad was going to go try to get his money. What I didn't understand initially, not fully, was that my purpose was to serve as the lookout and backup.

On the way there, my dad told me, "I got a tip that Earl was trying to leave town, skipping out on all his bills and all the bad checks he wrote all over town." It would take time for the banks to catch up with him, but we had quicker reaction time. This was not bank money we were talking about, which was insured, but my dad's personal money. It was always personal. The shared outrage simmered between us in the truck. How dare this son of a bitch try to steal that kind of money from us!

When we arrived on this weekday morning, the normally full

parking lot was empty except for two cars. A trucking company with no trucks? Had the company already gone out of business?

We jumped out of the truck and headed for the front door. My dad's hand was in the pocket where he kept his .38. He turned to me. "I need you to stay back, toward the door. Keep your eyes open."

Suddenly I felt like Michael Corleone in *The Godfather*, where he stood lookout at the hospital when a carload of thugs was coming to kill his father. Michael put his hand in his pocket like he had a gun, prompting the assassins to drive on past.

Inside the entrance was a hallway leading to an office with a desk, where Earl was hurriedly sorting through stacks of paper. A plump, sweaty man about my height but double my weight, he already had a furtive look, but as soon as he saw my dad stalking down the hallway toward him, he turned pale as cream.

"Got somewhere to be, Earl?" my dad shouted, hand in his pocket. "Where you headed off to?"

Startled, Earl flipped a sheaf of papers into the air. His mouth was moving, but no sound was coming out.

My dad stalked back and forth before Earl's desk. "So, you got my messages."

"Uh, sorry, what messages?" Earl said.

"You know the ones. The ones where I told you your employees came to my place and cashed their payroll checks with your signature on them. And they all bounced. Twelve grand worth. But you already knew that, didn't you."

Earl's voice faltered. "I'm not sure what you're talking about."

"Sure you do. You just wrote twelve grand worth of bad checks, and those are just the ones that affect *me*. So I figure you owe me twelve thousand dollars, plus the bounced check charges, plus some extra for my trouble to come down here and collect it."

Earl glanced over my dad's shoulder toward me hanging by door with my arms crossed, looking as stern as I could manage with my heart pounding in my chest. Throughout my life, I had learned the power of a fierce stare, tight forehead and squinting eyes, the kind that burns right through a person. The one that says "I'm serious and don't ever fuck with me." In that moment, he was a rabbit looking for the closest hole to bolt into, but if he tried, my dad would have him by the scruff of the neck in an instant. But Earl might not be alone. There were two cars outside. And when I realized that, my stomach turned cold and my pulse surged up my neck into my ears where it thudded like a drum. My senses kicked into overdrive.

The man babbled excuses, sweat sheening his plump forehead.

"Shut the fuck up," my dad said. "We both know what you're doing. You're trying to skip town." My dad's hand remained in his pocket, prominently in view. Earl kept glancing at it. "You might get away from the banks. You might even get away from the law. But you're not getting away from me."

Earl looked ready to collapse into a pile like a half-cooked egg.

My dad paced in front of the desk, glaring at him. "See, I got a feeling you're not as broke as you're trying to tell me."

"I—I—I really have to go," Earl said, his hands shaking so badly he dropped more papers. His eyes were feverish, darting.

My dad leaned over the desk and made his voice low and menacing. "Neither of us is getting out of here until you settle up."

"I don't want any trouble!"

"Too late. All you gotta do is cough up. I won't even call the police. You do know fraud is illegal, right?"

Earl's double-chin bobbed up and down.

My dad said, "I think writing twelve grand in bad checks is something like three to five. Hell, I could sit on you till the cops get here. Or I could make it so you're easy to catch." His hand squirmed in his pocket. By this time, he was well connected with the Hillsborough County Sheriff's Department, but he never turned to them for help when it came to these matters. He would never have called them, but Earl didn't know that.

"All right! All right!" Earl put up his hands. "Can I reach under the desk and get something?"

I tensed as the image of a shotgun burst into my brain, suddenly vigilant of where threats might emerge. I moved closer, and as I did so, the last of Earl's resistance deflated like a balloon. He knew better than to make any sudden moves. He may have pissed in his pants a little. I circled the desk to his flank, near where a bag of expensive golf clubs leaned against the wall.

He reached for a sack on the floor. The second he picked it up, I saw it had the heft and shape of a bag full of cash. Jackpot. But there could also be a gun in the bag. I pulled a three-wood from the set of golf clubs and gripped it.

Earl reached into the bag and pulled out stacks of cash, mostly tens and twenties, and placed them on the desk. Then he counted out twelve thousand dollars.

My dad said, "Throw in two more for my trouble."

Earl whined like a beaten mongrel, but he counted out two grand more.

Dad snatched the bag away from Earl, emptied it onto the desk, and stuffed the fourteen thousand dollars into it. Then he tossed the bag to me.

As we backed toward the door, my dad grabbed the bag of expensive golf clubs and slung it over his shoulder. "You're not going to need these anymore, are you?"

The journey to the truck felt like a thousand miles through enemy territory, exposed. Earl could grab a gun out of his desk. He could call for reinforcements. In the parking lot, I listened for the sound of any engine in case Earl was going to run us over. But my dad was cool as a cucumber salad.

As we slammed the truck doors and roared out of there, no pursuit came. A wave of relief dashed over me and I sagged against the seat beside the bag of cash.

"That's how we do it, Son," he said. "Very few people do what we just did. No one's that crazy. Word gets around that's how we collect debts. Word gets around, people know not to mess with us."

My guts were a wild mix of surprise that we had succeeded, exhilaration at getting away, draining fear for all the ways it could have gone wrong…and power. I was no longer watching my dad and his posse yield their might. I was now part of it. I had strength and power of my own. It had been my presence that pushed Earl over the edge. Had I not been there, with my dad and Earl one on one, it might have gone very differently.

I didn't know it then, but this experience became a bridge for me, a dance step where I learned my own power, my own strength leading me toward something I would have never expected, a combination of skills and talent that would eventually lead to my business success and place me at the doorstep of great wealth.

CHAPTER TWENTY

COLLEGE BOUND

THE TIME HAD COME to look toward the future, and college was in my sights. This plan had been set in motion since my birth. I would be the first Scarpo to attend college and could barely contain myself as I prepared to cross that threshold. The entire Scarpo clan was excited for me, especially my dad. Even though I was continuing to learn the bar hustle, I was also taking practice tests and sitting for the SAT and the ACT. I had long wanted to go to Florida State University in Tallahassee, but could I get in? Could I make it? What if all my friends got in and I was stuck in Tampa going to trade school or community college?

The truth was I wanted out of Tampa. I had to get out, and that drove me to push myself academically. Because of everything I had been through, everything I had seen and experienced, Tampa carried such a malaise that I felt uncomfortable living there anymore, especially knowing that all of my friends were moving away. This realization didn't come to me all at once, because I was doing what was expected of me as a good Italian son: following in the family business, learning the ropes, etc. But my aversion to the bar business was growing. I liked the hustle, the dance, but I didn't like what alcohol did to people, and I didn't like being a person who enabled that.

I must admit that I sometimes enjoyed the attention of the female clientele. As I grew into a man, they showered attention on me, almost competing among themselves for who'd be the first to date the owner's son. That they were doing this under my dad's watchful eye made it all the more surreal. Some of them were pretty and charming, but a little dinged by life, like a shiny Lincoln with a few hail dents or key scratches. But my dad paid close attention to whoever was paying attention to me. Among these women were a few grifters and various flavors of bad news, and he seemed to steer those away from me, with strong opinions about who was acceptable for his son. As a testosterone-ridden 17-year-old boy with sex being freely offered, I succumbed a couple of times with women whose difference in age from mine was still in the single digits.

As I began my senior year, however, my attention was seized by a girl I saw performing in concert chorus from my high school. When I saw her for the first time, my heart kicked against my sternum several times to get my attention. Whenever I spotted her at school, I couldn't take my eyes off her, but she was only a sophomore. I kept telling myself she was too young for me, too innocent for someone who had seen and done the things that I had.

Then we ran into each other at a lake bonfire party. Before long we started talking and getting to know each other. Her name was Lori, and within a few minutes I was enchanted. She was so lovely, with big blue eyes, tall and fair with wavy blonde hair and a smile that could light up a room.

Our first date was like all young teenager dates. I picked her up and took her to one of Tampa's iconic restaurants named CDB's. She was so easy to talk to, so innocent, so sweet, smart, and beautiful.

Hidden behind her shyness was a fun-loving, adventurous streak that drew me closer to her. She dreamed of being a rock star.

One date led to another and another, and soon we were an item. She came from a nice, church-going family who eyed me with a certain amount of well-placed wariness. I took things very slow with her because of our age difference. My innocence was long since gone, and I had no wish to bring her into my dark world.

As I moved through my senior year of high school, my two lives bifurcated and diverged further and further. That year went fast, burying me in sports and studying. I could sense a major transition on the horizon, like watching dawn coming, where the sun could break the horizon at any moment.

Tampa was my home, but it was time for me to get out and experience the wider world. Maybe I wanted to learn about the rest of the world and find out for myself if it was as dark as Tampa. I loved learning and expanding my knowledge in all subject matters. I may not be the smartest person in the room, but I am versed on many topics and can carry a conversation with anyone. I wanted to live a *big* life, not a cramped existence of quiet desperation like the barflies who worked hard and then came to Art's Lounge to fritter away every cent they made. Their vices had given my family affluence, but my sense of guilt over that was strong.

It was an agonizing wait, but when my college-prep test scores arrived, I was ecstatic to see I had done well on both the SAT and ACT. I immediately applied to Florida State, the only school I really wanted to go to—Go 'Noles!—and a few months later I received my letter of acceptance.

That was cause for celebration around the Scarpo house. We needed little excuse to throw a lakeside party, and all our family and friends joined us. Several of my friends, including Bobby, received their FSU acceptance letters at about the same time, making it seem all the more magical. The same great group of guys and girls that had become such a wonderful influence in my life, we were all going off on a great adventure.

This was my dream, a chance to not only make my own way, but also to see what normal really was. My high school friends represented the "normal" side of my life. I kept the nature of my other life secret from them, not only because my father demanded it, but also because I didn't want them to judge me. I was headstrong enough that if I had wanted to tell them all about hustling pinball games for money, toting sacks of cash, and selling Jack Daniels out the back door, I would have done it in spite of my father's prohibition. The truth was that the bar business made me uncomfortable in ways I wasn't prepared to acknowledge, and while I hadn't yet admitted it to myself, I couldn't wait to get away from that world.

By this time, Lori and I had been dating for a few months. We were solidly a couple. She was happy for me, but we both knew that Tallahassee was two hundred fifty miles away. My high school graduation day was bittersweet for both of us. Nevertheless, we were determined to make the most of our summer together before I went off to FSU. She would be old enough to get a work permit in the fall so she could get a job. Pretty soon she would be driving.

Meanwhile, I barreled toward my college experience with the pedal to the metal. A few days before classes started, I moved into a dorm named Osceola Hall with three other guys from high school, some of my best friends, including Bobby as a roommate and Art and Scott in the suite's other bedroom. The swell of pride and a sense of adulthood at having *my very own place* dizzied me.

In 1979, Osceola Hall was the most amazing place to live on campus, at least to me. In retrospect, it seems more like your typical freshman dorm with cinder-block walls and particle-board desks, but I was thrilled, probably because it was my first venture out of the house.

The one advantage Osceola Hall had over the other dorms was that it was private—and it was co-ed. Living with both guys and girls made for an interesting first year in college. The dorm also had its own kitchen and cafeteria, with three square meals a day. What more could I ask for?

As I walked around campus those first few days, the sense of vibrant *life* suffused me. The air was sweeter, the campus foliage greener, the students alive and friendly and just as excited and nervous and eager to make new friends as I was.

And even in the face of this, I couldn't help but feel like the darkness had followed me even there, hounding me. When I arrived, Florida State University was still deep in the shadows of one of the most notorious serial killers in American history. On January 15, 1978, less than a year before I arrived, Ted Bundy broke into an FSU sorority and attacked four young women, killing two of them, after which he entered a nearby apartment and assaulted another young woman, who survived but with permanent physical and emotional damage. A month later, he struck again, this time in Lake City, Florida. It was this crime that finally led to his arrest. As the investigation unfolded, he was ultimately suspected of thirty-six murders in four states, considered by many to be a manifestation of pure evil walking the earth. I could not help but think of Diana De La Paz, whose body had been found in the Cone Brothers pits, and Jonathan Kushner, a Tampa boy a couple of years younger than me who'd been abducted, molested, and killed when I was in the sixth grade. Lots of kids from school including me had joined the search parties for him.

I tried to put Ted Bundy out of my mind, but his crimes always lurked in the back room of my thoughts. My dorm and a local pub called The Phyrst were right next door to the Chi Omega sorority where Bundy had struck. Every day, I could see the back stairs he'd used to sneak in. For a few short months, this crime and its proximity to my new home haunted me, but I was determined to move forward as all the other students had. Clearly, evil was not isolated to the Tampa Bay area, it was like an octopus with far-reaching tentacles. Bundy's reign of terror stretched from Seattle, Washington, all the way to Lake City, Florida. A few years later, Ted Bundy was convicted of murder and sentenced to death. His evil and hatred toward women had been put on public display. As a young man, I struggled to make sense of this kind of rabid perversion. Florida law had recently changed, and cameras were allowed in the courtroom for the first time. It became a media circus with reporters from all fifty states and others traveling from distant countries. The world hated Ted Bundy, and his electrocution couldn't come fast enough. On January 24, 1989, he was strapped to Old Sparky and put to death at Florida State prison, thus bringing an end to one of the most notorious sociopathic killers in U.S. history.

I struggled to understand the theme or thread that bound all hatred and all evil. If you are born pure and innocent, with no evil, at what point did you change? At what stage in your life were you consumed?

Even though Bundy was in custody, there was still a chill in the air. Vigilance was high. Nevertheless, student life continued as it always does in such tragedies; as soon as classes started, the fraternity rush parties sprang up all over campus. Bobby and I found ourselves wandering from one frat house party to the next. This was all new and exciting for the kids from Lutz. We were pinned immediately by a fraternity, but we had no idea what it all meant, so we declined and began to do some research. We wanted to figure out which house would be the best fit for us. Some fraternities were too nerdy, some too stuffy, some too wild.

That first semester was a huge transition as I struggled to balance my personal life and my classes. I thrived in meeting new people, in learning new things, in discovering how the wider world worked, but I was still traveling back and forth to Tampa to see my family and Lori. In Tallahassee, I was swimming in temptation, stunningly beautiful college girls everywhere, but I was determined to hold on to my relationship with Lori. We cared about each other a great deal. Occasionally she would visit me in Tallahassee. It seemed to work.

By sometime during the second semester, Bobby and I found that we clicked best with the members of Pi Kappa Alpha, a.k.a. "Pikes." When the Pikes pinned Bobby and me, we spread the word to our circle of Tampa friends, and one by one, maybe a dozen in total, our friends joined us at Pi Kappa Alpha. Having those longstanding friendships continue not only to FSU but also into our fraternity house gave it a sense of home and continuity that made us feel like we immediately fit in. It was an amazing experience.

Joining a fraternity was a tremendous personal load; however, I managed to go through rush *and* Hell Week initiation *and* still maintain a heavy class load. I had only one chance here to keep my grades up. Bad grades would earn me a one-way ticket back to Tampa. My father would never tolerate me screwing around.

In Tallahassee and around my friends, I did not speak of my brushes with the mob or the multitude of brushes with darkness. Few of my fraternity brothers and other friends were even aware of the Mafia's pervasive presence in Tampa. All of them seemed to live normal lives. They came from suburbia, from all over Florida. Their diverse backgrounds fascinated the kid who'd spent his childhood plagued by gangsters and surrounded by rednecks, carnies, and gators. None of them, not even my friends from high school, except for Bobby, would have believed stories of my childhood, or even stories of things I had experienced over the last couple of years of high school, with my indoctrination into the bar business and my encounters with A.J.'s porn enclave. They would have thought I was a liar or a crazy person, or both.

Being around so many intelligent, motivated people boosted my confidence and drove me to excel. It seemed right to want to leave all that darkness in the dust on my journey forward. I was thrilled to be away from Tampa, thrilled to have survived its insanity, thrilled to be where I was. Many months had passed, and I was doing great at FSU. I was so proud of my accomplishments and was excelling in every way. My master plan of a top-notch education was underway and there was no stopping me.

But the darkness was not finished with me. Not by a long shot. No matter how far I traveled from Tampa, no matter how much focus and energy I put into my new life, the overwhelming shadow of danger and crime threatened to pull me right back in.

CHAPTER TWENTY-ONE

ONE CHANCE ONLY REPRISE

WE DON'T GET TO choose our formative moments.

As Bobby and I lay there in the vast palmetto grove, covered in another man's blood in the chill of a dark and dangerous night, my fevered eyes looking for signs of rattlesnakes, I was overcome by remorse for putting my best friend in mortal danger. A truckful of armed restaurant cooks was circling our patch of palmettos like vengeful sharks. Angry voices echoed within a few dozen yards of us. If they caught us, covered in their boss's blood, we were dead. Mosquitoes buzzed in our ears, in our noses, crawling over our arms, biting.

"I'm sorry I got you into this!" I whispered to him.

He hissed back, "It's okay."

I kept telling him, "I'm sorry!"

And he kept saying, "It's okay." Finally, he said, "Now *shut up!*"

All I could think about was how I had gotten us into this.

One minute I was well into my freshman year at Florida State, enjoying my new life as a young college student, the first in my family to go to college, newly pledged to an amazing fraternity.

The next minute, I was hiding in the palmetto bushes in the dead of night, hunted, praying for my life. The violence and darkness of my former life had come roaring back and threatened to consume not only me, but also my best friend. After finally managing to shed the fear, violence, and insanity that consumed so much of my life, after filling my life with things to look forward to, a brighter path, how could this happen? How did I get here?

~

I dated Lori through most of my senior year of high school. She was such a great girl, beautiful and sweet, two years younger than me, probably smarter than me, tall and fair with wavy blonde hair and a smile that could light up a room. She had a beautiful voice and loved singing in the choir. She had dreams of becoming a rock star, but first had to overcome her innate shyness.

We were both well aware that I was heading off to college. As with all high school relationships, the strain of separating at graduation tested the relationship in all directions. We were no different. Tallahassee may have only been two hundred fifty miles away, but it could as well have been Eastern Europe.

When I got to Florida State, excited to launch myself into new opportunities and experiences, I found myself breathing free in a way much like when the mob threat dissolved.

If anything, working the bar life with my dad had taught me how to be charming and engaging, which resulted in a near-instantaneous collection of new male friends—and new female temptations. The sheer multitude of stunning college co-eds dizzied me, so I often thought about breaking up with Lori, she was so far away. As much as I cared about her, the distance strained the threads of connection between us. But she was still a real connection to Tampa and to my old friends who hadn't left home.

We were in love, or as best that love can be at 19 years old, so we attempted the long-distance relationship. I came home on weekends and holidays, and we went out together, but I could feel it all slowly slipping away.

During one of those long breaks from college, I thought it would be nice to spend some extra time with Lori and planned an amazing evening at one of our favorite nightspots. Robiconti's was well known for its dinner, dancing, and live entertainment, and we always enjoyed spending time there. We both loved to dance, and she was always a big fan of the live bands and great music.

But from the moment I picked her up, I could see something was off.

She barely smiled when I arrived. She sat away from me in the car as if she didn't want to be touched. Her responses to my attempts at conversation were terse, practically monosyllabic.

I asked, "Is something wrong?"

She shook her head quickly and flashed me a smile. "So, how's school going?"

I shrugged and told her it was a challenge, but classes were going well, and I was excited about my fraternity. I was careful not to over-enthuse about how much I loved college life, since she was still stuck in high school.

When we arrived at Robiconti's, we found our favorite private booth and proceeded to order dinner. A live band was just starting on their first set, and in spite of her mood, I was happy to see her. I had missed her. Before long, the physical distance between us evaporated, but it seemed like the closer our bodies got, the more anxious she became. Nothing I said or did brought a smile or any light to her eyes.

The only conclusion I could come to was that my going away to college was too painful for her and the distance had taken its toll. Was she going to break up with me? That realization sent a shock-wave through me. Had she met another guy? If I knew anything by this time, it was that there are plenty of fish in the sea, but that's an easy thing to forget when one's sweetheart was sitting there just as lovely as she could be. Was it time for her to move on? Was it time for *me* to move on?

My curiosity became too much. I couldn't take this line of thought, but neither could I just charge in with questions.

I said, "Lori, things seem odd tonight. You've barely touched your food."

"Oh, what do you mean?" She wouldn't look at me.

"I've been trying to figure it out all night. Something is heavy on your mind."

She sighed a little but didn't answer.

"Has the distance been too much?" I said.

Her face flushed, and her eyes glistened.

"Do you...want to break up with me?" I said.

Finally, she shook her head. "No, that's not it, Tony."

"Are you sure?"

"No, no, no..."

"Then, I'm confused. What's wrong? You're not yourself." I tried to keep the frustration out of my voice, but she edged away from me.

Her glistening eyes burst into tears, and she blurted out a series of uncontrollable statements that were the last words I expected to hear that night. "They jumped on me! They hurt me! I've never been so scared in my life. I think they drugged me! They ripped my clothes off! They all... He, they..." She buried her face in her hands and sobbed uncontrollably.

Her words came in such a terrible rush of images and emotions that I sat there frozen. The terror in her voice stabbed me with a hot poker. My body felt like it was on fire. Dizziness washed over me.

People at nearby tables stared.

"Slow down," I said, as if I was desperately trying to understand the avalanche of information, "it's okay, please slow down." But I already knew what had happened to her. I could feel it in her pain. I could hear it in her words.

She caught her breath, still sobbing, trembling now. I slid my body next to hers and held her close. She cried against my chest, her shoulder shaking with each breath.

It had taken me two tries to get this right—Kathy and Susan. I had previously failed to help them, but I was not going to fail Lori. I whispered into her ear over and over, "It's okay, you're safe, you're with me now. No one is going to hurt you again."

When her burst of anguish subsided, she slowly pulled away from me, wiping her face, dabbing at her ravaged make-up with a napkin.

I said, "Please start at the beginning, and go slow so I can understand every detail."

She took another deep breath and gathered herself. I braced myself for what was coming. In the background, the band turned up the volume and the disco lights flashed in great spasms of blinding color. My head was spinning, but I tried to focus on her voice.

"I got a job a couple months ago, working at this restaurant near the University of South Florida," she said. She told me the name of the restaurant.

I knew it well because it was smack in the middle of my old Skipper Road neighborhood, close to USF.

"I thought it would be a way to make some extra money for gas and clothes," she continued. "Anyway, we worked really late hours, because of the college crowd. I was working there for about three months. Sometimes after work, we would stay late for a drink or we would go to the owner's house for some late-night partying. Pretty much everybody who worked there did it, and I liked my coworkers, so it was fun for a while."

Her voice slowed down. "But then, this one time, we went to the owner's house, Allen's house. I had a couple of drinks like always, but then I started getting dizzy, like *really* dizzy. I didn't know if I was getting sick or if it was all those hours on my feet or what, so I went to a quiet guest bedroom to lie down for a while."

Then her voice cracked again. "I must have passed out. The next thing I knew, there were three naked men standing around the bed. They were standing there, looking down at me. It was so quiet. All of my coworkers and the party guests had gone home. I was the only one there. I thought I was dreaming, but I think I must have panicked. I tried to get up, but I was so woozy. Allen pushed me back onto the bed, and they were all laughing at me. They grabbed at me and pulled my clothes off. I screamed, but that made them laugh harder. I screamed and shouted and cried. By some miracle, I was able to crawl off the bed and run for the bathroom. I got in there, locked the door, and hid in the bathtub. I was so scared, Tony. So scared. I felt like a rat trapped in a corner of the tub. They were on the other side of the wall laughing and beating on the door. Eventually they broke the door down. One of them grabbed me by the shirt and dragged me out, threw me back onto the bed. That's when they all piled on and held me down. I screamed and fought, but there wasn't anybody who heard me. They ripped all my clothes off. One of them must have got scared, because he went and stood in the corner, while the other two..."

The graphic description of that horrific night made my insides crawl, to a point where I was seething, threatening to throw my dinner back up onto the table. Those scumbags had spiked her drink with something. They had *planned* it. The blood was pounding in my ears, drowning out everything except the words she was speaking. My vision shrank to a tunnel. I almost couldn't see her. I begged God to help me maintain my composure and strength, because it was taking every ounce of strength she had to tell me all this. I had to be strong for her...and for myself.

She restrained further sobs to finish her story, but her voice shuddered. "I must have passed out from the shock or something. I woke up about an hour later, really confused, still naked. I panicked again, because I was afraid they were still in the house. I lay there, still as I could, and listened for I don't know how long. Turns out, they left to go late-night bar-hopping. I gathered up my things, tried to put my clothes back on, but my underwear was ruined. I went home, shaking like a leaf. I didn't tell my parents. I went straight to my room and didn't sleep a wink the rest of the night."

She took a drink of water to wet the growing hoarseness in her voice. "I went to the clinic the next day." The look of humiliation on her face told me she was reliving it all. "I needed to find out the truth about what they did to me. The clinic...they...confirmed bruising and...semen... The nurse kept asking me questions, but I just panicked again and wanted to get out of there. I didn't tell them anything."

I took a deep breath and kept my voice as calm as I could, but my stomach was clenching like a ten-foot alligator, a ball of primordial rage and fury. "Who were they?"

She swallowed. "One of them was the owner, Allen. One of them was Jeff, the assistant chef, the other was Ron, another of the cooks."

"When was this?" I asked.

"About a week ago. I never went back to the restaurant and never picked up my last check."

The sounds of the nightclub were blaring in my ears. This was no longer a night of fun and dancing. "We need to get you home," I said. My watch read about midnight. "It's getting late. Your mom and dad are probably wondering where we are." She was only a junior, and her parents were nice people but rightfully protective of her.

"Okay."

She took a few deep breaths, pulling herself together, wiping her tears, blowing her nose. In the car to her house, she was limp with exhaustion, staring vacantly out the window, as far from me as she could manage.

I spoke quietly, "It'll be okay, Lori. I promise it'll be okay. I'll figure this out. I'll handle this."

Then she spun on me, eyes wide, "What do you mean you'll handle this?"

"Like I said, I'll figure it out."

"Tony! He was my boss! He knows where I live!"

"It'll be okay. Please, please, trust me."

I pulled into her driveway. Throughout the drive, I had been trying to reassure her, but my brain was on fire with discarded ideas and plans, my body burning with the blood pounding through me, but something, a plan, was coming together. I was sure I was going to die of a heart attack before I could bring it into play. I walked her to the front door and gave her the warmest, most reassuring hug I could muster and just held her for a while. We both cried against each other for a while, tears warming my cheeks.

"You're not going to do anything stupid," she said, her gaze searching my face for evidence of my intentions.

"Trust me," I said. "Everything is going to be okay. I promise." She relaxed slightly.

"I'll be back first thing tomorrow to work through this."

She nodded and kissed me on the cheek. "Goodnight."

"Goodnight."

As I walked back to my car, the horror of her ordeal threatened to let that alligator in my belly loose. The law would never give her justice. I had plenty of time to think on the long drive back to Lutz.

I had to do something. More insanity cascaded through my imagination. All the bad things I had seen came boiling up, forming the ingredients of a very dangerous stew. Watching the discovery of Diana De La Paz's shallow grave, hearing the circumstances of her murder; my dad sitting naked, bruised, bloody in our bathtub, the thugs and gangsters he had beaten down; Bert's murder; the agony of Kathy's horrific abuse; Susan's degrading exploitation; the relentless ridicule Priscilla endured, all the poisonous underbelly behind Tampa's veneer of normalcy. All of those incidents had one thing in common. They were all built upon cruelty and greed, enacted by aggression and hatred upon innocent people. I could not help any of them. I could not stop any of it. I was too young, too incapable. A great sadness welled up in me, a sadness that had troubled me for years that God had placed me in situations where I could only observe all this awfulness, where I wanted to help but *couldn't*, where I was incapable, helpless, or lacked the resolve.

Lori was my girlfriend. It was my job to protect her, and I hadn't. I couldn't protect her because I was not here. I could not let this slide. I could not miss this moment of retribution. All the times my dad had snapped into Protect Mode—at least, the times I knew about—swirled in my mind, like the time he'd rushed out of the car and clobbered the man who'd said *fuck* in front of me.

The drive home gave me the time and space to sort through the storm of horrible ideas swarming my brain and come up with a plan.

Instead of pulling onto my dirt road, I made a last-minute turn and drove towards Bobby's house. I needed a sounding board, someone to tell me what I might be missing.

It was 12:45 in the morning, so Bobby was in bed, but he got up without questioning me. He could see I was amped up, supercharged with purpose. He knew Lori well. We had double-dated with Bobby and his girlfriend. As I told him what Lori had told me, the pain and horror on his face resonated with mine, amplified it. Then I told him my plan.

"You don't need just a sounding board," he said. "You need backup."

"No. I can't let you."

"Bullshit, Tony. You can't do this alone."

"No, Bobby. I can't get you involved."

"Too late. Doesn't matter what you say. Lori is my friend, too."

He got dressed and in five minutes we were heading south toward USF.

Neither of us had been to this restaurant before. It had opened since I moved away from Skipper Road. In the car, Bobby's refinements turned my plan into our plan. It was Friday night, which meant that the place would be packed with people, mostly college kids. We would blend in with the crowd. We knew the names of the men involved, and we had their descriptions.

Even through my seething rage, I was not blind to the risks. We could get hurt. We could go to jail. But the overwhelming weight of accumulated injustices kept pushing me forward. There was no turning back. Growing up in the bar business, watching my dad handle drunks and thugs, standing in my own living room poised with a shotgun to kill the first son of a bitch who came through the door, the deadly middle school war that almost happened, being around the mob, all those things prepared me for this moment. I had watched my dad for years, how he could explode into decisive action without warning, and more than anything, how he and his posse could take the law into their own hands. I had zero faith that Lori would see justice from the police. Sister Dorothy Barbara's teachings about forgiveness and compassion, the kindness I had learned from my mother, all softer notions like that fled like rabbits from the wolf of vengeance inside me. It was time to teach this rapist bastard respect. It was time to teach him a lesson he'd never forget. It was time for justice. My kind of justice. I couldn't help but think of Charles Bronson in the movie *Death Wish*. Tonight, there would be a reckoning. For Diana De La Paz, for my dad, for Priscilla, for Bert, for Dory, for Kathy, for Susan, for my mom, and now for Lori, I was going to go full-Mafia on this motherfucker.

~

We parked my dad's Lincoln two blocks away in an apartment parking lot, locked the doors, and walked to the restaurant. I barely felt the chilly night. We would go in, get a table, order food. We were customers, just like everyone else.

Bobby and I walked in and sat down, practically vibrating with tension and purpose. The place was like a Hooters crossed with a pizza joint.

The owner worked the kitchen with all the other cooks. The kitchen was visible from the open tables and booth seating. There was no back door. Customers could watch as the kitchen staff cooked and prepped. The owner was tall, maybe 6'4", athletic build. As soon as I spotted him, the pressure in my chest cranked a notch tighter.

We ordered salads and drinks from a pretty, college-aged girl—pretty and blonde, just like Lori. And we waited, every thundering heartbeat ticking past like movie frames in slow motion.

And then, the owner, Allen, went into the bathroom. One moment I was sitting at a hard bench table waiting to make my move and the next I was in the bathroom with the man who had brutalized my girlfriend.

I took a spot next to the rapist at the adjacent urinal. His height and build dwarfed mine. Stack Bobby and me together and we equaled about one of him. But I had righteous fury on my side.

My hands were trembling as I pretended to unzip. I said to him, "How you doing?"

He nodded vaguely at me.

"Your name Allen?" I said.

He nodded. "Yeah, why?"

"So you know Lori then."

He almost restrained a double take, a glitch in his awareness, mouth opening as if he suddenly sensed danger. "Yeah, why?"

"This is for her, you motherfucker!"

That's when I leaped on him and started punching.

~

We beat him into a blood-slick pulp.

I straddled his chest, punching and punching, wishing my hands were hammers, axes. I seized his throat and squeezed. This motherfucker was going to die.

But seeing his blood all over my best friend made me pause.

In that moment, the ramifications of what I was about to do had a chance to seep into the tumult of fire in me, perhaps like the night my dad had held a gun to a man's forehead to defend his own life.

After what seemed like minutes of punching, I lurched off and stood over him. "We gotta go," I said to Bobby, "we gotta get out of here."

The rapist was a moaning, crying wreck, choking on his own blood, spitting pieces of teeth.

I put my foot on his chest and said, "I'm going to let you live, motherfucker. But I'm coming back one day to finish you off. The next time you think about raping anybody, let the thought of this night pass through your fucking mind."

The belief that I would do exactly that settled into him. It was as certain as the next sunrise.

Then we ran for our lives.

~

Bobby and I waited in the dark, cold palmetto grove for several hours, until just before the sun came up. By now, the truck had stopped circling. The screaming voices were gone, leaving only the sounds of our breathing, the crickets, the frogs. The morning dew had settled on my hair and all over my clothes. It was long-since past the restaurant's closing time. No police cars showed up. Only when all sounds of cars and trucks had fallen silent for at least an hour did we make a move.

We rose up and peeked over the tops of the palmetto bushes, shivering, caked with blood and dirt.

No activity. No movement. No sign of the truck or our pursuers.

We hurried back to my dad's Lincoln, darting across every patch of open ground like G.I.s in No Man's Land. As soon as the car came into view, we rushed toward it and piled in. I would have to spend some time cleaning the bloody filth out of it. Bobby was covered with it, even his shoes. I must have looked just as bad. My hands were aching, my knuckles torn, stiff and swollen.

"I'm so sorry I got you into this," I said, feeling sick in the pit of my stomach.

"Shut the hell up and drive."

I revved up the Lincoln's big V-8 engine and eased out of my parking spot, hoping not to be noticed.

"What should we do with our clothes?" I said.

"We gotta throw them away," he said.

I nodded. "Before we get home."

"Yeah, my mom will lose her mind if she sees this."

So we stripped off our clothes and rode the rest of the way to Bobby's house in our underwear. We threw the clothes in a garbage can.

Dawn was coming when I sneaked into my house and cleaned myself up. I didn't get much sleep, because I was going to check on Lori in a few hours.

When the morning news came on, I watched to see if what we did had made the local news. Were there any witnesses? Had any reporters gone to the scene? But there was nothing, which seemed odd.

But then again, the rapist knew exactly why we were there. The last thing he would want would be to draw attention to himself, with police asking about a possible motive for the attack.

The next morning at about 11:00, I went to Lori's house.

She took one look at my bruised, swollen knuckles, glanced over her shoulder at her parents in the living room, and mouthed, "What did you do?"

Lest her parents get a whiff of anything serious in the air, we went for a long walk around her neighborhood.

As we walked alone, she seized my arm. "What did you do?"

"Bobby and I went to the restaurant—"

Her eyes bugged out of her head. "What did you *do?*"

"We beat the shit out of your old boss."

"*What*? Tony! He knows where I live!"

"Lori—"

"Oh, my God! He's going to come after me!"

"I took care of it."

"No, you didn't! *You* get to go away back to college! He's going to find me and finish me off so I don't tell anyone else!"

I took a deep breath and kept my voice calm, as reassuring as I could make it. "He'll never bother you again. I'll stake my life on it."

"Tell me everything," she said.

I told her the whole story. She listened intently, waves of emotion crashing through her: elation that some comeuppance had been delivered, the horror of reliving her own experience, terror that he would come after her, fear for my and Bobby's safety.

When I finished, I said, "He knows not to go near you ever again."

She clutched her elbows as she walked. "And how does he know this?"

"I told him I was going to let him live tonight, but someday I would come back and finish him off."

"What? Are you crazy?

"I taught him a lesson. One he will never forget."

She clearly didn't know whether to laugh or cry.

"Lori, trust me on this one."

"Why should I? God knows what they're capable of!" Her voice was shrill and brimming with panic.

I thought, *God, please help me. I've made matters worse. Please help me make this right for her. Please help me make it okay.* It seemed that my next words came out in my father's voice. "Because I went there to kill him."

She stopped and faced me, hands over her mouth. "You...you did?"

"I was choking him. My hands were around his throat. At the very last second, I let him live. And he knows that now. He felt it. Every corner he ever turns for the rest of his life, he's going to have a moment of fear that I might be there, hiding in the shadows to finish him. He'll never so much as look at you again. And he'll make that clear to his buddies."

She seemed to chew on this for a while.

"There's something I want you to do," I said. "I want you to be strong if you ever run into him again." In the 1970s, Tampa was a much smaller town than today, and it seemed that everyone knew everyone.

"And do what exactly?" she asked, voice quavering.

"I want you to say these words: 'You were allowed to live that night, but my friends are not finished with you.'"

"You're kidding. I can't say that!"

"Yes, you can. You're strong. 'You were allowed to live that night, but my friends are not finished with you.' Can you remember that?"

We walked the rest of the way in silence and eventually made our way back to her house.

I found out some time later that Lori's experience was one of a long pattern. Several of my female friends had also worked at the same restaurant and shared similar stories of after-work parties where drugs were freely passed around. One of the girls confided in me about her attempted rape, but it was thwarted when someone walked in. Apparently, this debauchery had been going on for some time, and Lori became an easy target, one of their latest victims. These men were not just gang rapists. They were *serial gang rapists*. The owner and his friends gave the girls Quaaludes or slipped them in their drinks. Quaaludes are a powerful sedative and muscle relaxant with hypnotic effects—the date-rape drug of choice in the 1970s.

As soon as I learned this, a jolt of vindication shot through me. I had put the fear of God into that scumbag. I taught him a lesson he would never forget. Let him live in his own prison of terror, like Lori and all the other young girls he'd victimized.

Nine months later, Lori ran into him at a mall.

He spotted her and immediately turned away, but she pursued him, pulling strength from deep within her soul. I can only imagine the guts it took for her to go through with this.

He wouldn't meet her eye, tried to pretend she wasn't there.

She said, "Hey Allen, remember me? The night my friends came to visit you, you were allowed to live, but they're not finished with you."

He froze in his tracks like a deer in the headlights of an oncoming semi. Sweat burst out on his forehead, and he started trembling.

Lori turned and walked away, and he practically ran out of the mall.

I feel no remorse for what Bobby and I did to that sorry piece of human scum. For several years afterward, whenever I drove by the restaurant, I smiled and said, "Fuck with me, you son of a bitch, fuck with anybody close to me, and you'll pay the price." At 19 years old, I was full of testosterone, secure in my badass-ness, but I had held another person's life literally in my hands. The rush of enormous power in that moment was not something I'll ever forget. I wouldn't change a thing, but I do fear how badly it *could* have gone, how it could have altered my entire life—if I had killed him, if we had gotten caught, if the guys with meat cleavers had caught us.

Over the next few months, I had a series of "come to Jesus" talks with myself. What I did could have altered the path of my life forever, and not just my life, but my family's. What I did was 100 percent Art Scarpo.

But I was not Art Scarpo. I was my own man now, trying to forge my own path.

Inside me were also the influences of Sister Dorothy Barbara and my amazing mother, Sandella Scarpo.

There were so many opportunities for me to head down the path toward a life of crime. I could have kept growing and selling weed, become a druggie like a few of my friends. I could have jumped into A.J.'s porn empire with both feet and wallowed in hedonistic abandon. I could have emulated all the gangsters. I could have jumped into the seedier side of my dad's business, embraced all that animal darkness, and become a king of it, carving out my own little empire in a world fraught with organized crime and corruption. But something deep down told me that those things were not for me. Maybe it was pride. Maybe it was conscience. Maybe it was the belief that I was destined for something better.

I never would let that animal loose again.

I got one chance, one chance only, to redirect the course of my life. I still had to extricate myself from my father's expectations of me following in his footsteps, but that was still to come.

I have no doubt, however, that I still know the darkness intimately, like I know my own shadow. No matter how far I've come in life, if something happened to my children or my wife, if someone hurt them, that carefully chained animal, like a monster in the basement, would come roaring free, break its bonds, and exact retribution on the perpetrators. But I might not be so lucky next time, and that's a feeling I can't shake.

CHAPTER TWENTY-TWO

THE COLLEGE YEARS

I SLEPT LITTLE FOR days afterward. Nevertheless, as Monday approached, I had to return to Tallahassee. Knowing what I had just done turned my insides into acidic Jell-O, even as the power of it energized me for days afterward. All my muscles felt tight, on edge, ready for more action.

But would the rapist go after Lori, try to silence her? Would he be able to connect a few dots and come after me? Was I going to be the hunted? These questions were all the sharper knowing that I was leaving her behind in Tampa.

The four-and-a-half-hour drive to Tallahassee always gave me the chance to transform myself from my Tampa persona to the person I was trying to become: the up and coming FSU student, the young adult, the new man with a new life. However, the vivid, viscous memories of what I had done plagued me the whole way there. Even in class, I couldn't help thinking about the smell of the man's blood all over me and Bobby, the way it caked between my fingers, the way his nose had snapped under my knuckles, the way I had literally held his life in my hands. Neither could I forget about what he and two other men had done to sweet, innocent Lori, and when those thoughts returned, I wanted to rush back to

Tampa, find him, and do it all over again. It was an oscillating mix of remorse and thirst for vengeance

I called Lori every day to check on her mental and emotional well-being. Like me, she wasn't getting much sleep, hounded by nightmares of terror, violence, and shame. I was happy to be her therapist from two hundred fifty miles away. The hardest part was maintaining my composure as she was telling me the most heart-wrenching things. I wanted to cry with her, and then go find that son of a bitch again.

"Every day that goes by without harm to you is a good day," I told her. "We just get through it, day by day."

The same went for me.

For maybe two months, I spent my dreams trapped in a palmetto grove with Bobby, unable to get out, surrounded by monsters circling, monsters coming up under our feet, monsters coming out of the palmettos. Then the nightmares stopped, my jangling nerves slowly quieted, and the haunting thoughts never came back.

As the weeks passed, I eased back into my routine. Fears and rage faded into the hubbub of classes and social activities, and as the razor edges of the emotions dulled, I was able to search my soul for who I wanted to be. It was a concerted, conscious process. I started going to Mass in Tallahassee, praying for guidance, thanking God for keeping me, Bobby, and Lori safe since that night. I still didn't regret what I had done. It felt very biblical, "an eye for an eye." After all, it had become clear that this guy and his friends had done terrible things to many young girls. The pride of vigilante justice still suffused me, and knowing that he would henceforth live in terror made it all okay.

Lori and I continued to date, but how could anything ever be normal between us again? Even though I think she appreciated my standing up for her, avenging her, knowing what I was capable of may have scared her a little. The distance part of the long-distance relationship took its toll. Months before we finally called it off, the writing on the wall became clearer and clearer, but we had been through so much together, we were simply reluctant to let each other go. What had happened was our private secret, Lori's, Bobby's, and mine. The story has never been told to another human being—until now.

I could have lost my life that night. I could have been responsible for Bobby losing his. My children would not exist. My mother would have lost her son. The good that I have tried to do in the world would not exist. These truths sunk into me and took root, fertilized by my lessons with Sister Dorothy Barbara, the influence of my devoutly Catholic mother. They forced me to consider whether I really was who I thought I was. How many people think they're faithful, self-identify as religious, profess to follow church teachings, but in reality, do no such thing? Here I was messing around with women in my dad's bar at 17, 18, 19 years old, messing around with Susan, messing around with weed and alcohol, working as a bartender and enabling people's worst impulses, carrying a .38 in my pocket, ready to kill anybody who came after the sacks full of cash I was transporting. Not the description of a good Catholic boy.

It's difficult to think about now, but by this time, my mother was confined to a wheelchair, barely able to function in everyday life. I wanted so much to help her, to cure her, but I couldn't, and watching that inevitable decline was like dropping my heart in a patch of broken glass every time I came home.

My sister Debbie lamented that with Dad still working insane hours, there was no man of the house anymore, no one to stand in the living room with a shotgun. She didn't have that kind of fortitude, and she talked constantly about moving out. Even after the pressure from the Mafia relented, we were still targets because my dad was a public figure with money. People still lurked around our house late at night, wanting a piece of what we had. What Debbie may have experienced around that house, I cannot say. She couldn't handle my mother's illness much better than I could, but she had to endure it longer.

The guilt for me was enormous, but kids that age are selfish, self-absorbed, and I was no exception. It was me, me, me, and I was out. For the first time, I had a life resembling "normal," one that I was making for myself.

In my fraternity house, we dressed in coats and ties, and learned how to serenade girls. It was a structured world of absolute normalcy: you eat, you study, you go to class, and when the time comes, you party. I loved collaborating with classmates and fraternity brothers. I loved being around people who were as smart as or smarter than me. I devoured all the knowledge I could get my brain on.

When weekends came, I cajoled myself to continue going home regularly, but it became easier and easier to find reasons to stay in Tallahassee.

On the weekends, I did return to Tampa, I worked in the bar with my dad. The more my relationship with Lori unraveled, the more I was tempted by the women who threw themselves at me in the bar. Women galore, like most people can barely imagine. And they all wanted a piece of the owner's son, their efforts made all the more surreal by my dad's presence. Then on Mondays I would go back to Tallahassee and find myself immersed in gorgeous co-eds. The contrast between the women in the bar and the women of FSU was stark. The college girls were intelligent, articulate, the marrying kind of girls, whereas the bar girls were rednecks, heavy smokers, many of them still attractive, but often on the rough side, many of them damaged almost beyond repair. This contrast high-lighted the fact that what had once been my normal world, into which my dad wanted me to follow him, wasn't all that attractive. It wasn't the world I wanted. Knowing that these bar women wanted a piece of me, all under my father's watchful eye, made it feel dirt-ier than I wanted any part of.

Knowing that if I failed out of school I would have to go back to work at the bar motivated me to study all the harder.

My father didn't know it yet, but college had given me a pathway out of the bar business. This realization came not as an epiphany but as a series of incremental, internal revelations. Going back to Tampa to work at the bar felt like falling backwards. I could have done it, but I didn't want somebody else's ready-made path. I didn't want to fall backwards. I didn't want to walk with one foot in the criminal world. It would have been the easiest thing in the world, the path of least resistance, but it led into a dark, dangerous bog.

∼

I had known since eighth grade that I wanted a degree in adver-tising. I loved the creative side of it. I loved the thrill of building a deal, and of closing a deal. Advertising, it turned out, was very much like the Dance, the hustle I had learned working in the bar, the basics of human nature and interaction, seizing an opportunity when it presented itself. By the time I entered my second year of college, I knew going back to Tampa to work in the bar was the last thing I wanted.

The advertising program accepted only thirty-two students per year, so even getting in was not a foregone conclusion for a solidly B-student like me. I knew I had to work my butt off, and I did. I mustered all the sheer grit and determination I could, I studied hard, I never missed a class, I talked to my professors dozens of times, sometimes camping outside their offices to plead my case. I made myself known to them; everything I could do, I did.

And when the letter came informing me that I had been admitted to the advertising program out of hundreds of applicants, I quietly exulted. I made it!

My family was happy for me as well. If my dad had known what this meant for my future, he would not have been so happy; he still didn't know that I was done with the bar business. I just didn't know how to tell him.

But when I was accepted into the advertising program at FSU, my life truly entered the track that would lead me into my own adulthood, a life that I would make for myself.

There were a number of professors in the Communications Department, but the head of the advertising program was a man named Dr. Edward Forrest, a throwback hippie from the University of Wisconsin. His full, white beard made him look like Santa Claus, but underneath the jovial exterior was a brilliant, razor-sharp mind and a blazingly creative soul. It was 1981, and he took me under his wing.

When I entered his class, he told me, "From now on, you will only go to class half the time. The other half will be for creative thinking, out-of-the-box thinking, focus groups. As your lab, you're going to start your own ad agency, build it from the ground up."

"You're kidding me!" I said, thrilled at the prospect that my entrepreneurial bent would be used to attain my degree. The first two years of college had been the endless grind of core classes and exams.

"Can you dig it? You're going to pitch your services to local businesses, in collaboration with Florida State University. Any money you make, along with your classmates, we'll pool together to fund the betterment of this program."

I said, "That sounds amazing, Professor!"

"I'm only offering this special project to about a dozen students. Do you think you're up for that?" One of the reasons I was so excited about this program is that graduates often went on to work in the big Madison Avenue advertising firms. The idea of moving to New York thrilled me to the crown of my head. Now Dr. Forrest was telling me that he'd hand-picked li'l ol' solid-B me to join this elite group of a dozen students. When he told me who the others were, my jaw dropped. He'd mostly named all the students I had already identified as the geniuses of the program. I must have swelled with pride to half again my normal size.

"I'm more up for that than anything in my life," I told him.

So it began, and it changed the course of my junior year. I was spending half as much time as my peers in class; instead I was out there bird-dogging new clients for our fledgling ad agency. Most of our clients proved to be banks. I found myself pitching our services to bank executives all over Florida. We got the jobs because we were go-getters; they were amused by the fact we were college students, and doubly so because we were far less expensive than typical ad agencies. That hustle my dad had taught me, that sharp sense of human behavior so necessary to work the bar industry, the steps of the Dance, served me well, and pretty soon, inexpensive as we were in the wider realm of advertising, we were making shocking sums of money. Outside of our program, our peers were going about the standard educational grind, struggling for their As and Bs, but we were already out there doing it. By the end of our junior year, we had more clients than we knew what to do with. We had complete freedom to do what we needed to do. In truth, a bunch of college students had just launched a real live ad agency, and we were going like gangbusters.

I knew the advertising business was lucrative, but I had never realized just how lucrative until we started getting paid for our ad campaigns. All that money went into a pot feeding back into the program.

But Dr. Forrest was not motivated by money. He just wanted to see us out there in the real world, making it happen for ourselves, in many ways making it all up as we went, the ultimate test of hands-on education.

The first thing we did with all that money was throw an enormous party at the end of the school year, just for the twelve of us and Ed. By this time, he had become a friend, a true mentor.

Over the course of my junior year, I made a number of high-powered contacts in the business world, and the prestige of Florida State's program gave me a toehold in New York. I joined forces with a travel agency, becoming a kind of partner, which allowed me to put together a trip for myself and sixteen of my classmates to go to New York on a kind of exploratory trip over the summer. I set up meetings at Philip Morris, *Time-Life Magazine*, Ogilvy & Mather, BBDO, Foote, Cone & Belding, and others. Many of these companies employed alumni from Florida State.

When we all arrived in New York, sixteen of my cohorts and I, young and fresh and all dressed to the nines, these companies gave us the red-carpet treatment, extensive tours of their facilities, even lunch and dinner.

I fell head over heels in love with the Big Apple. It felt more vibrant and alive than any city I'd ever visited. It made Tampa and Tallahassee look like bruised, half-rotten, shriveled apples. The joy of it all heightened my senses, filled my eyes with stars. The food tasted better, the colors looked brighter, Times Square was a scintillating fever-dream. We were blown away by the brilliance of Broadway shows. I was going to move to New York someday. With all of the successes on my resumé, I felt like a shoo-in.

The goal of this was to give my cohorts experience and the opportunity to pitch themselves to these big, prestigious companies, but I had another motive as well. Because I was the facilitator, the lead man, it was a way for me to make myself known to these companies and solidify my standing through repeated exposure. These companies would know who I was, and they would remember me.

And it worked. I was tapped to do some contract consulting for Philip Morris on their major national campaigns, and my aim was to transition to a full-time permanent position for them after graduation. I also worked for the Adolph Coors Company as their young adult marketing coordinator when the beer company began to expand into the Florida markets. Because the drinking age back then was 18, they wanted full exposure on all the Florida college campuses.

As all of this unfolded, I felt unstoppable. I had opened the doors for my classmates at some incredibly powerful places—and I was still just a college student. At 21 years old, I had sat in on board meetings with CEOs, CFOs, and presidents of large corporations that had hired me to do their advertising.

When senior year came around, all of us looking ahead toward graduation, Ed dropped a bomb on us: "I don't know that we're going to continue this for another school year. I feel like you've accomplished everything I wanted you to do, and then some."

But abandoning it felt like an enormous waste that would squander everything I had accomplished. I jumped up immediately. "No, please! What we're doing is so great, I want to continue on." We still had jobs to do, clients to serve.

He looked at me and at the rest of us. "All right, Tony. I'll let you and three other students keep going. You can use the lab and the department facilities. But don't let it get in the way of the rest of your studies."

We readily agreed, and the four of us carried on. I was part owner of a real advertising agency, a successful one, as a senior in college. We continued working for our existing clients, again, mostly banks.

As we continued our advertising business over senior year, I must admit that the staggering sums of money we were making, coupled with the flush of the New York trip, went straight to my head. I let the ad agency work get in the way of the studies. I didn't need to study. I was already practically guaranteed my dream job. My grades quickly floundered. By that point, exams and papers felt like busy work, unnecessary backtracking, because we were already out there doing it. By the end of first semester, my grades were in the toilet, and I was in danger of going on academic probation. Ed pulled me aside one day after a particularly abysmal final exam.

The anger on his face was plain, all the more shocking in a man who looked like Santa Claus. "You had *one* goal!"

"I know, I know," I said. "I'm sorry—"

"You promised you would keep your grades up!"

"Yeah, I know but..."

"You're letting me down. You're slacking. You're letting everything go to your head."

"You're right, and I'm sorry about that." I shrugged. "The money is just too good."

He knew how much we had made the previous year, so no doubt he had an idea how much we were making this semester. "Give me a figure. Five thousand? Ten?"

"About twenty," I said with no small amount of pride. "Apiece." That was enough to put me through grad school.

"If you want to stay in this program, it's over."

"What!"

"You heard me."

"That's bullshit, Ed!"

"What's bullshit is going back on your word. You're here to *learn*."

I just stared at him for a moment, feeling a mixture of anger and shame.

Then he hit me with another bomb. "Look, Tony. I'm launching a new master's program, and I wanted you to be a part of it. You and two or three others have exceeded my expectations, but I can't justify bringing you onboard if you tank your grades."

I stared at him for another long moment. "You're kidding me."

He shook his head with slow disappointment as I stared at him.

If I let this opportunity slip out of my fingers, I would never forgive myself, so I decided, right then and there. "I'm really sorry, Ed. I promise it'll never happen again."

"No advertising agency. You got to let it go."

I took a long, deep breath, let it out. That was a *lot* of money. "Okay."

He grinned then. "You are going to be my lab rats for this new Master's in Marketing and Advertising. You're my guy, Tony."

I went out of that meeting with my feet barely touching the earth.

So, we closed the ad agency's doors and returned our attention to being students. The second semester I turned everything around and busted my butt in all my classes.

But my family knew nothing of this new advanced program, nor of the successful ad agency, nor that I had my sights set on moving to New York. The ad agency was money I had made all on my own, and I had told no one in Tampa about it.

My father was expecting me to graduate, come back to Tampa, and join him in the bar business. The whole Scarpo family was waiting for an invitation to my graduation ceremony, but I decided not to go. I was going to go straight into grad school and get an MBA, and I had the money to pay for it.

When my dad discovered that I had in fact graduated but told no one, he was furious. "The whole goddamn family has been waiting to hear, all this time, when your graduation is! The first Scarpo ever to go to college. Everyone is so proud of you! We all wanted to see it! And you didn't even invite us! I spent all this money, and I didn't even get to see my boy graduate."

"I'm sorry about that, Dad." I finally had to tell him, "I'm not coming back to the bar."

"What?" he said. "What are you talking about? It's time to come back to work." His face took on a darker shade of crimson, because I think he knew something like this was coming, like a bull poised to lock horns.

"Not only am I not coming back to work, I've owned my own advertising agency in Tallahassee for two years. I'm going to grad school to get a Master's in Marketing."

"I'm not paying for that." He glowered at me.

"That's fine," I said, shrugging. "I made a lot of money. I don't need you to pay this time." I had made enough to set myself up well. I owned my car outright. My colleagues and I had bought a modest house in Tallahassee. The costs of my tuition and books were well in hand.

He looked at me for a long time. "So, what, you're gonna pay for your own master's degree?"

"That's the plan."

"You're not going to come work at the bar."

I knew I couldn't, but I still couldn't say it with the finality it needed. "Not now. Not just yet." I was about to move into another level of education, one of the most exciting programs I could imagine. The taste of my own money was like the finest steak dinner. There was no way I was going to come back to the bar business.

But I still had no idea how I could tell him that, or what would happen when I did.

CHAPTER TWENTY-THREE

UP IN FLAMES

I PRACTICED THE CONVERSATION hundreds of times in my head, imagining how it might go.

I would say, "I'm sorry, Dad, but I can't go into the bar business with you. I don't want to take it over."

He would cross his arms, clench his teeth, and raise his voice. "Why the hell not?"

I couldn't even begin to give him all the reasons, because there were so many. It took me years before I finally understood them myself, piece by piece.

So I would say, "All those people that got out of line, the ones that you had to be tough with and beat the hell out of, the dozens and dozens of customers who drank too much and you had to teach a lesson and left them bruised and bloody, they're going to come back for me one day—and I'm not interested. I'm not you, and I'm not interested in fighting your battles from the sixties and seventies."

Hours of drinking hard liquor made a short man grow ten feet tall by the end of the night. At times, there was no choice but to use sheer brute force to get them under control. I was not a fighter and did not like the idea of constantly looking over my shoulder.

I would tell him, "I'm just not going to do it."

His face would be unreadable, a basalt block with magma surging behind it. He would be angry, of that there was no doubt, but the anger would come from hurt. He had done everything he did, fought all of those fights for me, for my sisters, for his family. And I was going to throw it back in his face.

I often wondered when that day would come, dreaded it, steeled myself for it.

But then something happened no one could have expected. The unimaginable.

Not long after the dust-up between my father and me after my undergraduate graduation, during the summer before grad school began, I received a horrible phone call in Tallahassee.

"The bar's gone," Dad said, barely able to speak. "Everything's gone."

"Dad! What happened?"

I had never heard him more disheartened in my life, not even when he was sitting in a bathtub full of bloody water. "The bar's gone. Burned down last night."

"Oh, no! How bad?"

"To the ground. It's all gone."

"Was anyone hurt?"

"Thank God, no, nobody got hurt."

"How'd it happen? Somebody coming after you?"

"No, it was bad wiring, an electrical fire. Fire marshal said the fire spread nice and slow until it hit the stock room and package store. Then bottles exploded like the Fourth of July."

I could imagine the ball of blue flame that must have ripped through the building when the liquor caught fire, making short work of the entire structure after that. "You had it insured, right?"

The silence on the other end of the line dropped the bottom out of my stomach. Finally he said, so quietly I could barely hear him, "I...uh...I'm not sure. And if I did, I'm sure it's not enough."

Normally, he kept his business wired tight at all times. He paid his bills, took care of the employees, and made sure everything ran smoothly.

In a quiet voice, he said, "I think I forgot to increase the old insurance policy from years ago. I'm pretty sure we're underinsured."

After everything he'd been through, all the danger and struggles, the mob, Bert's murder, now that he was at the height of success, the entire world he had built for himself was nothing but ashes. With the nature of the check-cashing business, tens if not hundreds of thousands of dollars in cash must have been turned to cinders. All that work, all that cash, all that energy and effort, now lying in a heap of smoking ruin, made me sick to my stomach.

"I'll be there this afternoon," I said and hung up the phone.

I sat down at the kitchen table and just looked at the floor for at least a minute. *Holy shit, what on earth am I going to do?* This was a big, big deal. I knew what I *had* to do, but that clashed with all of my plans and dreams.

But first I had to do one thing. I sought out Dr. Forrest on campus and found him in his office.

He greeted me cordially, but the look on my face must have told him that something terrible had happened. "Tony, what is it?"

"I think I have to go back to Tampa."

He looked at me for several moments. "I take it you're talking about leaving the program."

It was like a cold knife in my side after everything I had

accomplished. I sat in the chair across his desk and leaned on my knees. "I think so. I'm not sure, but...it's bad. It's really bad."

"Tell me what's going on."

"My dad's business just burned to the ground. He didn't have enough insurance on it. Everything he's spent his life building is just gone. I don't know if we'll be able to rebuild. All I know for sure is that my family needs me right now, and they might need me for a while. I have to sort through this."

"So you don't know if you'll be back in the fall."

I nodded slowly. "I don't know when I'll be able to come back, period."

He rubbed his chin thoughtfully. "You're a valuable part of this program, Tony. I'd hate to lose you. I know you have to get home to your family, but you're going to have the whole summer to think about this. The semester starts in late August. You'll have a better idea of the situation then."

I felt a modicum of relief at that. Maybe I could get everything ironed out and still come back, so I thanked him and got myself ready to hit the road for Tampa. As I walked out of our little house, with all my belongings in hand, I stopped and looked back. Would I be able to return? My insides were a sick stew of guilt, regret, and yearning, as if the fire in Tampa had burned my life down, too.

On the drive back to Tampa, I had four-plus hours to reflect on my future, unable to stop the dread that the future I had so enthusiastically built for myself was about to crash down around me. My dad was relentless. After this, he would want me there. I needed to be there for my family. How could I possibly refuse?

When I walked into the house, the nursing home smell made me want to cry, churning up great clouds of guilt inside me. My mother was confined to a wheelchair now, barely able to manage herself. My sisters were her caregivers and took care of her daily needs, children and parent switching roles. We went through several live-in nurse's aides with the hope that one would work out long term, but it was always a revolving door of different personalities. It broke my heart just to look at her in that condition. I jumped right back in to assist with my mother's care. One can never understand the hardship and pain that a family endures when a loved one is sick or physically handicapped. In our case, Mom's MS had found its way through her entire body, turning her into a quadriplegic who was unable to feed herself or go to the bathroom alone. She was completely dependent on me and my sisters, but she was our mom, and she was in pain, and we had to help. There was never a debate; this was now a time to be selfless and offer love and support at every turn.

My dad was sitting in the living room in his chair, staring at the wall, empty-eyed. When I walked in, he stood to greet me with what looked like tremendous physical effort, as if he was climbing out of that bathtub full of blood.

We hugged each other. He was still a man hard as a brick.

Then I hugged my sisters, and my mom, and I just let myself be immersed in the lake of collective sadness, coming up for air occasionally with snippets of conversation about inane things. My mom and my sisters were asking me about grad school and Tallahassee. My dad just sat in the living room, silent, shell-shocked.

Later that day, I drove him over to the bar—or rather, where it used to be. There's finality in seeing a catastrophe for oneself. As I got out of the car in the parking lot surrounding a blackened, smoking pile of bricks and charcoal timbers, more sadness washed over me for all the hours I had spent inside, the work, the fun, the memories. Recognizable carcasses of various things poked from the rubble. A melted pinball machine. The shattered surface of a pool table. The blackened bones of barstools, chairs, tables. Glass everywhere from exploding liquor bottles.

My dad was looking toward where the safe used to be. I could see the blockish shape of it, melted and deformed as if in a forge. No way any cash inside could have survived.

It was a day of sadness and sighs.

My dad had no idea what he was going to do now. He had lost everything, and he still had a family to support, a severely ill wife with enormous medical bills. It was like a close family member had just died unexpectedly. We were in shock. Aunts and uncles came over to lend their support, along with my dad's friends, his posse. Almost like a funeral, they all brought tons of food.

The grieving went on for a day or two, but as time passed, I got restless, itchy. No one was offering any solutions. My dad had turned into a zombie, going through the motions of getting up and pretending to be alive, but at times he barely registered what anyone said to him.

All my life, he had been the man with the answers, sharp and decisive, but now, I couldn't get anything out of him. He had survived beatings and assassination attempts and bounced back as strong as ever, but this had gut-punched him all the way to the core.

"What are you going to do, Dad?"

"I don't know."

"Come on, there has to be something!"

Silence.

The itchiness in my spirit increased. I had just spent two years in a wildly creative realm. I had just built a successful advertising business from the ground up.

I grabbed a swatch of butcher's paper that we used to wrap meat, then grabbed a pencil and started to draw.

I drew the shape of the lot. I sketched in where the bar had been, its interior layout. From memory, I knew its rough dimensions.

Before long, my efforts snared Dad's attention. "What are you doing?"

I said, "You know what? We had this place for how many years? I never liked where the check-cashing booth was. We were always sitting ducks. I also didn't like the liquor store. It was way too small. You never had an office. Somebody could have burst through the back door and we'd have been slaughtered. We don't need to worry about selling whiskey out of the back door anymore, because Sunday sales are legal now." While I spoke, I drew.

He stood there and watched me draw and draw.

"You know another thing? You never had live entertainment. You've got to have a bandstand, a stage."

"Well, I really never liked live entertainment," he said.

"All the best clubs have live entertainment. It's all about the music, Dad. It brings people in and they love to dance."

"What about the people that just want to drink in peace?"

I sighed and kept drawing, but the more I drew, the more he edged forward.

"We put the check-cashing booth here," I said, "along with a couple of nooks for guards, so they can see everything. If something happens, you just need to duck in here, and there would be protection with guns coming out of the shadows. We put your office here, with a *fireproof* safe. All this space in the back parking lot, we don't need that for a drive-thru anymore. We can make the package store five times bigger."

He sat down at the table and studied what I was sketching.

"So, you know you got all these lines of credit from the liquor salesmen. They'll set you up with stock. You know you'll pay it off in a heartbeat."

He nodded. "New stock wouldn't be a problem."

"What about that safe deposit box full of cash you showed me, way back when?"

He blinked as if coming out of a trance. "What about it?"

"All of us kids are growing up. The Trafficantes are gone. We're not going to get kidnapped anymore. Let's get as much as we need out of there. Can we do that?"

A long pause, then he said, "I guess we could." His face started to brighten, like a match flame struck in a black void.

By this time I had drawn a rough sketch of a new building, complete with features the previous bar did not possess.

"Tomorrow," I said, "I'll call an architect and see about getting some plans drawn up."

"But—"

"Dad, how many people do you know?"

"A shitload."

"How many of them are carpenters, builders, electricians, plumbers?"

We said it together. "A shitload."

"Dad, these are your people. Half of them would lay down in front of a train for you, and the other half would blow up the tracks before the train got there. I'll bet you could get Jerry and his bull-dozer down there by tomorrow afternoon."

He leaned back, crossed his arms, and rubbed his chin. The bulldozer treads were starting to rumble in his brain.

~

Myself, my dad, and all the men who had been loyal to him for years, these southern-fried rednecks and working men, stood beside the still-smoking ruins of Art's Lounge, next to a bulldozer, a loader, and a dump truck. We didn't even have to ask for help. These guys just showed up with "What do you need me to do?" already on their lips.

The rubble and old foundation were gone within a day. As things started to happen, my dad re-emerged from the depths of his despair and became more and more like himself again. He was out there doing things, moving, making things happen.

What was different this time was that *I* was making it happen, too. I worked with the architect to finalize the design of the new bar—complete with a bandstand. I worked on PR and advertising campaigns to let the community know that we were going to come back stronger and better than ever.

The old bar had been built in the 1950s, but we were coming back with something bigger, better, modern. It was a testament to true teamwork and family, the way that happened.

Over the summer, construction began on the new building, and by August, it was clear that my dad was back in the saddle, excited for the future, thriving on the idea of building something bigger and better than it was before. Amid all the hard work and organization, my own footing started to feel firm again. My dad was looking to me for guidance and camaraderie. We were building something together, and he couldn't have done it without me. We worked nonstop, seven days a week, morning, noon and night for three to four months. Watching that building rise, from concrete foundations to stud walls to rafters, filled me with satisfaction every single day.

By this time my mother and sisters and most of my aunts knew that the bar business was not for me. My dad and all of his brothers, on the other hand, hoped and wished and prayed that after graduate school I would return and take over the business. It was the Italian way. I think my dad knew all along that I was not cut out for the bar business, that I had set my course toward other things, but that didn't stop the wishful thinking nor the tension every time he was reminded of my real intentions.

I'll never forget the way he looked at me when I told him I was going back to college. I had a master's degree to finish.

He didn't yell, he didn't scream, but the expression of horrible disappointment on his face almost broke my heart.

I said, "Dad, I got to do what I got to do."

And so as the new school year rolled around, I went back to Tallahassee. My actions had made a difference. The bar was bigger and better, and I helped bring it all together.

Like many times before, I had to say goodbye to my mother. It got harder and harder as her illness progressed. Even though she was happy for me, when it came time to leave, she would always cry and ask me when I would return. The guilt of leaving her behind always stayed with me and became a hidden sadness that never left me alone. I realized the burden placed on my sisters in my absence and tried my best to comfort them by phone. It was an awful struggle to leave that world, knowing that it may be the last time seeing my mom. My sisters deserve all the credit for taking care of her; without them, she would have been placed in a nursing home at an early age. But they were just young girls, probably as scared as I was, but they endured and sacrificed in a way that few people can understand.

After Debbie married and moved away, the total responsibility for my mother's care fell upon Antoinette. I have never seen or met a stronger person in my life, not even my dad. During her final years and long after her death, my mother Sandella left a lasting impression on all of us and her spirit continues to live on through my sister Antoinette.

I returned to Tampa in the autumn to help with the Grand Opening of the brand-spanking-new Art's Lounge, which was a huge success, packed with friends and family and customers old and new, all the familiar names from my childhood, my dad's clan and many more. All there to support our family. I reveled in the glory of working beside him and pouring drinks for all our loyal customers. And the band stage was a perfect addition to the new space, being used for the first time. Everyone danced the night away.

When I came back on holidays and summer breaks, I walked into that place with an incredible smile, my chest swelling with pride. When I saw a band up on the stage, I nodded with satisfaction. *I* had done that. That was *my* bandstand.

When our sparkling new building got the business rolling again, Dad's previous empire became a double empire. The check-cashing business alone exploded to over a million dollars a month. I was happy for him, proud that we had pulled it all together and rebuilt.

~

Charging toward my destiny in the Big Apple, I blasted through my graduate program in only one year. Looking back, I have no idea how I managed it. As I neared completion of my master's thesis and graduation loomed, I started the interview process with the various large companies I knew from the advertising business and from my trip to New York. I still yearned for Madison Avenue; that was my dream.

Together, my dad and I had rebuilt his empire from ashes. We had worked as a team in a way that he always wanted. We had worked with the architect, the builders, the designers, the suppliers to create a bigger and better empire, this time with my fingerprints all over it. We had both loved every minute of it.

And then I went back to my own life, pursuing my dreams and trying to make it on my own. The world was now mine and I was ready to make my mark, or so I thought.

Chapter Twenty-Four

A Diamond in the Rough

IN MANY WAYS, my life had long been planned for me. My father would raise his son, teach him the bar business, and have him eventually take over all that he built. But that was not the plan I had for myself.

Ever since I was in eighth grade, I had wanted to enter the field of advertising. Madison Avenue sounded like the most exciting place in the world, and that's where I was aiming my trajectory.

These two conflicting plans could only diverge.

Throughout my year in grad school, I was trying to build upon the contacts I had made in New York as an undergraduate, aiming for a job at one of those prestigious advertising firms or big companies.

But after I graduated with my master's, no jobs were forthcoming. I couldn't understand why. My resumé was stellar. I had already helped create a successful ad agency while I was still an undergrad. I had partnered with a travel agency to organize trips for not only me and my classmates, but also the students coming up behind us. But this was 1983. The economy was in shambles and was only slowly recovering; nobody was hiring.

Meanwhile, the pressure on me from my dad was constant, like a coastal wind that never died.

I finally received a job offer from a small, New York-based advertising firm, but with a starting salary of only about $30,000, this was not a happy event. I had done my research. I knew what it cost to live in Manhattan, as well as each of the other boroughs, even New Jersey. To have any kind of life, I would have to commute a couple of hours in each direction, just to afford to live, unless I wanted to live college-style with six guys in a roach-ridden matchbox in the armpit of a Queens back alley. I was used to watching hundreds of thousands of dollars flow through my dad's bar. There was no way I was willing to live in New York City on that kind of salary, especially after how much money I had made throughout my college career.

As soon as I heard that number, after all my hard work and high hopes, the sky crashed down around me.

I just sat there, repeating to myself, "There's no way. How could this be happening?"

So, after graduation, I moved back to Tampa. To say I was floundering would be an understatement. This was not part of the master plan. Accepting the dissolution of my dreams took some time, complicated by the fact that, by this time, I had been away from my family for going on five years. The guilt became a weight so enormous I couldn't escape it. My mom was entering the final stages of her illness; she didn't have much time left on Earth. I told her, "I can't be away from you anymore." It was one of the saddest moments of my life.

Debbie was long married and out of the house. My sister Antoinette was therefore taking the brunt of caregiving for my mom. Antoinette was suffering terribly with the burden of single-handedly taking care of our mother. I saw it on her every time I walked in the house. She looked far too old for someone barely out of high school. She had no life of her own, few friends, no prospects, but she did have a very loyal and loving boyfriend who went on to marry her. They are still together to this day.

With the new and improved Art's Lounge, my dad was back to working like a dog, raking in piles of wealth, more than anyone needed, but by this time, there was no such thing as enough for him. He had to have it all. He still pressured me to come work for him, but I couldn't do it anymore, even after the success we had in rebuilding the bar. So, I started looking for a job in Florida.

I remember giving my resumé to a headhunter, who thought it was impressive. He arranged for an interview with General Electric. GE apparently agreed with him, and pretty soon they offered me a job, with a great salary, company car, and some nice perks, an incredible compensation package for a kid right out of college. But there was one stupid, horrible caveat. They wanted me to be in sales. I hated sales. And they wanted me to move back to Tallahassee to handle the North Florida/South Georgia territory for their consumer electronics division—TVs, VCRs, camcorders, audio equipment. But with my options limited, I took the job. Maybe I could learn to love being in sales. It would have been a great job for someone interested in sales.

So, after spending six months in Tampa and helping out around the house, I had to tell my mom that I planned to move away again. It broke her heart, and mine, too.

GE sent me to the Dale Carnegie Institute for training. They sent me to GE headquarters for training. They sent me to a major electronics show in Las Vegas. Before I knew it, I was traveling extensively, getting the finest training from a blue-chip company. I told myself, *You don't like being a salesman? Shut the hell up, Tony. Appreciate what you've got. Nothing about your work is exciting, but you're being given all this incredible knowledge, and all you have to do is sell your quota.* Meeting my quota was a breeze, because consumer electronics practically sold itself. I stood to make at least triple what I would have been making on Madison Avenue, and with housing in Tallahassee a fraction of the cost.

The first major trouble with moving back to Tallahassee was that it was no longer my college town. All my friends had graduated, and many of them had moved elsewhere. The parties were over. We were adults now. I came to hate Tallahassee almost from the moment I came back. The guilt of leaving my mom again ran too deep. My only other option at that point was going to work at the bar, though, and I had long steered myself away from that path. My Big Apple dream was gone. I couldn't bear to live so far from my mother anymore. Even Tallahassee felt like a stretch.

To crank up the family tension even tighter, the relationship between me and my dad had deteriorated to the point that the tension between us was palpable. His internal conflict must have been immense, because on the one hand, I was a success with a master's degree, soon to be working for one of the world's largest companies; on the other hand, I had betrayed him, turned my back on the family. He must have been in some way happy to have raised an independent son, but my actions went so strongly against Italian tradition that it saddened him, which emerged as a kind of passive-aggressive bitterness and hostility.

The tension between us lasted at least two years, and even during that time he was hoping secretly that things wouldn't work out with GE and I would come home to Tampa. He was always quick with the back-handed comments about my foolishness for not tak-ing over the empire and all that money. I had a good salary plus commissions, but he laughed when I told him how much I was making compared to the cash flow at the bar.

In other Italian families across Tampa, the kids all went back to their families' little empires, and they became wealthy very quickly—but under their fathers' control. That could have been me, right out of grad school. But that wasn't for me. My entire ex-tended family thought I was insane.

So I worked at GE, but my heart was not in it. The drive to do something else gnawed at me constantly. The entrepreneurial spirit kept pulling me elsewhere.

Adding to my disillusionment with corporate America was the way GE and other companies like it treated their employees. Gone were the days when a man would get a job, work there for forty years, and retire with a pension and gold watch—if those days had ever really existed at all. GE actively recruited college graduates like me and used them to replace the people who had been there for twenty years, because they could pay the kids a fraction of what they were paying the people who'd given a huge chunk of their lives to the company. I found it unspeakably sad and depressing.

The more my dissatisfaction grew, the more I researched, soul-searched, and prayed. What did I want my life to look like? Who did I want to be? Who did God want me to be? What business would stoke my entrepreneurial spirit?

~

Since my job at GE required little brain power, I had plenty of free time to churn through resources and books, building a base of knowledge that might free me from my corporate bondage. I studied the lives and practices of an array of successful people. What made them tick? What kind of people were they? What constituted a true entrepreneur?

Eventually, however, there came a day when I simply had enough. It could have been a particularly rough weekend in Tampa seeing my mom's decline. It could have been one more mind-numbing meeting. But I gave my boss a two-week notice.

He looked at me like I was insane. "Tony, no one ever resigns from General Electric. We stay here for life."

My next thought was: *Yeah, until you lay me off in twenty years and hire a kid fresh out of college.*

After that: *Maybe I am crazy, but I've seen enough. I'm never going to work for anyone else again.*

I had made enough money to sustain myself for a little while, so I took that opportunity to continue my research and reflect on what I wanted to do.

Sometime during this period, I encountered three books that would change my life. Each one of them rang me like a gong.

The first was *The Art of the Deal* by Donald Trump, long before he ever dreamed of running for president. I happened to be in a bookstore and picked it up soon after it was released. I was still yearning for New York. I had been inside Trump Tower, and he was this larger-than-life personality all over the press. The way he described the art of the deal reminded me of the Dance, the same dance I had learned at my dad's bar and in business school. I found his descriptions of negotiating skills and the way to handle real estate fascinating. One insight from the book that stuck with me was the story of how, when he was trying to acquire bank financing to refurbish and develop one of his properties, he instructed a crew of bulldozers to move enormous piles of dirt around the property every day, just to make it look like there was activity. A piece of property that sits dormant and unattended makes potential investors apprehensive, but seeing things happening sparks them to act, to jump into the project, to lend money. Business was, in many ways, all about perception.

The second book was Tony Robbins' *Unlimited Power*. Like Donald Trump, he was all over the press and television. I saw his story on *60 Minutes* or *20/20*, and it energized me to pick up his book. The way he inspired people with his charisma and energy fascinated me. I was building the courage to launch my own venture, to build upon my existing skills to be a successful independent businessman. One of the major tenets of Robbins' philosophy was to "take action," meaning you could spend your whole life thinking about doing something or being somebody, but until you acted, nothing would materialize. I later went to see him speak and spent the extra money for a front row ticket. He was an amazing motivational speaker, and I sat there in the front row, thrilled, inspired, soaking it all in. I came away from that event energized, but my enthusiasm was still undirected. I felt like an armed cruise missile searching for a target lock.

It didn't happen all at once, but the target slowly resolved, like emerging through a fog.

I saw an article about the diamond industry. The diamond business—literally for the entire planet—was controlled by one company: De Beers. It was the world's largest monopoly, strictly and meticulously controlling the mining and distribution of *rough*—the term for uncut diamonds. How had De Beers become a global monopoly? Something about that story sparked my interest, so I went to the library in search of everything I could find relating to the diamond industry, and I found a book called *The Story of De Beers,* a history of the company, its founders, and the diamond industry itself.

The more I read about how the diamond industry worked, the more my target came into focus. The profit margins were so huge that if I could sell a diamond for *half* the normal markup, I would still make a huge profit. Everyone in the diamond industry, from De Beers to the cutters to the jewelers, all made huge profits. For a simple chunk of carbon dug from the earth, the same element as charcoal and graphite, the profit margins were so enormous it seemed they should be illegal. Over the course of almost a century, De Beers spent hundreds of millions of dollars in marketing to convince Americans that every engagement and wedding ring *must* have a diamond in it. In Europe, people still wear simple gold wedding bands, but Americans had to have *diamonds,* and they were willing to spend fortunes small and large to acquire them.

Somewhere in those three books was my future.

The diamond industry was one of the most profitable, with huge profit margins and sustained demand. But it was also one of the opaquest.

As I walked through the malls past all those jewelry stores, contemplating my future, I flirted with the idea that that might be the path I was seeking.

I started writing notes, shuffling them into the beginnings of a business plan, drawing from my recent education and experience with advertising and marketing. Maybe I could do this.

There was only one barrier in my way, but it looked insurmountable.

I was not Jewish.

De Beers controlled the distribution of rough, uncut diamonds, but every single diamond cutter was Jewish, most of them Hasidic Jews living in Antwerp and Tel Aviv. Antwerp, Belgium was the historical home of the diamond cutting trade, although during and after World War II, many of those people fled the Holocaust to Tel Aviv. Every single diamond released to the consumer market came from De Beers and went through the Jewish gem cutters before it arrived at the jeweler, many of whom were also Jewish. It was a close-knit clan. You were either invited into it or born into it. I was neither, a young Italian Catholic kid from Lutz. I had a ton of street smarts but the wrong kind of surname. Furthermore, I knew nothing of gems, precious metals, or jewelry. Fortunately, the last deficiency was fixable.

But I had to come up with my own business model.

~

My business plan did not involve opening a jewelry store. I would open an office specializing in diamond engagement rings only, where buyers could come, by appointment, and I would teach them about these precious gems. Each customer would get personalized service and learn about the four Cs: *cut, color, clarity,* and *carat* weight. Because I would not have a huge store and its attendant inventory, my overhead would be almost nonexistent.

The markup on diamonds was so enormous that I could sell at deeply discounted prices and still make a profit. Customers could get bigger, better diamonds for less money. But I still needed a way into the industry.

A term little used in everyday conversation but critical in the diamond industry is *sightholder*. A sightholder is a company sanctioned by De Beers as a bulk purchaser of rough diamonds, the only companies authorized to do so. Today, fewer than ninety sightholders exist worldwide, all of them Jewish-owned.

This was one of the first things I discovered as I was poring through the jewelry industry trade publications, trying to learn who the players were and how to contact them.

Every telephone number had a New York area code. I started calling. From New York, my phone calls were re-routed to Antwerp or Tel Aviv.

The conversations went something like:

"Hello, I'm starting a jewelry company in Tampa, Florida, and I'm thinking about buying diamonds from you, gold, settings, et cetera."

"Excellent!" the voice would say in a French or Israeli accent. "What is the name of your business?"

"I don't have that yet. Right now, I'm just gathering information."

"That is fine. What is your name, sir?"

"My name is Anthony Scarpo."

There would a slight pause, then they would laugh and hang up.

Every time, the moment they heard my very Italian name, I would hear a *click*.

Over the course of about three months, I made dozens of phone calls, all ending in a dismissive *click*. I found myself at a loss for how to talk to them. Even after months of studying the industry, I was still learning how to talk the talk.

What they didn't realize is that I was just as driven as my father. I had learned it from him. I was never going to be told "no" just because I wasn't Jewish. They controlled all the gem cutting, but I *would* find a way in.

At somewhere around Phone Call No. 50, a man named Jacqui Ekstein picked up the phone at Eknam Diamond, with offices in New York and Antwerp.

I launched into the pitch that by this time I could have given in my sleep, fully expecting to be disconnected in midsentence.

The voice that responded was slow, cultured English with a slight French-Belgium accent. "Tony, slow down a bit. Talk to me. Do not waste my time. Just tell me what you're trying to accomplish."

His smooth drawl slowed me down, made me deepen my tone and explain what I was trying to do. It was like talking to someone from South Georgia.

He listened quietly for a minute or two, then said, "Oh, my friend, you are wasting your time. No one will do business with you. Do not get into this business."

"That's what I keep hearing. A lot."

"Who is your jeweler?"

"I don't have one yet. First I need a diamond source."

"Who's going to study these stones for you?"

"Again, first I need to find a supplier."

"Tony, Tony, this is not how the business is done."

"That's what people keep telling me. But I already have a client, someone ready to buy a stone."

I had created business cards for my still-imaginary business, with just a phone number, a Mailbox USA address, and "Diamond Importer" printed under my name. I had recently run into a woman from my high school class, and when she told me she was engaged I gave her a card. Soon after, she called me and asked if I could help her with a diamond. She was my first glimmer of a customer.

I said, "Jacqui, I think I can sell a two-carat oval diamond."

"What do you mean? What is the make? What is the color? You have to be specific with me about this."

I answered his questions as best I could, feeling woefully out of my depth the entire time, but I was also a believer in the adage: *fake it till you make it.* Why he stayed on the phone with me, I wasn't sure. Maybe he had an Italian girlfriend once.

He said, "Tony, what are you doing trying to get in this business? It is not for you."

"Look, Jacqui, I'll never know if I can do this if you don't send me a stone."

"I'll tell you what I'm going to do. You send me a check for $5,000. I send you the stone. If you sell the stone, I cash the check. If you don't sell the stone, you send it back to me, I tear up the check."

I didn't have anything to lose. And I didn't have $5,000, so it was going to be a bad check—unless I sold the stone. "Thank you. That sounds great to me."

This was my introduction to another of the cornerstones of the diamond industry—trust. Hundreds of millions of dollars are exchanged on a handshake. Your word is your bond, and your reputation is everything. Your *name* is everything.

I sent him the check, and he sent me the diamond. I mail-ordered all the accoutrements for displaying a diamond—the tweezers, the loop, the stand, the light, the polishing cloth. I had also invested in a handful of simple solitaire settings. Then I set up a meeting with the old classmate in the office of a friend who worked for an attorney. The attorney happened to have several open offices, so it all looked very professional.

I didn't know what the hell I was doing, sitting there with all this stuff. All I knew was the retail price, my cost, and that that two-carat rock sparkled like crazy.

When the customer and her fiancé walked in, I turned on all the charm I could muster, and spent about forty minutes educating them on the specifics of the diamond—and then most importantly, the price. She took another long look at that stone, sparkling on its bed of black velvet, and her eyes teared up with joy and she clasped her hands to her chest, gushing. Her fiancé took one look at her and said, "We'll take it."

I said, "Excellent! You're going to be so thrilled. Wait here."

Then I immediately ran outside and down the street to a jeweler who I'd begged to set the stone for me. I gave him the traditional solitaire setting, and he grudgingly set the stone while I waited. Strangely, jewelers are not diamond people. They're just jewelers, people who make jewelry, create things. They're not terribly skilled at selling diamonds.

With sparkling treasure in hand, I ran back to the office and presented the customers their stunning new wedding ring. They wrote me a check on the spot, and when they left, all of us—well, maybe not the fiancé—were floating on air. I had made maybe $1,000 profit in five minutes on this ring and saved them thousands of dollars at the same time.

When I got Jacqui back on the phone, I said, "You can cash that check in two days."

"You are kidding." His voice told me he thought I was full of shit.

"No, I'm absolutely not. You cash that check. Pretty soon, I'll be calling you again."

I could hear him smile a little. "Very well, Tony."

Everything evolved from that moment. I rented out my own private office space in a professional building, and I was in business.

I put a great deal of thought into my business name. I knew that it had to evoke trust and confidence, but most importantly it had to be special to me. The name that I kept coming back to was Anthony Louis Limited. I wanted to honor my family, specifically both of my grandfathers, Antonio Scarpo Sr. and Luigi Ciccarelli. In the diamond business, name was everything, and nobody was going to steal mine from me or tell me it was "less than" because it was Italian. I knew they were looking down on me with both pride at what I had already achieved and curiosity about whether I could really pull this off.

Little did I know that Jacqui Ekstein was the suave and savvy Casanova of Antwerp. He was a few years older than me, but had a full head of luxurious dark hair, tiny gold-rimmed John Lennon spectacles, and a smooth Belgian demeanor. After our first transaction, we hit if off quickly, becoming like brothers from another mother. We spoke to each other often, sharing stories and little triumphs.

I spent the lion's share of my budget on marketing—that was something I *knew* how to do. I didn't concern myself much with keeping much inventory of ring styles and settings. The real money was in the diamonds, and for that I used Jacqui's inventory. I never kept diamonds on hand, because everything was done on a telephone handshake. If I needed a stone, he shipped to me immediately, then I paid him immediately. Not unlike my dad's check-cashing business, hundreds of thousands of dollars began to flow *through me*, and I kept my cut. I never owned any diamonds.

Jacqui took me under his wing, introduced me to the Jewish families, flew us both to Las Vegas for the largest diamond industry show in the world, the Jeweler's Circular Keystone, billions of dollars in diamonds and other precious stones under one roof. The armed security at this event was like walking up to Fort Knox.

He told me, "Tony, you need to learn. Everything you're doing right, you're doing by accident. You want to be big in this business, you need to learn." So I did my best to learn everything I could as quickly as I could. I was starting to make some money, but I was still a minnow swimming with killer whales. The truth is, I felt very stupid for a very long time. I had to learn the ropes from these Jewish families.

The strongest word in the diamond business is *mazal*, a Hebrew word meaning *fortune,* but in this context, it meant *sold*. Every negotiation is finalized with a handshake and a *"Mazal!"* Even today, millions of dollars in cash and stones routinely change hands to the sound of *"Mazal!"*

Just because I was Jacqui's protégé did not mean I was accepted, however. Nearly everyone I met treated me with barely concealed disdain. I was encroaching on *their* world, and there was no way they would ever accept me, a Gentile, into their clan. But they would accept my money.

That first girl from high school spread the word about me. I contacted all my fraternity brothers and high school friends, most of whom where now young professionals of marrying age, and they came to me. Then they sent their friends to me. Another customer stream surprised me. One might not expect the working people who frequented Art's Lounge would be in the market for a $4,000 diamond ring, but Bill the electrician might have some rainy-day money squirreled away for his thirtieth wedding anniversary, or Frankie the truck driver might want some sugar for his girlfriend. They all knew me, and word got around.

I built my business by recognizing that I would be dealing with couples, and men were clueless about diamonds and jewelry. Men didn't want to deal with catalogs and showrooms. I brought them to my office to *teach them* about diamonds, one on one, so they could feel informed, and then the sale became an understated side effect.

When a man called me, the conversation usually went something like:

"I'm thinking about asking Holly to marry me, and I want a diamond engagement ring."

"Oh, wonderful, Joe. That's fantastic!"

"I'm thinking about getting her a diamond."

"What size?"

"Uh, maybe one carat?"

"A round diamond? Square?"

"Uh, yeah, a round diamond kind of like my mom's."

"Okay, a round diamond, one carat. What kind of budget range are you thinking of?"

"Oh, I don't know, Tony. What do these things cost?"

"Something like that typically runs between two and six thousand dollars."

He would whistle or give a long pause.

I would say, "Would you like to make an appointment? You can come to my office, I'll teach you all about diamonds. We need to educate you first. Then, if you like, you can look at some stones."

The mix of relief and trepidation was always there. "Let's do that."

So then Joe and his fiancée would come in, pick a stone, and I would give them their choice of maybe five settings, and then have the stone set for them.

Jacqui taught me early to never show them only one diamond—show them three, representing a range of quality and pricing. Every diamond is graded and priced on the four Cs: cut, color, clarity, and carat weight. He would send me a range of stones via registered mail, fully insured. I would sell Joe one of the stones and ship the other two back to Belgium. If the diamonds were large enough, worth more than the maximum insured amount of $25,000, Jacqui would bring them to me personally. Every time he brought me a diamond, I sold it. I worked with Jacqui over the course of about a decade, by the end of which my word was good throughout New York, Antwerp, Tel Aviv.

As my business grew, there came a time when Jacqui couldn't supply all my needs, so I was forced to branch out. He allowed me to drop his name when necessary, and that opened doors just enough for me to meet another global diamond cutter. Then that introduction lead to another and then another, and so on. Finally, after all this time, when Anthony Louis Limited called any major player in the diamond business, the phone calls were answered.

My company name became a fixture in the diamond industry and all over Florida, a testament to those two Italian men who had made it in America, who were proud to be Americans and proud of their names. I had come far in a short time, and I credit my heritage and the perseverance ingrained in me from the start.

But that doesn't mean it was an easy process. I was shocked to find myself negotiating with diamond suppliers in a way not unlike how my dad dealt with liquor salesmen. What was strange was how this Dance dovetailed perfectly with the way the sightholders already did business. The dance steps were familiar: vitriolic verbal fanfare interspersed with personal moments to relax the tension, loudness to the verge of yelling at one another, then a pause, then hammering at each other again. But we didn't fight too hard, because we both knew we were going to make money. It was only a question of how much. I was still an outsider to them, but my reputation preceded me. In the end, they respected me and wanted my money.

Once the business was starting to roll, I used all of my well-earned skills at marketing and advertising to expand my clientele beyond my circle of friends and their friends. There was one market I yearned to tap. Tampa had been, for a very long time, a breeding ground for millionaires. Even nowadays, there seems to be a higher percentage per capita of millionaires in Tampa than almost anywhere in the US. Those folks do love their sparklies. But they did not yet know about me, and I didn't know how to reach them. One effective marketing avenue I stumbled upon early, however, was advertising in local theaters as part of the pre-movie slide show.

In a testament to the efficacy of pinpointed advertising campaigns, it so happened that at a Sunday matinee, a lady saw my advertisement. She called me on Monday morning to tell me she had seen my ad and that she and her husband were looking to upgrade their diamond. We had a pleasant conversation, and she told me what she was looking for.

First of all, I rarely received phone calls from women. Ninety-nine percent of the time, my calls came from men seeking knowledge and a good price.

Secondly, she said she wanted a six- to eight-carat flawless diamond.

As I absorbed what she had just said, my mouth fell open. Was she joking? Pulling my leg? I wasn't even sure what a stone like that would cost. Easily over a million dollars. I took a deep breath and slowly moved forward with some prequalifying questions, realizing if I pressed too hard, she might push back. Something in her voice felt very real, very authentic.

"Ma'am, I've never received a request like this, and this is an unusual call for someone living in Tampa, Florida. Do you mind if I ask you what you do for a living and who is your husband?" I said.

She had a sweet, cultured Southern accent. "I don't mind if you ask at all. Have you ever heard of Gatorade?"

"Indeed I have," I said.

"Well, my husband is one of the inventors and was a former professor at University of Florida," she said.

I knew that several of the inventors lived in the Tampa Bay area, were a part of the city's high society, and one or two of them were professors at the University of Florida, so there was something in her voice that rang true.

We talked for a bit, and she told me her name was Gretchen. She was kind, patient and had a great wit about her. She may have sensed this was a huge opportunity for me and seemed to relish the thought of giving me the business.

I thanked her very much for her phone call, and I told her I would be happy to help. I would have some diamonds to show them the very next day.

Except that there was no way I would be able make this deal using my normal methods. I had no diamonds on hand, and had never even seen a diamond of that size except on display at the Las Vegas JCK show.

Plus, I couldn't show them just one diamond. I had to show them several. And Jacqui couldn't provide me with a group of stones of that size and quality.

Thanks to Jacqui, I had made some inroads with other diamond cutters in New York by this time. They still didn't like dealing with an Italian, but they knew my money was good. When I told them what I was after, and that the sale was a done deal—it was only a matter of degree—they dispatched a Brinks armored truck from New York to Tampa with a little black box of diamonds inside.

My heart was pounding out of my chest until that truck showed up the next morning, right on time. Waiting patiently with my snub-nose .38 tucked away, I was not taking any chances. I had been down this road before and knew that such a delivery involved great risk. But on top of that risk was the sense that I was stepping into a whole new realm, a quantum leap. An *armored truck* had just driven *all night*, all the way from New York, to bring *me* a diamond. If I could pull this off, everyone in Tampa's high society would soon see that diamond, and they would hear exactly where it had come from. Lots of millionaires in a relatively small pond. Word would spread. Armed guards brought the little black box to my office. I couldn't resist. I opened the box. One look at those amazing gems and my heart pounded even more. My mouth went too dry to whistle. I had only ever seen such gems at Jeweler's Circular Keystone in Vegas, and only then behind bulletproof glass and security systems. I had never had the opportunity to handle one before, *feel* that eight-carat weight. A Round Brilliant cut of that weight is 1.3 centimeters in diameter.

Gretchen showed up promptly for her 2:00 p.m. appointment. She brought with her an air of being accustomed to royal treatment. Floridian aristocracy was real, and she was firmly embedded in it.

When we opened that box and the gleam and sparkle of those stones caught the light, she lost her breath. A thrill shot through me. If I didn't screw this up, I had her. My hand trembled as I picked up the first stone with a special tweezer.

As a university professor, she was a highly intelligent, educated woman who brooked no nonsense, which made her easier to deal with; she knew what she wanted, but she also wanted to learn. She seemed to appreciate the fact that I was a straight shooter and that I wanted to teach her about diamonds first and foremost.

The diamond cutters in New York had sent me some incredible stones, and we spent the afternoon examining them in fine detail. She adored them all and found the decision difficult. She finally settled on a six-carat flawless diamond, a stone that was almost a million dollars at retail. By this time, I had brought on a designer, and we had prepared a number of beautiful samples to show her how we might set the stone. She sat with me and my designer for another hour designing a magnificent setting suitable for such a stone. We would custom-make the setting and I would deliver it to her personally in one week's time.

A week later when the ring was finished, I made an appointment with her and her husband, Dr. Dana Shires, at his office.

I was punctual as always, but he was already checking his watch. Gretchen was there as well, dressed to travel.

"Good thing you arrived on time," he said. "You have four minutes before we have to leave for the airport. I have to catch a flight to California."

A hand squeezed my heart. Could this deal fall through, after everything I had been through?

Feeling a bit rushed, I said, "I think you're going to love it, sir."

Then I opened the little black velvet box.

And there was that stone, sparkling like a thousand tiny mirrors catching the afternoon sun, free of any impurities, born from millions of years of intense subterranean heat and pressure, smashing together carbon atoms from the bones of dinosaurs, from stardust, into a perfect lattice, then heaved near the Earth's surface by tremendous forces, dredged from the crust by the hands of men, gleaming like I'd captured a star in my hand.

She gasped and clapped her hands. "Oh, *Dana!*" The look on her face was like the sudden emergence of the sun. Bringing that kind of joy to people truly never gets old.

Dr. Shires glanced at his Rolex. "If she loves it, then I love it! Will you take a personal check?"

I had never accepted a personal check that large from anyone in business, but I took one look around his magnificently furnished office, took one look at this incredibly wealthy man, squared my shoulders, and said, "Sure. No problem."

I stood silent as he pulled the ring from the box and slid it gently onto her finger. I will never forget the look on both of their faces, like it was their wedding day again.

Those expressions were the root of my business model and the core of my business philosophy. If I could bring that much joy and happiness to a couple, then my journey was well worth it.

In that moment, I knew I was doing exactly what I was meant to be doing with my life.

As I walked out of that office with that check in my hand, the sun was warm on my skin. My whole body radiated with warmth, my heartbeat racing, every nerve-ending electric. I couldn't wait to tell somebody, anybody. As I got in my car and pulled away, I shouted my elation through the sunroof. People must have thought I was crazy, and they would have been right. I cranked up the music. I danced in my seat, hooting and hollering with exultation.

Just as I expected, word spread like wildfire through Tampa's high society. From that point forward, my phone never stopped ringing. My customers continued to be young couples who could barely afford a half-carat, but now also old-money Tampa gentility, as well as everyone in between. That sale put me on the map.

I had created a business with its own unique model. My dad was still slinging drinks and cashing checks, serving people, but I was serving people, too. I was bringing them joy, and every time it happens it still brings a tingle to my body, warmth to my face, filling my heart with pride for what I built, and with happiness for being able to bring that joy to someone. Both of our niches, my dad's and mine, were very personal, very interpersonal. We were making people happy, having a great time, and reaping our own rewards.

Not bad for a kid from Skipper Road.

Epilogue

Never Let Them Steal Your Name

WHAT'S IN A NAME?

My whole life has been an answer to that question.

My dad stood up as my best man at my wedding a few years ago. It was such a powerful moment for me, because he actually stood up and gave a speech, which was unprecedented. He's always been incredibly personable and amiable with people one on one, but he'd never done any form of public speaking.

In the speech, he didn't talk about the rough patches our relationship had been through, or how I had defied his wishes and broken his heart, or the terrible things we went through. In his long-adopted Southern accent, he talked about my two beautiful daughters, his granddaughters, my success in the diamond business, and how proud of me he was for everything I had achieved. He talked about Anthony Louis Limited, the company I started on my own and named after my two grandfathers, Antonio Scarpo and Luigi Ciccarelli. He talked about his father, and my mother's father, how they had come to this country with nothing, the things they went through, and how proud they would be of me. I just sat there and stared at him, half in shock that he was speaking in front of a huge crowd, but I listened, my eyes tearing up, a lump in my throat. When he finished there was great applause, and I got up and hugged him. Even in his eighties, Art Scarpo was still a brick of a man. Crumbling at the edges, perhaps, and a bit worn at the corners—eighty-three years of hard living will do that—but still a proud brick of a man.

As I sat back down, I couldn't help but think about his admonition to me, way back when I was a boy: "Never let them steal your name."

My grandfathers' names and my father's name had formed the foundation upon which I built mine. That one simple sentence formed the core of our lives, the seed from which everything grew, for all of us. Tony's Tavern. Art's Lounge. Anthony Louis Limited. Your name is everything in the bar business, just as it is in the diamond business.

It seemed our family had always been plagued by the dark underbelly of humanity, in many ways tempted by it. I had always tried to resist it, to varying degrees of success in my younger years.

I grew up hearing the story of how my mom and her sisters were raised in part by the nuns in the Catholic Church. Her mom died while she was a young girl, and her father was an immigrant who spoke very little English. For me and my sisters, our mother formed the core of all goodness, all that's good in Catholicism. My mom and Sister Dorothy Barbara formed the foundation of all kindness and compassion in my life. My dad formed the core of what was strong, immovable, resolute. For some reason, the temptations I faced were stronger than most other people face—money, booze, drugs, crime, women—and I spent a lot of time thinking about why that had to be.

Where was the moment where I turned away from the darkness

for good? The dark side may still exist in me, as it does in everyone, but I make choices every day to embrace the light, to seek the divine. Was it the moment I chose to not take a rapist's life? Was it the moment I was struck by a car and sent spinning high into the air?

Is it possible that I briefly died that day on my bicycle, spinning like a helicopter toward the heavens? It might have been three seconds, or it might have been three minutes. I don't know for certain, but I have a strong sense that I did. I can still see the vivid colors surrounding me, suffusing me during that terrible, pivotal moment. Was I saved? Was it just not my time? Did God have a plan for me? Does He still? I don't know the answers to those questions, but just asking them makes me consider larger questions.

Is a person's life destined from the beginning?

Is it all a major plan, laid out by God from the moment of conception? Catholic scholars and theologians have considered and debated the notion of free will for almost two millennia.

Is there anything you can do to alter your destiny, or is every choice you make preordained by a cosmic entity for Whom all Time is already known?

Or...

Do we have control?

Do we have a say-so in the direction of our lives?

Is the power of choice real or an illusion?

Can one choice alter your destiny, or was that, too, part of the Grand Plan?

How close are we with and to God? What is our relationship with Him? Does that even matter?

What if all this, my life, my story, has been a test? I'm the first to admit, much of this might sound unbelievable, or like something from fiction or film.

What if in that moment after impact with that car, with my pulverized body flying through the air, my spirit slipped away and kept spinning toward Heaven, where I was gently embraced for three seconds, three minutes, three hours, and then released back to Earth, where I would be tested throughout my life to choose good over evil? Could I make a difference in this world? Could I be an instrument of good? Did God put Sister Dorothy Barbara in my path to guide me toward the light at the most critical moment?

I think these thoughts, and then some part of me rears up and says, *Tony, that's absurdly far-fetched.*

But I still see that bike accident and all those beautiful, coruscating colors, and feel the spinning like a helicopter as vividly as if it just happened, even though it was forty-eight years ago.

I believe in the eternal struggle between Good and Evil. I believe that all of us are born good but many of us are pulled to the dark side and embrace evil. We can all point to those who have embraced pure evil, such as Ted Bundy and all the ruthless killers, greedy swindlers, and heartless pedophiles that lurk among us. As long as humans exist, there will be those who embrace Evil. There are forces constantly tempting us, dragging us toward darkness. I've felt this pull on more than one occasion, and I see it happening to others all around me; it is not to be laughed off. The power to resist that pull lies within each of us, in our conscience, in our relationship with God. For the strong, it's an easy task. Those who lack sufficient faith or internal fortitude find resisting the pull more difficult.

Experiences that would leave some people crying in a corner, I have treated as moves in a chess game between Good and Evil on Earth, and in my own soul. Each move, a masterful placement on the chessboard of life.

I believe the path I took, both the good and the bad, was a part of a journey that would prepare me to take care of my mother as her illness ultimately paralyzed her. It also prepared me to take care of my two daughters as a single father, to raise them and teach them at a time of great difficulty and stress.

The path to goodness can lead to great things, where your life can make a difference, where you can help people and have great influence—but it's *never* the easy path. The easy path is the road most traveled; it does not offer challenges, nor does it tempt you. Those who have experienced difficulties in life know the hard path, the one that twists and turns and throws up roadblocks along the way.

My grandfathers knew that challenge; they were well aware of the hard road. My dad knew that pain and difficulty. And now, I know what that road looks like. The temptations and evil that surrounded my young life threatened to destroy my innocence, and holding on to that was my biggest test.

Did I pass the test? Did I survive? Ask those who know me best. Ask my Mom or Dad, ask Debbie or Antoinette, ask Madelyn or Sister Dorothy Barbara. I believe they all would say I passed.

THE END

ACKNOWLEDGEMENT

I wish to express my sincere gratitude to the following people for their support, love and inspiration as I pulled from the memories of my past and wrote them down on paper. I spent ten years contemplating and one full year writing, researching and collaborating to fulfill a dream and to share my experience with the world. As I embarked on this project, I met Mark Graham of Mark Graham Communications and his writer Travis Heermann. I would like to thank them both for believing in my story and sharing my vision. I would especially like to thank Travis Heerman for lending his creative spirit, talent and writing skills to help bring my story to life. You provided a voice that has been hidden away for years. I would like to thank my Dad, my mother Sandella, and my step-mom Madelyn for their love and support and believing in me. The story of my childhood, my early teenage years and all that I learned are, in large measure, because of those three amazing people. I want to say thank you to Sister Dorothy Barbara, an inspiration and guiding light in my life. Without her and her love of God, I may have fallen into despair. My sisters Debbie and Antoinette deserve special credit for putting up with me and my mischievous wayward pranks. Their love and devotion to our mom, in her many times of need cannot be adequately expressed. To my sister Diane, I hope this book brings a better understanding of the early years. So much of my passion for the written word and a full understanding of the English language is credited to my lifelong mentor and friend, Mr. Harold Givens. I believe he would be proud. And lastly, to all the people who passed through my life, walked through my doors and shared in my amazing life experiences, thank you. Each one of you helped shape the man that I am today.

Made in the USA
Middletown, DE
13 November 2019